Fire Within

Fire Within

A Civil War Narrative
from Wisconsin

Kerry A. Trask

The Kent State University Press
KENT, OHIO, & LONDON, ENGLAND

© 1995 by The Kent State University Press, Kent, Ohio 44242
All rights reserved
Library of Congress Catalog Card Number 95-1706
ISBN 978-0-87338-587-9
Manufactured in the United States of America

This is an on-demand reprint of the paper edition
published by the Kent State University Press.

Library of Congress Cataloging-in-Publication Data
Trask, Kerry A.
Fire Within : a Civil War narrative from Wisconsin /
Kerry A. Trask.
p.   cm.
Includes bibliographical references and index.
ISBN 0-87338-519-5 ∞
ISBN 978-0-87338-587-9 (pbk.) ∞
1. Manitowoc (Wis.)—History. 2. Wisconsin—History—
Civil War, 1861–1865. I. Title.
F589.M2T73   1995   95-1706
977.5'67—dc20

British Library Cataloging-in-Publication data are available.

for
Emily and John Peter Trask

What of the faith and fire within us
Men who march away
Ere the barn-cocks say
Night is growing gray,
Leaving all that here can win us;
What of the faith and fire within us
Men who march away?

—Thomas Hardy, "Men Who March Away"

Contents

Preface

*W*HAT HAS NOW become this book began with a very simple idea. Some years ago, in a well-intended effort to foster a stronger, more historically conscious sense of place among the people of my adopted hometown, I decided to put together a brief impressionistic talk about the first soldier from Manitowoc to be killed in the Civil War. I had run across his story, almost by accident, while cranking through some microfilm reels of old newspapers and had been struck by the profound emotional impact that individual death had made upon the entire community. At the time I knew little about either the Civil War or the city's early history, but my intentions were also modest—just a couple mildly amusing jokes and a colorful, fast-paced recounting of that interesting, somewhat ironic little story would suffice, I figured, to get their attention and fill the gap between the dessert and the rush for the exits that is part of the civic group and service club ritual. I would use such occasions and that long-forgotten casualty of a bygone battle to create among my listeners a better sense of the relationship between the past life of this particular place and the bigger, much better known events of the national experience, and by so doing make the significance of the smaller part more apparent.

I tried it and it worked. But it also worked on me. After having spent much of my professional life thinking and writing about eighteenth-century America, I suddenly felt a need to know a great deal more about the Civil War and the history of this place.

At first there was nothing systematic about my response to that impulse. I had no long-term goals or major projects in mind—

maybe a few more short talks or a brief nonscholarly article or two. But material—really rich, untapped primary stuff—just kept coming my way, much of it brought to my attention by people I did not even know who would stop after my talks to tell me of some old letters or a diary written by an ancestor of theirs who had been in the Civil War. Then, in correspondence on a related matter with Paul Hass of the _Wisconsin Magazine of History,_ he suggested I look at the papers of James S. Anderson.

It was not until quite a while later, when in the State Historical Society's manuscript collection working through some dense material on the Great Lakes fur trade, that I took time out to read some of Anderson's letters. I was amazed. They were so full of life, so filled with the sights and sounds of the war and with a young soldier's wonder and concern. But not until on sabbatical leave at the William L. Clements Library in Ann Arbor did I think of writing a book about Anderson and his hometown comrades. What sparked that idea was the picture on the dust jacket of James M. McPherson's newly published _Battle Cry of Freedom,_ which I noticed while browsing in a bookstore during a noontime break from the papers of Jeffery Amherst and Thomas Gage. It was a picture of Union soldiers pressing forward, rank upon rank, over fallen bodies, into clouds of smoke, toward a group of Confederate troops who appeared determined to hold their ground. Above those Union ranks waved the royal blue flag of the Fifth Wisconsin Volunteers. That was Anderson's regiment. There they were, the hometown boys, caught in time upon that cover, and I felt a strong desire to write their story and bring that picture at least part way back to life.

I wanted to write a book my students might wish to read. Most of them are about the same age as the young men who went off to Shiloh and Vicksburg, or those of my own generation who failed to survive freshman English and ended up in the firefights of Southeast Asia. "All wars are boyish, and are fought by boys," observed Herman Melville, and if that is so (certainly the part about being fought by boys, and now by girls as well, is accurate enough), then our students, maybe more than anyone, ought to understand the true nature of war. I hoped my attempts to recreate a sense of how the Civil War looked and felt amidst the dust of the march and heat of the struggle would help with that.

It was also my intention to write "local" history and recount the experiences of "ordinary" people in a fashion that would interest the general reading public and to do it in part by pointing to the broader implications of these small pieces. To that end I wove together a variety of personal perspectives and wartime experiences resulting in a narrative that reflects the passions of the times and describes some of the conflicts encountered by both men who marched away and people who remained at home.

In this endeavor I came to count upon the generous help and sound advice of colleagues and friends. Assistance came in many forms. There was, for example, the interest and encouragement of my good friends Deborah and David Douglas, as well as that of Mary Anne Ciavatta, Monica and Greg Hirte, Tom Skubal and Rosemary Krummel. My colleagues at the University of Wisconsin Center in Manitowoc, particularly Martha Schuh and our dean, Roland Baldwin, lent support by twice granting me the Kay Levin Faculty/Staff Professional Development Award. That helped pay for typing and maps. On projects like this there are always the debts of appreciation owed to the indispensable but often anonymous librarians. In my own case I am especially grateful for the polite and professional help received from the staff members of the Manitowoc Public Library, the librarians and archivists at the State Historical Society of Wisconsin, and the considerate people at the University of Wisconsin–Milwaukee's Golda Meir Library, who gave me extra time to work with some of their special collections materials.

Lynda Dvorachek made an invaluable contribution. She is Rosa Kellner's great-granddaughter and the present keeper of Rosa's wonderful journal. One night, after finishing another of my talks, she came up to the podium as I was packing up my papers and told me she had an old Civil War–era journal written by a young Bohemian woman. She wondered if I might be interested in looking at it. I was immediately curious, of course, but it was some time before I was able to make my way to the Dvorachek farm to see what Rosa had written. I was astonished by the richness of the journal and recognized that Rosa Kellner's thoughts and observations would add a vital dimension to the story. I am therefore exceedingly grateful to Lynda and her mother, Mrs. Catherine Cyr, for permission to use material from that journal in this book. Lynda also tipped me off to the Mead Holmes letters. Besides that, I want to say here how much I always enjoyed the time spent just sitting around her kitchen table, talking together about history and life and the importance of roots.

Paula Robbins, a former student of mine who has gone on to a successful career in cartography, drew the maps. I admire her professional skill, enjoyed this chance to work together, and appreciate her generous and enthusiastic help. Special thanks go to my good friend Ellen Nibbelink, with whom I talked at great length about this work during our early morning walks along the lake when she still lived in town. Ellen did the photography.

In writing anything of much length over an extended period of time, it becomes impossible to maintain much objectivity. After a while you wonder about the quality, clarity, and even the appropriateness of what you have written and realize you need the brutally honest reactions of impartial readers. Gail Fox plowed through a very premature draft, but encouraged me nonetheless. William Mulligan Jr., now at Murray State University in Kentucky, who knows a lot about books and good writing, gave the whole manuscript a close and careful reading before I considered sending it to any press. He offered advice and considerable encouragement. So, too, did Frederick J. Blue of Youngstown State University, who evaluated the manuscript for The Kent State University Press.

It has been my good fortune to work with John T. Hubbell and his staff at Kent State. They have all treated me with uncommon courtesy, especially senior editor Julia Morton, whom I sometimes pestered with small questions, and assistant editor Linda Cuckovich, who, with good humor and considerable skill, has helped me attend to many important details. Most of all, it has been my privilege to become acquainted with so thoughtful and learned a gentleman as John Hubbell, whose wise counsel, sharp editorial eye, and faith in the project enabled me to produce a far better final draft than I could otherwise have done. Of course, the faults and errors that remain are entirely my own.

My best critic and most steadfast supporter has been Susanne Skubal. She is a woman who possesses an unusually fine sense of the creative powers of the language and a perceptive feel for how it works. We frequently talked long and late about *Fire Within,* well before I ever conceived of it becoming a book. She was always straight with me when I sought her opinion, and although we sometimes disagreed, her opinions counted for a great deal. Susanne read every line of every draft, and her insights and suggestions made each successive effort a better piece of work. Throughout the project (and all those that came before) she believed in me and my ability to do the job. Furthermore, she bore the inconveniences and irritations of the whole process with remarkable patience and affectionate good humor.

As much as I am indebted to Susanne, it is our children, Emily and John Peter, to whom I dedicate this book. They, more than anyone, shared with me those summers of manic mood swings. They were great companions and constant reminders of what is truly important in life. We have lived together here along the lakeshore and watched the ice come and go and the lilacs bloom and fade for more than a dozen years now, and in that time they have each been for me a loving source of inspiration and hope.

Prologue

What is a historical fact? A spent shell? A bombed-out building? A pile of shoes? A victory parade? A long march? Once it has been suffered it maintains itself in the mind of the witness or victim, and if it is to reach anyone else it is transmitted in words . . . and it becomes an image, which, with other images, constitutes a judgment.
—E. L. Doctorow, "False Documents"

FROM A DRAFTY TENT in northern Virginia, Corporal James Anderson wrote home in mid-January of 1864 to his parents in Manitowoc, Wisconsin. He had just turned twenty-two and had been soldiering since the very beginning of the Civil War. He complained only briefly about his conditions, and then requested that they take good care of the diary he was enclosing as well as all the letters he had so faithfully sent them since first leaving with the Fifth Wisconsin Volunteers: "I intend if I ever get out of this term of service to write an account of my three years campaign."[1]

The letters and diaries were saved. But his account, like that of most soldiers who served in the ranks, was never written.

Perhaps James Anderson's story remained untold simply because he was an ordinary soldier—certainly no hero, at least no winner of medals or high rank, but one of a great armed multitude. Men like him were usually lost in the enormity of that struggle. It was a war different from those that had preceded it, having more in common with World War I than with the American Revolution or even the Napoleonic Wars, and was the first military conflict in which the power of the industrial system was turned to the brutal business of mass destruction and death.

We know a great deal about the magnitude of the Civil War, its character, its major figures and events, as well as its terrible costs. But much less is known about the farm boys, mill hands, and store clerks—the boys like young Anderson and his comrades—who came pouring out of the country's small towns and rural regions, down dusty roads to march in the ranks and fight from Bull Run Creek and Shiloh to Vicksburg and Cold Harbor. They were taken into the armies, trained, and transformed into cogs in what Hamlin Garland called "a vast machine for killing men."[2] And more of them lost their lives than all the soldiers who died in all this country's other wars combined.

Walt Whitman predicted that little would ever be written or even remembered about such ordinary men. The story of "the actual soldier . . . with all his ways, his incredible dauntlessness, habits, practices, tastes, [and] language," which Whitman regarded as the story of the "real war," would soon be forgotten, he feared. "The real war will never get in the books," he declared, regretfully concluding that "its interior history will not only never be written—its practicality, minutiae of deeds and passions, will never even be suggested."[3]

Fortunately, that has not been entirely so, due in large part to the fact that the American Civil War was also the first major military struggle in which large numbers of ordinary soldiers were able to read and write. Some of them were highly articulate individuals who wrote of their experiences in detail and with considerable insight, and, as a result of their often plain-spoken observations, we can still come to know or at least sense how the war looked and felt at the dirt level. There it was a different war from the one orchestrated and observed by the political and military leaders. Down where the boys were, where they lived and died and lost their limbs and sometimes their minds, patterns and strategies were usually unclear, often virtually imperceptible. For those in the ranks, soldiering consisted mostly of long, monotonous periods of waiting and numbing routine, interrupted often without either warning or explanation by long marches to unknown places with unfamiliar names. Sometimes, along the way, they collapsed from exhaustion, and sometimes the marching ended with more waiting and wondering, or sometimes in the cold convulsive chills or burning fevers of sickness, or with the deadly clash of combat amidst smoke and noise and fire. Too often it ended in sudden death.

Widespread literacy among the troops permitted their perspective on the war to be recorded and retained. That, in turn, has helped democratize the story, and in time, has allowed new images and attitudes about the war, and modern warfare in general, to take shape and emerge in the public mind.

At an early point in his career, Winston Churchill complained that "from the moment Democracy was admitted to, or rather forced itself upon the battlefield, War ceased to be a gentleman's game." Certainly once "gentlemen" lost their almost exclusive control over what was written and remembered about war, it became readily apparent that it was no game at all. But before that, throughout the long centuries before soldiers could write and ordinary people could read, war was usually depicted as being the most manly of all human endeavors. Warriors, whose bold and bloody deeds were exalted in literature and history, were the heroes of Western civilization. Through archetypal figures such as Achilles and Beowulf and red-crossed knights, the aggressive, violent, and often savage qualities of Western maleness were held up for generations of youths to admire and emulate. For a succession of centuries the myths of warrior heroes cast a powerful spell on the entire culture, inspiring sons to eagerly march off to battle, cheered on by fathers and willingly offered up by mothers in the belief that somehow regeneration and new beginnings would magically spring from the death and destruction. And in America there were those who agreed with Thomas Jefferson that "the tree of liberty must be refreshed from time to time with the blood of patriots."[4] Consequently, during war, perhaps more than in any other times, myth merged with experience to create within the collective imagination a dramatic, if distorted, vision of reality.

Those distortions were amplified by rituals and ceremonies that had always been integral parts of warfare and that transformed it into pageantry on a grand scale. The rites of war concealed the ugliness of naked violence, making brutality seem glorious and suffering noble. And within the spectacle, as the participants were called upon "to imitate the actions of the tiger . . . [and] disguise fair nature with hard-favor'd rage," each soldier, no matter how humble or ordinary, was made to hope and then believe that he might somehow come to play the hero's role.[5]

The martial pomp and ceremony and those same beguiling myths stirred deep and ancient feelings and most surely cast their spell on the members of Anderson's generation. That was particularly so during the first hot flashes of war fever, which flared up during the excitement-filled spring days immediately following the attack on Fort Sumter. The green, unworldly adolescent boys were, as always, the most susceptible. They were so full of youthful energy and naïve notions, and were especially eager to escape the dull routine of uneventful communities or the drudgery of isolated farms. They set off with high expectations of adventure in far-off and exotic places where they would have their chance to prove their manliness.

Soon enough, observed Mark Twain, they were changed, changed in radical ways, "from rabbits into soldiers" or, as Ambrose Bierce put it, changed from something only slightly more than children into "hardened and impenitent man-killers." Gradually they grew tough and indifferent to their own discomforts and to the pains of others. Eventually, wrote Twain, soldiers engaged in "the killing of strangers" against whom they felt "no personal animosity," "strangers," he said, "whom in other circumstances, you would help if you found them in trouble."[6]

Upon reaching the place of battles—"the place of blood and wrath," as Stephen Crane described it—the newly fashioned soldiers found themselves both seduced and terrified by what awaited them. Death was there, its presence betrayed by its unmistakable stench. It was everywhere, stalking everyone. There, if they were "good soldiers," the boys themselves became the instruments and agents of death, and for them killing became a vocation. But in this war the killing of men did not much resemble the purposeful slaughter of hogs or the butchering of beef cattle on autumn farms back home, for on the battlefield where, said Farley Mowat, "all was dark and bloody and the great winds of ultimate desolation howled and hungered," death came in cruel and random ways, with furious noise and with blood and brains and body parts scattered all around, taking, as Ernest Hemingway later observed, "the very good, the very gentle, and the very brave impartially."[7]

For the sake of survival, gentle, more humane qualities had to be suppressed to make way for the ascendancy of more primitive drives and reflexes. The soldiers had to take on the "indifference of wild creatures." They had to toughen up and adjust so as to become able, as Bierce put it, "to sleep on hills trembling with the thunder of great guns, dine in the midst of screaming missiles, and play at cards among the dead faces of their dearest friends." But that required more than the suspension of a sense of horror, more than the suppression of fears, for those who endured and survived often came to be like predators, living beyond the realm of reason and outside the boundaries of good and evil. "By the animal instinct that is awakened in us we are led and protected," wrote Erich Remarque, who survived the perils of the World War I trenches. In describing that instinct he made it clear that it was not a deliberate thing: "It is not conscious; it is far quicker, much more sure, less fallible than consciousness."[8]

It was also on the battlefield, observed Mowat, that "the line between brutal murder and heroic slaughter flickers and wavers . . . and becomes invisible," where innocent lads come face to face with the dark side of their own nature and the truly malevolent character of war. In the midst of combat, as Philip Caputo later discovered in Vietnam, "weeks of bottled up tensions would be released in a few minutes of orgiastic violence," sweeping one up to a "precarious emotional edge, experiencing a headiness that no drink or drug could match." J. Glen Gray experienced that during World War II and claimed that the "headiness" or "manic ecstasy" often produced in soldiers "a delight in destruction" and a "monstrous desire for

annihilation" that far surpassed "mere human malice" and did so
with such emotional intensity that it seemed to him as if they were
"seized by a demon and . . . no longer in control of themselves."
In some cases it was like being in the presence and under the spell
of what Stephen Crane called the great red, "blood-swollen god."
There muscles grew tense and almost instantly stronger, hearts
pounded harder and faster as sweat and adrenaline flowed, making
"the medieval images of hell and the thousand devils of that imagination believable."[9]

The whole monstrous thing drove men on, pushing them to
their limits and beyond, wearing them down, using them up. And
all the while there was the fear, the cold gnawing dread of death
and dismemberment, of the enemy's bayonet and the surgeon's saw,
of what was happening and what might yet occur, as well as a whole
host of fearful concerns about one's own weaknesses and limitations.
To endure, the soldiers closed ranks, becoming members of "a
mysterious fraternity born of the smoke and danger of death." They
were fused together into companies and regiments and were made
members of a "subtle battle brotherhood" that sheltered them from
the "onslaught of nothingness" and in which their separate selves
merged to become parts of the collective personality of the unit.
For that they would willingly die.[10]

It was a metamorphosis that made of a boy someone and something much harder. And as that occurred, and their time as soldiers
grew, they came to have less and less in common with the people
they had left behind. Once the parades had passed, most of those
who remained home were soon enough reabsorbed in their own
affairs. In time many stopped writing, stopped sending packages,
and actually seemed to stop caring about those who had marched
away. Even when there were expressions of interest and concern,
they somehow rang hollow and insincere, for how could those
with decent food, dry beds, and the pleasant sweet-smelling company of women ever really understand and therefore truly empa-
thize with the lot of the common soldier? And how could the
soldiers, whose lives were both miserable and endangered, not grow
to envy and even resent the advantages and comforts enjoyed by

those who remained at a safe distance from the struggle? Such circumstances often generated a morose sense of alienation, so that some soldiers came to actually despise the very society they risked their lives to defend.[11]

Among the men themselves, as heat and pressure built, the interior realities of the struggle strained against external appearances and intervened between the old romantic illusions and the harsh and ugly stuff of actual experience. Many found it increasingly difficult to bring their own moral views and values into line with the necessities of the battlefield. They struggled, often in vain, to reconcile their powerful instinct for self-preservation with their abiding fear of being thought cowards by people whose good opinions still mattered to them. Consequently, deep and disturbing conflicts were set in motion within them, as within their companies and regiments. Duty clashed with self-interest as the boys who had set out with hopes of becoming heroes grew increasingly concerned about surviving. Along the way the power of the old myths never completely loosened their hold. And new myths—those of common men and their battles—emerged to contribute even more confusion to their inner conflicts of high ideals and base passions.

Similar conflicts arose within towns and villages far away from the war front. In the beginning there had been, in most cases, unity and agreement at home. But as the war went on and demanded far more than most people had ever anticipated, the strain began to show. Volatile mixtures of idealism and fear, self-interest, self-sacrifice, grief, and guilt accumulated and exploded causing communities to fracture and pull apart along fault lines that had been there before the war but had temporarily been obscured by a shallow consensus. In northern settlements, particularly those in the Great Lakes region, internal divisions had existed for some time as Catholics and Protestants, native-borns and immigrants, Democrats and Republicans had all pushed and competed to shape those communities, especially those recently settled, according to their own designs and aspirations. In such places, life at close quarters often bred as much contempt as affection and, with the added pressures and passions of the war, disagreements sometimes took on malicious qualities.

People tried to hold things together and recover a sense of common purpose. In most cases communities relied heavily on rituals and ceremonies, and on a highly conventionalized and sentimental rhetoric to restore the old myths or make new ones. Sometimes unity, at least of a superficial sort, was restored. But success was usually fleeting, and for most people, both at home and on the march, the Civil War became a series of very difficult internal conflicts, each within the other, within the nation, within communities, and within the private heart as well.

All of that—the transforming nature of the struggle and the war within—was reflected in the experiences of young James Anderson, his comrades, and his home village of Manitowoc. The Civil War was the great history-altering event that linked them to the bigger, broader life of the nation. On the eve of the war 775,881 people were living in Wisconsin. About a third were native-born. The rest, in almost equal proportions, were either from the New England–New York area or immigrants from northern Europe—especially from the German states, the British Isles, and Scandinavia. Others came from Upper and Lower Canada. Although often in conflict, the war gave them a common historical frame of reference, a shared sense of participating in something of very great significance, and that experience shaped the generation that, more than any other, fashioned the state's character and collective identity.

In 1860, a large majority of Wisconsin's people lived on farms, and less than 20 percent of the population resided in communities of more than twenty-five hundred inhabitants. There were then only twenty-four such settlements, of which Manitowoc was one. It was located along the west shore of Lake Michigan, about a hundred miles north of Milwaukee, and at the time of Abraham Lincoln's election had a population of 3,065 people. It was a lumber mill and shipbuilding village consisting of a collection of log-and-plank buildings and huts clustered around the mouth and along the banks of the Manitowoc River, which meanders through the pine forests of northeastern Wisconsin for about forty miles before reaching the lake. It was an unassuming village far removed from the important places and developments of the day. But news of the Confederate attack on Fort Sumter abruptly changed that. The village, like the rest of Wisconsin, responded enthusiastically to President Lincoln's call for volunteers, and by the time the fighting was finished, 2,467 men from Manitowoc County had served in the Union's military forces.

That was an unusually strong display of commitment, especially for a newly settled county of only slightly more than twenty-two thousand inhabitants. Yet in so many other ways the wartime experiences of James Anderson, and the others like him who left the lakeshore to take up the fight, as well as those who stayed at home, had much in common with the experiences of the other people and communities of the Great Lakes region. In the basin of the lakes and along the rivers flowing into them, a new regional culture was taking shape, similar in many ways to the way of life in the Northeast yet with distinctive qualities and characteristics. So too, it had its own regional slant and perspective on the war. The war would also quicken that cultural transformation. And when the conflict was over and the people emerged from what Whitman called the "lurid interiors" of the war,[12] they were different from what they had been before, having different visions of the future, a new sense of themselves, and a deeper awareness of the dark and tragic dimensions of human existence.

CHAPTER ONE

A Place to Begin Again

American social development has been continually beginning over again on the frontier. This perennial rebirth, this
fluidity of American life, this expansion westward with its
new opportunities, its continuous touch with the simplicity
of primitive society, furnish the forces dominating American
character.

—Frederick Jackson Turner,
"The Significance of the Frontier in American History"

*T*HE YELLOW GLOW of a lamp burnt late in an upstairs window
of the Williams House Hotel, an imposing three-story brick
building on Manitowoc's main street. Inside, on the night of April
18, 1861, Rosa Kellner sat writing friends and recording the events
of the day in her journal. She also listened to the many sounds that,
since suppertime, had filled the usually quiet village streets.

Rosa ran the hotel with her sometimes less-than-dependable
younger brother Leopold, or "Labolt" as she affectionately called
him. She had been in charge since their older sister Anna and her
husband, Samuel Williams, had departed for Texas that previous
August. Samuel was dying of tuberculosis. Once a tall and robust
man, he deteriorated at an alarming pace, the cold, damp Lake
Michigan climate only hastening his decline. Eventually, the dry
warmth of the Southwest seemed his only hope for survival.

Rosa had never wished to become an innkeeper and had moved
to town initially only to help her sister and Samuel. She was willing

Figure 1. Rosa Kellner, seen here in her early twenties, observed and recorded her impressions of the war at home. (Courtesy of Lynda Dvorachek)

to do what she could for the sake of family, but from the very beginning Rosa found the work unrelenting and exhausting. In May of 1860 she wrote in her journal: "I feel very tired doing all the work alone [and] how I wish we were all safely stowed away in some pretty white cottage instead of keeping a public house for there is always work and so little time to improve our minds." The burden of it all became much worse once Anna and Samuel left her completely in charge of their establishment, which also contained a tavern and dining hall. Leopold was expected to assist her, and he sometimes did, but even with his help she found her situation almost overwhelming. "I am 18, Labolt 16, how will we get along [running] a public house and [we are only] two children to take care of it, may God give us strength to do our duty," she scrawled on a journal page.[1]

Rosa was a member of a large immigrant family from the Bohemian region of the Austrian Empire. Altogether there were fourteen of them who left the family's home village of Neumark in the late summer of 1846. Their crossing was a rough one, and the sailing ship on which they came was in a serious state of disrepair when they finally docked at Beauport, a small French Canadian village on the St. Lawrence River, a few miles downstream from Quebec City. The Kellners remained there for the better part of three years, and it was during their sojourn in Lower Canada that Anna met and married Samuel. The Williamses operated a mill in Beauport, and Joseph, the oldest of the Kellner boys, worked for them. He, as well as his sisters Barbara and Mary Ann, both of whom were older than Rosa, married in Quebec, and while there, John, the last of the Kellners' children, was born in early January of 1847. By then Mrs. Kellner was forty-seven years old, and Joseph Sr., the family patriarch, who had served in the Austrian imperial army during the Napoleonic Wars and fought in the Battle of Dresden in 1813, was sixty-one.[2]

While they waited in Canada, Michael, the second oldest son, went on to Wisconsin. The rest of the family landed in Milwaukee and joined him in Manitowoc County in May of 1849. Old Joseph was a tanner by trade, but in Wisconsin he purchased land a few miles northwest of Manitowoc, up near French Creek, and became a farmer. His son Joseph acquired another farm right across the road from his, and Michael bought and cleared a number of acres a few miles north of that. In time, Michael built a shingle mill, opened a general store, and eventually operated a grist mill at what became known as Kellnersville. By 1860, all of them, including the sons-in-law from Canada, seemed to be prospering, and the aging parents, along with the younger children, had taken up residence in "a pretty white cottage surrounded by a sweet garden," which Rosa said was "beautiful compared to the old log house" they had lived in until 1857.[3]

Rosa was by then a tall, spindly, plain-looking girl with a fine mind and affectionate nature. Her relationship to Anna, who was seventeen years her senior, was especially close, and at one point she wrote in her journal: "Dear Anna, she is very different from my other sisters, more kind, more considerate, more like a dear mother." Rosa also cared deeply for Samuel, describing him as "more than a brother, almost a father." When he became ill she pitched in and worked harder than before, even though her own health was far from robust, and when Anna and Samuel departed for Texas, she became still more conscientious in her attempts to hold the business together.[4]

The hotel was a busy place. It was in the midst of the village, just two blocks south of the river and on the northwest corner of Franklin and Eighth streets. Farmers who came to town and passengers off the boats that docked in the harbor congregated there. Rosa was an observant and inquisitive girl, and the Williams House Hotel provided her with an excellent place from which to watch the passing parade of village life.

On Wednesday, April 17, news of the attack on Fort Sumter reached Manitowoc by steamship and immediately produced a commotion. The lakeshore had emerged from the isolation and confinement of the long northern winter. The weather was growing warmer, the harbor was finally free of ice, and ships were running again. People were once more coming in from the surrounding countryside. Since Abraham Lincoln's election and the secession of the Southern states, suspense had been building, but when the message of the attack reached the village, the mounting anxiety gave way to a sense of relief. People in the streets and taverns speculated about what would happen next. Most of them believed that the rebellion should be crushed. As the agitation increased,

Figure 2. The Williams House Hotel, owned by Rosa Kellner's brother-in-law, Samuel Williams, and her oldest sister, Anna, was managed by Rosa during their two-year absence in Texas. (Courtesy of the Manitowoc Public Library)

Gideon Collins, the village president, announced there would be a public meeting in the courthouse the following evening. There they would decide what Manitowoc's response to the crisis should be.

"I heard the tramp of heavy boots continually. They were going to the war meeting," wrote Rosa in her journal that Thursday night, April 18. All day long men and boys had seemed unable to talk about anything else as they waited impatiently for the meeting to begin. When it finally did, it was "attended by several hundred persons" from the village and surrounding area who packed themselves into the building's largest room. There, throughout the evening, the "vast assemblage" was whipped into a frenzy by a succession of impassioned speakers. Among them was Charles Esslinger, who delivered a fiery harangue in German. Temple Clark, a rising political star in the local Democratic party, declared that although he had not supported Lincoln's election, "the time had come for true men to be united" behind the president and his policies. There was also a Mr. Anderson, perhaps James's father, who took to the podium and shouted that the "traitors . . . should be hung as Tories in the Revolution were." Each time a speaker finished there was wild applause, and then another would rise to offer his condemnation of the South and secession. The crowd passed a series of resolutions by thunderous voice votes, but then, after much time and talking, Perry P. Smith, one of the community's original settlers, went forward and spoke. He chided the audience and sternly asserted that the speech making ought to finally give way to some action, and that rather than mere words the situation demanded men—"men that will fight, men enough to go down and wipe the [*damn*] rebels off the face of the earth." A roar of approbation filled the hall and it was unanimously decided that Manitowoc would raise an infantry company for the war. Another meeting, they determined, would be held that Saturday night, and men would be asked to sign up. The crowd was exhilarated by its own decisiveness, and after the meeting everyone poured out into the cool spring darkness, where they were joined by a brass band. Torches were lit and they all "marched through the principle streets to the music of stirring airs," reported the *Manitowoc Herald.*[5]

Next morning, when Rosa learned of the decision to form an infantry company, she boldly wrote: "If I were only a boy tomorrow with other brave men I would enlist and let those Southern traitors see what northern men can do!" She was caught up in the emotions of the moment and felt so strongly about the dramatic turn of events that she seemed to resent the limitations of who and what she was. "Why, Oh why am I a girl? If I was only free!"[6]

James Anderson was free. He was nineteen and had just finished school that spring. He had taken work in Ben Jones's lumber mill on the south bank of the river but did not intend to make the sawing of logs his life's work. Like Rosa, he too became caught up in the emotions of the developing events, and when the call came during the Saturday night meeting, James was among the first to surge forward to enlist. He later boasted that he had been "fourth or fifth on the list" of volunteers.[7]

Anderson was a tall, thin, light-haired Scottish boy who had been born in the Kelvin Haugh district of Glasgow on Christmas Day 1841. His father, John, who was once described as "a man of good education [and] an unwearied reader of good books," was then a calico printer in that city's textile industry. But before taking up that demanding trade, he, like so many other young Scots, had been a soldier in the British army. John Anderson had grown up in Stirling, a substantial community to the north of and in between Edinburgh and Glasgow, a place of ancient battles where a great thick-walled castle, once considered the strongest in all of Scotland, stood high upon the cliff above the town. Mary Stuart had been crowned there and for a time had made Stirling Castle the royal residence before events compelled her to seek asylum with her cousin queen in England. John Anderson too had left his home there for foreign places, departing in December of 1822, at the age of eighteen, to serve in the Seventy-first Highlanders Light Infantry Regiment. During the next seven years he saw duty in India, Ceylon, and the British West Indies. His superiors rated him "Very Good" at soldiering, but in 1829, and still at the rank of private, he had apparently had enough of army life and rather than reenlisting, he once again returned to Scotland.[8]

Scotland was then a poor country of struggling people, of uprooted crofters from the harsh highland countryside who had been pushed from the land, where they were replaced by large flocks of more profitable sheep. At the very time when their miseries were increasing, their numbers were multiplying at an alarming rate. The population was increasing, at least in part, because more people were being vaccinated against smallpox and because the nutritional conditions of the lower classes were improving due to widespread cultivation and consumption of potatoes. However, the population growth made the already wretched social conditions even worse, and that, in turn, made Scotland prime recruiting territory for the British army. For many young men the chance to march to the pipes behind the Union Jack was greatly preferred to the dismal prospects of remaining mired in rural poverty or the surrendering of themselves to drudgery and early death in the mill towns to the south. But not all who wished to serve were taken, and many landless young men had few choices left other than migrating to Edinburgh, Glasgow, or the English industrial cities, where they would engage in a desperate search for wage labor. If they found work and were able to endure the exhaustion and monotony of the mills, they might then, if they properly disciplined themselves and enjoyed considerable good luck, eventually save enough money to escape to the colonies or perhaps even off to the rising opportunities in the United States.[9]

The flight from the countryside and the massive, if unplanned, growth of textile manufacturing turned Glasgow into one of the great urban monstrosities of the British industrial revolution. During the first forty years of the nineteenth century, its population exploded from about thirty thousand inhabitants to well over three hundred thousand, and by 1840, at about the time when John Anderson married Harriet Sibree, the inner city had become a grotesque slum sprawling for miles along the foul and polluted banks of the River Clyde. Of the three hundred thousand people living there, nearly 80 percent were impoverished workers who lived among what Friedrich Engels described as the "endless labyrinth of narrow lanes and wynds . . . [in] old, ill-ventilated, towering houses crumbling to decay, destitute of water and crowded with inhabitants, comprising three or four families (perhaps twenty persons) in each flat." It was a city full of smoke-belching foundries and factories, constant noise and motion, foul sewage-strewn streets, and great stinking heaps of manure and garbage. Also, according to Sir Archibald Alison, nearly thirty thousand miserable people there were "every Saturday night in a state of brutal intoxication." Drunkenness seemed their only means of numbing the pain and escaping the near hopelessness of their circumstances. Glasgow was the second largest city in the entire British Empire, but by 1839 conditions within it had become so atrocious that the much-traveled English social scholar J. C. Symons wrote: "I have seen human degradation in some of its worst phases both in England and abroad, but I can advisedly say that I did not believe until I visited the wynds of Glasgow, that so large an amount of filth, crime, misery, and disease existed in one spot in any civilized country."[10]

It was from all of that that the Andersons fled in 1852. John was then forty-eight years old, Harriet his wife, thirty-five, and young James was just a boy of eleven. There were three other children: six-year-old Jean, little Harriet, who was then just four, and an infant boy who died shortly after they reached Wisconsin. They arrived in September, and after the squalor of Glasgow and the crowded discomforts of the long Atlantic voyage, Manitowoc County must have seemed like an unspoiled, and nearly unoccupied, promised land.

"It is a land which has but awakened out of a sleep of thousands of years and reveals many, many traces of its primeval conditions," wrote Westphalian immigrant Gerhard Kremers, who settled near Manitowoc Rapids in 1848. Just a few years earlier, John M. Berrien, a civil engineer conducting a survey of the Manitowoc River region for the War Department, reported: "Its valley is fertile, and abounds in valuable timber of all kinds, especially pine."[11] When the Andersons arrived it was a place still more wild than settled, where the trees stood dense and towering and the forest stretched back mile upon unbroken mile from the lake. And among its shadows wolves still howled in the darkness, especially when the white smoke of cabin chimneys rose straight up in clear, cold, windless winter nights.

The Andersons brought with them few worldly goods, but John had managed to save sufficient funds to cover the cost of their voyage as well as the purchase of a homestead in Kossuth Township, the same area northwest of the village where the Kellners had settled. The Andersons were a little east of them, not far from French Creek, in a part of the county still only sparsely occupied. Some French Canadian families were living along the creek, and near Michael Kellner's place there was a cluster of Bohemian farms, but otherwise there were few other white people in the area. There was, on the other hand, a substantial Indian community on the Neshoto River, to the east of the Andersons. At least that village was there during the warmer part of the year, for its inhabitants, most of whom were Ojibwas, came and went, appearing and disappearing, with the annual round of the seasons. Each year they would appear out of the emptiness of the winter forest in early March and would first make camp near the west bank of the river in the midst of a large grove of maple trees. There, observed young James, "their ponies would graze and grow fat and sleek after their winter's privation," and there the women of the band would tap the trees, collecting and straining the clear sweet sap through old blankets into black caldrons that simmered and steamed over low and steady fires for days at a time. When sugar making was through they packed up and crossed over the river, where they resurrected their bark hut community, and there, in time, when the cold was finally gone, the women planted extensive gardens of corn, beans, pumpkins, and squash in the black silt left behind by the spring flooding. "Each family seemed to have its own tract, which the women industriously worked with their hoes throughout the season," observed James. The band's leader was a man named Katoose. Anderson said he was very friendly toward the settlers and described him as being "tall, with a large frame, very spare in flesh, well past middle life, but with nothing of the decrepitude of age." Katoose and his people remained in their Neshoto River community until harvest time, making occasional trips to Lake Michigan to spear and dry whitefish, or to Manitowoc and Two Rivers to trade. Then, just before the snow fell, they packed their ponies and again headed northward, vanishing into the vastness of the leafless forest.[12]

During his first summers in Wisconsin, James and the Indian boys played together in the woods, sometimes hunting small game, he with his single-barrel shotgun and they with their bows and arrows. It was a wondrous time and place, and although he did not understood the language of his playmates and they did not understand his, they all managed, he said, to communicate well.

Besides his playmates, there was one particular Indian who caught his attention and imagination. His name, at least the name he used among the settlers, was John Williams, and about him, said James, "there was a good deal of mystery." Williams didn't live in the village with the other Indians. He stayed to himself, living in the forest with his wife, and had almost nothing to do with Katoose's people. He was an impressive man. Anderson said he was "tall and well formed, with fine features" and "at all times neatly dressed in a fine suit of buckskin—hunting shirt, leggings, and moccasins." Over his shoulder and running diagonally across his chest he wore a broad, black, leather belt studded with brass buttons, and at the end of it hung a large sheath-knife. In many ways, at least for the impressionable young Scottish boy, Williams much resembled the mythical "noble savage," in that he was an unusual mixture of primitive simplicity and refined civility: a skilled hunter who frequently provided Mrs. Anderson with fresh venison, but also a man who "spoke excellent English" and whose "table manners were better than most white men." Williams often ate dinner with the Andersons and discussed a wide variety of interesting subjects on those occasions. He was obviously a man who had seen something of the world, but he remained a mysterious figure who revealed almost nothing about himself or the life he had once known. Where he came from he kept a secret. Just a couple of summers after the Andersons settled in Kossuth, Williams vanished without a trace.[13]

That same summer, the other Indians living in the area departed, less mysteriously but also for the final time. Their last large gathering met at the Neshoto River village site in the early autumn of 1853. James estimated that there must have been at least five hundred tribesmen there on that occasion. They talked and ate together, and one evening events took a dramatic turn when they all put on special regalia, painted their faces and bodies with black and colored stripes, and built a huge fire around which they circled and danced throughout the night. It was the young men who did the dancing—those who in former times would have been warriors—and the women and old men beat out a constant cadence upon the drums and wailed out mournful chants into the darkness. Through it all young James sat among the shadows along the edge of the circle watching the painted, near-naked forms rhythmically moving in the blazing light of the fire. There he huddled close to an old man who, he said, "was too feeble to take part in the violent dancing" but whose "eyes would flash and his voice grow strong as he rolled out the guttural notes of the chant." As the old man joined in, "he seemed to be recalling the warlike traditions of his tribe." It was all very exciting and it made a powerful impression on Anderson's young mind. But when the sun rose, the dancing stopped, the fire was allowed to sputter out, and the camp returned to normal. The people lingered on for just a few more days and then were gone for good.[14]

Some other Indians groups continued to make summer camps in other parts of the county for a few years after that, some far up the Manitowoc River near the Calumet County line, and another band, led by a chief the French called LaChandelle, spent the warm months in a village on the river near Mishicot. Also, until the end of the 1850s, Indians continued to travel to Manitowoc, where they traded at Peleg Glover's post, on York Street down near the lake. They trusted Glover because he spoke their language, and because of his own mixed French and Indian ancestry. In 1858 or 1859—Anderson was not sure which—a large flotilla of birch-bark canoes came down the lake, propelled by large crews and carrying tons of cargo. The paddlers were Menominee, and when they landed in town they camped for a few days along the river's north bank, just down from Glover's, and traded fish oil, baskets, maple sugar, and pelts in exchange for blankets, gunpowder, and metal goods. But once their business was through, they too departed. "It was a picturesque sight when they started on their homeward journey, paddling their large fleet of canoes over the smooth lake in the morning sunshine. That was the last great band of Indians that visited Manitowoc," Anderson later recalled.[15]

By then, life along the lakeshore was changing. The Andersons had moved to town in 1855, after giving up their struggle to cut a farm from the forests of Kossuth Township, and in Manitowoc they rented a "small but very clean" house—not much more than a shanty, in fact—down on the river flats at the west end of Chicago Street.[16] John, then in his early fifties, managed to find at least part-time employment in the B. Jones and Company sawmill. Once again they had become poor and landless folks, but being in the village at least gave James and his two sisters the chance to continue their schooling, and it also made it possible for Mrs. Anderson, who was then chronically ill, to receive regular medical attention.

Manitowoc was a place where nature and culture came together in both conflicting and creative ways. Its first settler, in the spring of 1837, was Benjamin Jones. Jones was originally from Massachusetts and had migrated to Wisconsin after having lived for a long time in upstate New York and then in Chicago. He and his brother William had opened a store in Chicago in 1833, and soon after the organization of the Wisconsin Territory and the opening of a federal land office in Green Bay, Jones purchased, at $1.25 an acre, two thousand acres of land on either side of the Manitowoc River. That was in 1836, and the next spring Ben Jones came up the lake by schooner with a work crew. During that summer the workers built a house for Jones and his family close to the lake, just north of the river, and put up some rough shanties for themselves. They also laid out streets, surveyed quarter-acre house lots, and constructed a sawmill, a warehouse, and got a good start at building the National Hotel. That same summer a boatload of "colonists" arrived from the Windy City, and before fall were joined by other people moving in from the east.

Where Jones's village took shape the sandy shoreline of Lake Michigan curved inward in a long even arc from Two Rivers Point on the north to the mouth of the Manitowoc River and then outward again to South Point just beyond where Silver Creek entered the lake. The Manitowoc River, after flowing through flat terrain

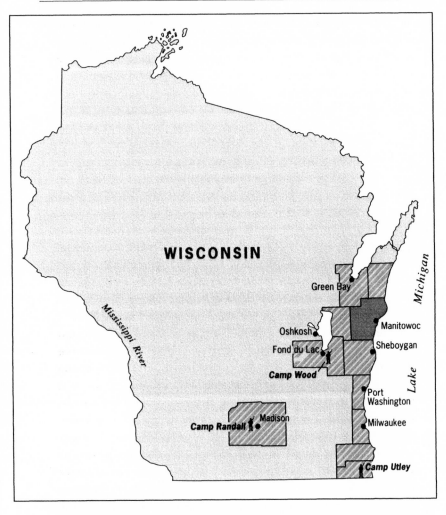

Figure 3. Wisconsin, showing the counties along the Lake Michigan western shore. (Map by Paula Robbins)

for nearly thirty miles, descended 262 feet in its final 15 miles and then merged with the lake. It was an almost ideal stream for moving logs and driving mills, and that, along with an ever-increasing demand for lumber in Chicago, seemed to guarantee the settlement's success. There were other sawmills, each with its own cluster of workmen's shanties, beginning to appear about the same time in other parts of the county. One was upstream at Manitowoc Rapids and another farther west near Cato Falls. Then to the north, first at Two Rivers, and after that about eight miles up the West Twin River as well as at the confluence of the Neshoto River and Johnson Creek, other mills were erected and their work crews were soon engaged in cutting the region's white pines into planks and beams.

However, it seemed that no sooner were the sounds of axes heard in the forest than a financial panic struck the country, sweeping westward and causing the collapse of businesses and banks. As a consequence, by the onset of winter most of the mills in Manitowoc County had shut down and most of the people who had settled there during the summer had departed. That setback, though severe, proved only temporary. Soon Chicago's insatiable appetite for lumber and cord wood revived the county's infant economy, and by 1849, when John Schuette set eyes on the village for the first time, it had begun to flourish in a modest way.

Schuette was from the German province of Oldenburg. He and his family had spent their first Wisconsin winter with friends from the old country in Cedarburg, near Milwaukee, and in early spring he had walked north along the beach in search of place to settle more permanently. It was during the first week in May, and he initially caught sight of Manitowoc from a hill just south of town. Immediately impressed, Schuette described the village as being "nestled in a half moon valley, bounded by the blue lake on the east, the north, west, and south [by] a rising embankment, the river running through the center, [with] a few vessels loading with lumber and shingles [and] a sawmill . . . with its saws wafting . . . the pleasing hum of industry." The rest of the family arrived by steamboat on the nineteenth. The Schuettes stayed and started a store.[17]

Gerhard Kremers had landed there the previous summer, coming over from the village of Vluyn near Dusseldorf, and he reported in a letter to the folks back home that Manitowoc consisted of about fifty clapboard cabins and had some "fairly good stores, several good inns, and an English school," along with "2 physicians and 1 apothecary shop." It was still a simple, rough-hewn place, and Gustaf Unonius, a Swede who was the village's Episcopal priest in 1849, complained that most of its inhabitants were "crude uncultivated laborers" who, he asserted, gave the place a "spirit of brutality, savagery, and lawlessness." Nevertheless, he continued, it was "one of those embryonic western towns which resembles boys in their teens, subject to many bad habits, yet full of life, vitality, and hope for the future."[18]

During the next dozen years some of that hope began to be realized. Between 1850 and 1860, the village population increased from 756 to 3,065, and by the eve of the Civil War, Manitowoc had ceased to be just a crude collection of huts along the wild rim of the lake. It had become a modest center of civilization and commerce with a jail and a poorhouse, 646 houses, five churches, four breweries, at least thirty saloons and taverns, four newspapers (one of which was published in German), three public schools and a private academy, two bookstores, a library, a theater, and an impressive new brick courthouse that had cost more to build than those of either Chicago or Milwaukee. It was a settlement that smelled of freshly cut lumber and wet sawdust, of salt fish, wood smoke, and the yeasty aroma of fresh fermenting beer. The village had become a busy port as well as a market center for the whole county, the population of which had also exploded during the decade of the 1850s, increasing by more than 600 percent, from 3,702 to 22,416. There were a number of hotels in town to accommodate people who were coming and going from farms and lumber camps or from off the boats that docked in the harbor. The National Hotel, Thomas Windiate's two-story Windiate House, and Samuel's Williams House Hotel were the biggest and best of the lot, and all had livery stables attached or close at hand. John Schuette, Perry P. Smith, Osuld Torrison, and J. E. Platt all had general stores. The Barnes brothers and T. C. Shove ran banks at opposite ends of town. The community also had a growing number of industries. The Smalley brothers, for example, ran an iron foundry on the north side of the river, close to the lake. Louis and Eugene Sherman operated a tannery and in 1859 processed and shipped out five thousand pounds of finished leather. In 1860, J. N.

Figure 4. The village of Manitowoc in 1860. (Map by Paula Robbins)

Perry built a large ashery, also north of the river, and there he and his workers manufactured soap, candles, and potash. Of even greater importance were the mills that lined the river's south bank, from Tenth Street down to the lake. A few hundred yards in from the beach stood Robinson's grist mill. It had its own dock and plank platform along the river. West of that, around Eighth Street, was the

Nollau sawmill, then Guyles's, followed by Beardsley's, then Ben Jones's, and finally, upstream near Tenth Street, was the Pankratz and Schock Lumber Company mill. All, except for Robinson's, were surrounded by logs, piles of lumber, and small mountains of sawdust and slab wood. By wartime they were all driven by steam engines, the stacks of which puffed out clouds of smoke that rose above the town and drifted out over the lake.

Much of the community's life and activity were oriented toward the lake, which both connected it to and isolated it from the bigger world beyond. There "the water [was] exquisitely clear, cool, and of a beautiful sea green tint," said G. C. Wellner, who settled in Manitowoc as a boy in 1858. Out from shore it deepened and darkened, gradually changing from green to cobalt blue. At the village, two sturdy timber piers extended out from the ends of Quay and Franklin Streets on the south side of town, and another from the foot of Chicago Street north of the river. Just back from the beach, not far from the north pier, stood a brick lighthouse flashing out its signal every two minutes through the lens of its oil lamp, and right next to the pier there were big black heaps of coal as well as the sheds and warehouses of the Goodrich Steamship Company. Rows of weathered fishing shanties, built upon piles, lined both river banks near the mouth and jutted out over the water. Also, near where the river met the lake, on the south side where a low marshy stretch had been filled in with dirt and sawdust, William Bates had a sprawling and cluttered shipyard. There was another yard, run by G. S. Rand, just west of the Eighth Street drawbridge on the north bank, and still farther upstream, on the inner side of the river's last large curve, was C. Sorenson's shipyard.[19]

William Bates, who worked with his sons, was the first shipwright on the Lakes to design a schooner specifically suited to the peculiar conditions of the Great Lakes. His ideas all came together in 1852 in his creation of the *Challenger*. It greatly resembled a clipper ship and was a sleek, long, two-masted vessel with a shallow draft. Graceful, fast, and amazingly maneuverable, the *Challenger* became Bates's prototype for a whole series of schooners built in the Manitowoc yard, schooners like the *Clipper City* and *Manito-*

woc, which became almost legendary for being among the fastest and most beautiful ships on the lakes. But besides the schooners, Bates completed by the spring of 1861 two side-wheel steamships, the *Union* and *Sunbeam.* Toward the end of April, Rosa Kellner walked down to the lakefront to watch one of them launched: "It was a beautiful sight. How the huge bird glided down and the blue waves laughed joyfully as she touched them."[20]

Ships such as those, with puffed white sails or smoke billowing from black stacks, seemed to come and go constantly throughout the navigation season, which lasted from April to November. Most often they ran between Manitowoc and Chicago, a round-trip voyage the schooners usually completed, with stops along the way, in about a week. Without the stops, and with strong and steady winds, vessels like the *Clipper City* could make the same voyage one-way in fifteen to twenty hours. The much less majestic steamships churned and plowed along the same route but did so on more dependable schedules carrying much larger cargoes.

During the shipping season of 1859, a total of 1,077 ships docked and departed from Manitowoc's harbor—371 sailing vessels, 430 sidewheel steamships, and 276 propeller-driven ships—and that same year Manitowoc exported on those vessels cargos worth a total of $25,965,000. Most exports were wood products: 11,467,154 board-feet of lumber, 76,702,000 shingles, 66,000 barrel staves, 193,000 cedar posts, 120,000 pickets, 13,663 cords of firewood, 9,000 railroad ties, and 60,000 pounds of pearl ash. But besides that there was fish, mostly whitefish netted in the cold, deep, offshore waters and salted and packed in barrels. Nearly all were sent to Chicago, where they sold for about six dollars a barrel, and that year 2,250 of them were shipped there. The cutting of trees prepared a way for the commencement of farming. In fact, many of the logs processed in the village mills were cut and hauled to town by farmers clearing fields. By wartime, however, agriculture still remained in a somewhat underdeveloped state, carried on mostly by German and Bohemian immigrants who still plowed with ox teams among the stumps. Yet by 1859, those farmers were harvesting enough grain to make the grist mill profitable, and although most of what the farms produced was locally consumed, that shipping season Manitowoc exported twenty barrels of wheat flour, along with 3,810 bushels of oats, 1,195 bushels of timothy seed, 992 bushels of potatoes, 4,500 pounds of maple sugar, and 300 pounds of butter.[21]

In 1860 the village, although busy and growing, was still a place with few frills and little color, a settlement of unpainted wooden buildings bleached silver-gray by the sun and rain. Within the settlement the streets ran north and south parallel to the lake and westward back from the shoreline. None was paved. Therefore, during dry spells clouds of dust arose from them, kicked into the air by winds and walkers. When it rained or the snow melted, there was mud, often ankle deep, churned up by the hooves of horses and oxen and the iron-rimmed wheels of the wagons they pulled. Pigs freely roamed about foraging for refuse, rooting in the muck, wallowing among the puddles. But along Eighth Street, which was the main street, boardwalks flanked the shops and offices on either side and there, at least, pedestrians were able to remain above the mire.

The core of the town's culture had been brought out from the Northeast, from upstate New York and New England, by the people who became the village elite and who, naturally, were eager to have Manitowoc be as much like the communities they had left behind as possible. However, during the 1850s there were other people arriving from the Old World with different languages, religions, and cultural values who added some powerful new elements to the cultural mix. In fact, by 1860 a clear majority of the people living in Manitowoc—53 percent of them, in fact—had been born outside the United States. Nearly a third were Germans, the largest number of them coming from the states of Prussia and Mechlenburg and others from Baden, Bavaria, and Saxony. There were also large numbers of Irish, Bohemian, Norwegian, and English immigrants who ended long journeys on the piers at Manitowoc. There they were joined by smaller groups who had left homes in Upper and Lower Canada, France, and Scotland, and various prov-

inces of the Austro-Hungarian Empire. All came to Wisconsin
looking for fresh starts.

Within the village itself, almost all the people from New England and New York settled north of the river. They comprised
about 15 percent of the town's total population of 3,065, but their
influence was greater than their numbers. Among them the British,
Scandinavians, and Canadians mingled, and they made up almost
another 15 percent of the population. All of the bankers, and all
but one of the clergymen, along with most of the lawyers, physicians, substantial merchants, and "gentlemen" lived on the north
side. So too did most of the servants, sailors, tavern keepers,
fishermen, and schooner captains and mates, along with Fred
Randolph, the village's only liquor distiller. But most of the latter
lived close to the waterfront, whereas the "better class" of north-
siders had their homes upon the hill. Also on the north side, but
down along the shore, there was a cluster of crude shanties collectively known as "Irishtown."

On the other side of the river, in the growing neighborhoods to
the south and west, lived most of the Germans and Bohemians, who
made up nearly 38 percent of the entire settlement. Although most
men among them were laborers, lumbermen, and teamsters, a considerable number were highly skilled artisans—carpenters and coo-
pers, blacksmiths, masons, printers, tailors, cobblers, shipwrights,
and seamstresses, along with fewer numbers of tanners, brewers,
cabinet makers, confectioners, apothecaries, and brick, harness,
wheel, and wagon makers. Many had fled regions undergoing in-
dustrialization, where the factory system diminished the demand
for their skills. At the time, Manitowoc was a place of modest
opportunity for such people, a place where they could set up their
own shops and small businesses, and where, as one observer noted,
"no one was very rich nor helplessly poor" and those willing to work
hard could make a decent living. Besides job skills, the community
was fully literate and according to the census information of 1860
almost everyone in town, both male and female, north side and
south, could read and write. Therefore, Manitowoc had risen well
above being that place of "crude uncultivated labors" once found so

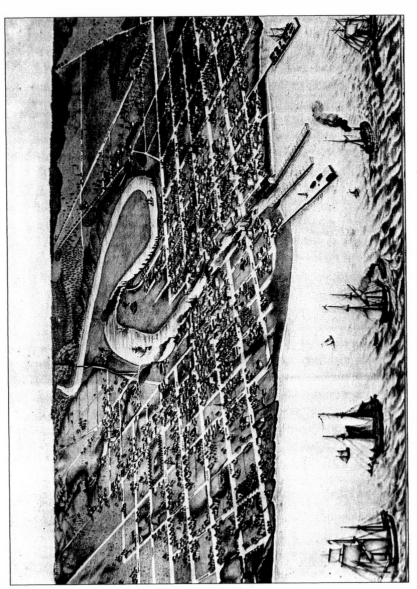

Figure 5. This etching of the village of Manitowoc was made in 1868.

wanting by the likes of Gustaf Unonius, and by the autumn of 1858, one newly arrived settler was delighted to find that most of the people there were "plain, frugal, thrifty, and exceptionally intelligent, representing the best class of immigrants."²²

It was a young community, and not only because its history—what little there was of it—was brief. In 1860, more than half the people living in Manitowoc (53 percent) were under the age of twenty, and the average age of those older than that was just thirty-five. Within that mature population, men and women were fairly evenly represented—779 men and 689 women—which was somewhat unusual for a logging and lumbering settlement so near the frontier. Most of those men and women were married to one another and lived together in modest-sized families. There were, in 1860, 641 married households, 516 of which had children, and the average family size was about five members.²³

Before the Civil War, the village was in fact full of children. It was a good place to raise children and a pleasant one in which to be a child, especially a boy. That was certainly the opinion of G. C. Wellner, who spent most of his own childhood and youth there. For boys, he remarked, "it appeared as if the village were built for their especial delight," and, "in truth," he added, "the boys found everything after their own heart[s]." During the warm summer days, when school was out, they spent much time in the water and on the beach. They fished from the piers and the platform behind the grist mill, as well as down between the logs floating on the river. In late summer they picked berries, sometimes carrying pails and working their way upriver all the way to Manitowoc Rapids. The boys also played in the forest, which, before the war, "even contiguous to the village, was as yet surprisingly untouched by the hand of man," said Wellner. When winter came and winds blew cold and hard from off the lake, they skated on the frozen surface of the river, rode their sleds down the hills on either side of town, and engaged in rousing snowball fights.²⁴

It was indeed a pleasant place, but it was not completely without its dangers and tragedies. In June of 1860, for example, little seven-year-old Erick Erickson drowned while swimming in the lake, and early that same fall Margaret Ripling, then only six, fell into the river and lost her life in its cold and muddy depths. That December, Ellen Ryan burned to death when her family's house caught fire. She was just three. In fact, that year 231 children died in Manitowoc County. Many had only begun to live, and the average age of those who managed to survive their first year but died later in childhood was only four. Nearly half were victims of scarlet fever. Fear of that illness played heavily on parents' minds once the chill of winter was in the air, and it was not until spring that they again ceased worrying about its often-fatal consequences. In between, the fever could become the merciless killer of babies and growing children, particularly among the many families still living in one-room cabins, where it was impossible to isolate the sick. In some cases, like that of the Zahn family, care-worn and exhausted parents sat helplessly by, watching one flushed and delirious child after another convulsively succumb to the sickness. The Zahns, who lived south of the village in the township of Memee, lost six of their children to scarlet fever in 1860. Within the village itself, seventy-six children died that year, thirty-six of them from scarlet fever.[25]

In contrast to the sad plight of the children, only four adults died of scarlet fever in the whole county during that same time. In fact, out of a population of more than twenty-two thousand, only seventy people over the age of fifteen died in 1860, and just nine of them were residents of the village itself. The leading causes of adult deaths were tuberculosis (twenty cases) and childbirth (eleven cases)—in fact, a full one-third of all female fatalities were the consequences of their efforts to bring new human beings into the world.[26]

The general youthfulness of the adult population must have, to a considerable degree, accounted for those remarkably low mortality rates. Good water, simple but wholesome food, and plenty of exercise must have also contributed to the healthful conditions that prevailed throughout the region. However, the deaths that did occur may suggest, or even reveal, something about other aspects of life in mid–nineteenth century Manitowoc County.

For example, in February of 1860, fifty-nine-year-old Hannah Packard was shot and killed by her son-in-law John Gage. Gage,

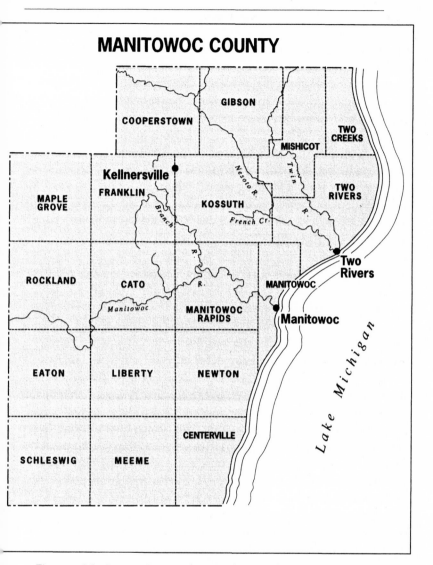

Figure 6. Manitowoc County, showing the townships into which it was subdivided. (Map by Paula Robbins)

who lived in the western part of the county, in Eaton Township, had been involved in a very heated argument with his wife, who, finally unwilling to tolerate any more verbal abuse, left with the children and went to her mother's place nearby. In time, Gage went after her, and on reaching Packard's he pounded violently on the door and demanded to see the children. His terrified wife refused to come out, refused to allow the children to see their father, and so Gage persisted with his angry demonstration. Eventually, Mrs. Packard lost her patience and threw the contents of her chamber pot and a kettle of boiling water on him. That only increased his rage, and rather than going away, Gage retaliated by firing his rifle through the door. The shot struck Mrs. Packard in the left breast, killing her instantly. Gage himself was then hit in the neck by a shotgun blast fired at him from close range by his own wife. Although he managed to pull himself together and flee the scene of the battle, John Gage was later arrested in Calumet County.

In March that same year in Kossuth Township, Catherine Shenfeldt, a fifteen-year-old Bohemian immigrant girl, thought to have become depressed over the long dreary winter and the unending drudgery of farm life, hanged herself from a tree. At about that same time, the *Manitowoc Pilot* reported that an unnamed Bohemian farmer, also in that same area, was killed by a pig "while laying out of doors in a state of intoxication." Israel Ruige, a twenty-year-old Canadian fisherman living in Two Rivers, froze to death in his boat that April. In June, John Rose, a young English lumberman, was caught and crushed to death in the machinery of the Manitowoc sawmill where he worked. Also, that winter, Jemima Reynolds, who had migrated to Mishicot from New Jersey, died of convulsions brought on by eating opium. It was also recorded that in early summer, Ena Halverson, a Norwegian woman living in Manitowoc, quietly passed away in her bed from "old age." That was then still something of a rare occurrence.[27]

Much of the community's life went on in isolation from the rest of the country. The lake, although it connected the village to the bigger world beyond, was a natural barrier, especially in the winter when the ships remained moored in port. Also there was, as Wellner said, "the endless line of forest, north and south, shadowy and mysterious," which nearly surrounded the village with an "overpowering solitude." The roads inland, such as they were, were often impassible and no telegraph or railroad lines connected the community to the outer world until after the war. Even the mail was expensive and irregular.[28]

All that forced confinement did not necessarily contribute to an atmosphere of tolerance and social harmony within the settlement. In fact, it often fostered conditions and moods in which many of the ordinary frictions and irritations of life and ethnic and class differences seemed only more exaggerated. Gustaf Unonius observed just that early on in the town's development and remarked: "Between the people of the two sides of the river there is a spirit of strife and jealousy. . . . Each wanting to make his side the principle and most trafficked part of the new community. From this cause there arose parties and disagreements which resulted, among other things, in a problem communicating between one part of the town and the other." "It was," he concluded, "one of the meanest little rivalries, and it was encouraged mainly by the big landowners on either side of the river."[29]

That internal enmity led, in 1853, to a great row between the north and south sides over where the new courthouse ought to be built, and that same year the non–English-speaking residents also raised angry demands that the county publish all its official business in German, Norwegian, and French, as well as in English. In both cases ethnicity played an important role, but it was not the whole story. In addition to those divisions there were conflicting value systems, which made cultural differences more antagonistic.[30]

In the 1840s, when author Margaret Fuller toured the lakes, she observed that the people on the boats heading west "were almost all New Englanders, seeking their fortunes," and carrying with them, she said, "their habits of calculation, their cautious manners, [and] their love of polemics." They were an industrious, serious, and emotionally tight people determined to rise in the world while, at the same time, bringing order to the wild country into which they moved, and were inclined to be self-righteous about those intentions. They came believing in the power of hard work, education, and the capitalist market system, and with the stern conviction that self-improvement and improvement of the land could never be achieved without severely restraining and repressing one's passions and appetites. Theirs was an orderly and productive view of life, and in time those Yankees, along with their close cultural cousins from upstate New York, were reinforced and reassured about the rightness of their views by the pietistic Protestants who joined them from England, Scotland, Norway, Upper Canada, and some of the German states.[31]

Although they felt certain about this new errand into the wilderness, they were soon challenged by those who migrated into the western Great Lakes region from the more traditional and communal Old World societies in which there was a more easygoing, less emotionally repressed approach to living. Immigrants from Catholic folk cultures, such as those from Ireland, French Canada, and many of the German provinces were, in contrast to the settlers from the northeastern states, inclined to be somewhat less zealous in their pursuit of worldly success and individual self-improvement. Furthermore, their cultural traditions permitted and, indeed, encouraged a joyful and even passionate communal celebration of life's special occasions. That was plainly observed by Fredrika Bremer, a Swedish writer who visited eastern Wisconsin in the autumn of 1850 and while in Milwaukee noted: "The Germans in the Western States seem, for the most, to band together in a clanlike manner, to live together, and amuse themselves as in their fatherland. Their music and dances, and other popular pleasures, distinguish them from the Anglo-American people, who, particularly in the West, have no other pleasure than 'business.'"[32]

Both ways of living and looking at life were present within Manitowoc during the decade preceding the war, and as the village grew they became sources of increasing internal tension and stress. Also, due to the patterns of settlement within the community, the river became a clear line of demarcation between the contrasting worldviews. The differences encouraged conflict, and the differences found expression in the intensely partisan character of local politics, which, in turn, made elections occasions of considerable discord. For a while the Democrats dominated the scene. They decisively carried the county for Franklin Pierce in 1852. By 1856, however, the Democrats' hold on power began to slip. Immigrants were arriving in ever-increasing numbers and the Republican party, which gave clear and forceful expression to the Yankee middle-class worldview, had been formed. The Republicans, led locally by Ben Jones and Perry Smith, gathered considerable support from native-born, British, and German Protestant voters, and although James Buchanan still managed to win in Manitowoc County with 1,907 votes, John Frémont made a very strong showing with 1,177. The next time around, the Republicans won. They campaigned hard in 1860, using every occasion to push their cause. During that year's Fourth of July festivities, for example, two companies of firemen, escorted by a brass band, marched down Eighth Street and stopped in front of the Williams House Hotel, where they "let out some grand hurrahing for Lincoln." That September, Carl Schurz, "the great republican speaker," as Rosa called him, came to town to campaign for Lincoln and other party candidates. He stayed at the Williams House and addressed some large and enthusiastic crowds. In the election itself, Abraham Lincoln carried Wisconsin by twenty-two thousand votes more than his three opponents, and in Manitowoc County he edged out Stephen Douglas by 2,041 votes to 1,947. In the village itself his victory was much more decisive, winning there by a margin of 480 votes to 221.[33]

As the partisan competition had intensified, so too had the rhetoric, and no one in town was more vehement in that regard than Jeremiah Crowley, the Irish Catholic Democratic editor of the *Manitowoc Pilot*. His political passions were often vented in vicious editorial outbursts, and he commonly referred to the Republicans as "fanatics and abolitionists." Above all others, his favorite Republican target on the local scene was Sewall W. Smith, the Protestant editor of the *Manitowoc Tribune*. Smith, a nativistic New Yorker and a veteran of the Mexican-American War, was the quintessential secular Puritan—proper, responsible, and hard-working, as well as haughty, humorless, and intolerant—and Crowley characterized his newspaper as an "outlet of vanity, envy, hatred and malice." He also declared that the local Republican party was "dictated [to] and controlled by one or two gentlemen living on the North Side of the river," suggesting that it was a tool of the local elite and an instrument of class domination. But Crowley's contempt was not reserved for Republicans alone. He also came to despise fellow Democrat Charles Fitch, originally from New Jersey and editor of the *Manitowoc Herald.* In the 1860 election, Fitch came out in support of John C. Breckinridge. Crowley was a Douglas man and accused Fitch of being anti-Catholic and anti-Irish and of taking the position he did in a deliberate attempt to "create schism and prejudice in the Democratic Party on the grounds of nationality." When Lincoln carried the village, Crowley blamed it mostly on Fitch and his "clique," who, he declared, were primarily responsible for "the internal dissention which prevailed" among the Democrats.[34]

After the election, when a national crisis was precipitated by the secession of the Southern states, Crowley held Lincoln and the Republicans fully at fault. They were, he said, all fanatical adherents to "Black Republicanism and Know-Nothingism," and were, in fact, more interested in "plunder than principles." Furthermore, he was convinced that the intersectional troubles would never pass away until the "fanatics and abolitionists of the Northern States retracted the wrongs committed upon the people of the South." Crowley was in sympathy with the Southerners, but felt certain that the Republicans were too arrogant and ignorant to initiate the kind of actions necessary for resolving the conflict. Therefore, he assumed the nation would soon break in two, but hoped that when it did, the rupture would not result in violence. "We pray that not a drop of our nation's blood may be spilt in civil war. If the worst comes, let it be a peaceful dissolution," he wrote in the spring of 1861.[35]

Most villagers did not agree with Jeremiah Crowley on that. Although they too wished to avoid bloodshed, they shared neither his sympathy for the South nor his conviction that Lincoln and the Republicans were entirely to blame for the crisis. They waited in suspense, hoping cooler heads would prevail, but when Southern guns fired on Fort Sumter, they seemed relieved, even glad. Their time of tense anticipation and fearful wondering was at an end, and they finally knew that civil war was a certainty. Nevertheless, Crowley continued to stubbornly persist in the opinion that the political dispute need not be transformed into an armed conflict. Even during the emotionally charged public meeting in the courthouse the night of April 18, Crowley rose and took exception to "the rash and impolite language" used in the anti-South resolutions being passed. At one point in that meeting, when a speaker called Jefferson Davis "a double dyed traitor," Crowley jumped to his feet and shouted back: "He is not. He is the bravest man that ever lived!" But before he could say more, "his voice was drowned in a perfect torrent of groans, hisses, and yells," reported the *Tribune*. That night the people of the village made their sentiments unmistakably clear and by so doing must have caused even Jeremiah Crowley to reconsider his position, for the very next day, to the surprise of many, he announced in his paper that "men and means must be furnished, and the government sustained at ALL HAZARDS."[36]

A short time later, in the April 22 edition of the *Tribune*, Sewall Smith observed with considerable satisfaction that "the feeling of opposition to the traitors is shared by almost everyone." He declared: "A greater revolution in public sentiments has never been seen any where, than has taken place within the last three days." Everyone, it seemed, was rallying to the Union cause, as even young James Anderson remarked in his diary: "The cloud at last burst," he wrote, "and the storm came with all its fury . . . [and] all partisan feelings were crushed for the time and all classes quit their business and rushed to arms."[37]

CHAPTER 2

Rites of Passage

Squads gather everywhere by common consent and arm,
The new recruits, even boys, the old men show them how
    to wear their accoutrements, they buckle the straps
    carefully,
Outdoor arming, indoor arming, the flash of the
    musket-barrels,
The white tents cluster in camps, the arm'd sentries
    around, the sunrise cannon and again at sunset
Arm'd regiments arrive every day, pass through the city,
    and embark from the wharves,
How good they look as they tramp down to the river,
    sweaty, with their guns on their shoulders!
        —Walt Whitman, "First O Songs for a Prelude"

*T*HE PAST WEEK has been one of uninterrupted excitement, produced by the thousands of rumors furnished by the dispatches
from all the scene of actual and expected hostility," wrote Charles
Fitch in the *Manitowoc Herald* on the second day of May 1861.
Since first hearing of the outbreak of fighting, the people of the
village had been preoccupied with the subject of war. A series of
boisterous meetings were held at the courthouse in the evenings,
and during the days, observed James Anderson, "nearly all labor
was suspended [as] men gathered on street corners to discuss the
situation." At times it seemed that people became emotionally
carried away with the whole business, and even Sewall Smith, who

Figure 7. Private James S. Anderson of Company A, Fifth Wisconsin Volunteers, as he appeared while at Camp Randall in the early summer of 1861. (Courtesy of The Manitowoc County Historical Society)

was himself caught up in the excitement of the developments, noted: "The feeling is too intense and it is continually heightened by the news which is arriving from the South."[1]

People were eager to find out anything about what was happening, and each wished to be among the very first to learn any news that they could then pass on to others. Events and rumors of events seemed to carry equal weight, contributing to a rising tide of emotion and an outpouring of self-righteous rage. Citizens condemned the Southerners for bringing about the "dissolution and tearing into fragments of the best government on the earth," and the tone of their declarations became ever more fierce and strident. Fitch's editorials reflected the mood. He called for harsh reprisals against the Rebels: "The time for conciliation has passed. The time for submission and endurance is gone and the hour of resistance, united and vigorous, is upon us." He particularly called on the youth of the town to rise up and "avenge the BLOOD" of the brave men who had already fallen at Fort Sumter. Indeed, Fitch became somewhat obsessed with the war, denouncing secession as "a heresy that must be drowned in blood" and proclaiming that the broken nation would require "the sacrifice of fraternal blood to restore it to its primitive strength and grandeur."[2]

Out of that same mood there arose images of the South as a crude and cruel region inhabited by a dangerous and depraved people. Smith did much to create and embellish that imagery, asserting that Southern society had displayed "a growing tendency to lapse back into barbarism." It was, he said, a society unlike that of the North, for in those hot and lazy regions there were few schools and almost no respect for learning, and there, he added, "the masses are growing up in ignorance and vice." As a consequence, unruly men resorted to "violence and bloodshed, rather than calm discussion and courts of justice to settle their disputes and difficulties." In fact, concluded Smith, "all classes are impatient of restraint and indulge in a reckless and lawless disregard and contempt of all institutions of society or religion which obstruct the free exercise of their passions and their prejudices."[3]

According to Smith's picture, Southerners were destitute of nearly all the strengths and virtues most admired by the age, especially by those who adhered to the worldview brought west from New England in which order was equated with virtue and emotional repression with respectability. Thus, the people of the South were a people of bad, even evil character, devoid of self-discipline and emotional restraint. To Smith and his readers it seemed apparent that passions, impulses, and appetites had free rein throughout that lower section of the country, and that spring people like Smith became increasingly worried about the expansion of the rebellion and the northward spread of the South's moral contagion. Decadence and disorder could advance and increase, dissolving decency and destroying the very institutional structures necessary for the survival of a proper, civilized way of life. "The combined malignity, depravity, and cruelty of all the fiends of the infernal regions seem to have become centered in the Southern mind," declared Smith. "The rebels," he continued, "have boldly thrown off all claims of humanity, Christianity, and civilization and now stand before the world in the garb of cowardly and brutal murderers, thieves, and outlaws who seek by intimidation to accomplish what they have not courage to attempt otherwise." Sewall Smith loudly led the call for the men of Manitowoc to rise up and march forth to destroy those evil traitors who threatened "to deluge the land with blood."[4]

This image of the South allowed villagers to think well of themselves. The coming of the war gave them an outlet for the venting of repressed emotions as well as the redirecting of hostilities that had accumulated within the community itself.

But besides all that, as Jeremiah Crowley pointed out, the war was also seen to be "a glorious opportunity for . . . young men to distinguish themselves" by demonstrating how strong and courageous they were in taking up arms against their nation's enemies. In the meetings held in the courthouse, all of which took on the characteristics of religious revivals, men attempted to do just that by jumping up to confess their devotion to the Constitution and proclaim their willingness to become martyrs for the preservation of the Union. And many rushed forward to add their names to the lengthening lists of volunteers. At one such meeting, fifteen-year-old Martin Adams, a teller at the Lake Shore Bank who was visibly moved by a warm rush of patriotism, rose and denounced the "blood thirsty traitors" and then went on to inform his attentive listeners of his own brave intentions. "I do not court death," he said, "but I do feel as if to die in vindication of my whole country's honor, it would be a glorious death." Then, although only a frail boy, young Adams joined the company and by so doing must have made it extremely difficult thereafter for other lads, especially the older, more physically rugged ones, to hold back when urged to enlist.[5]

By the end of the first week of May, ninety-six men had volunteered to serve in the Manitowoc County Guards. Those who then signed on were among the very first of the nearly two and a half thousand men and boys who eventually left the county to participate in the war. Temple Clark described the outfit as being "made up [of] the pick from . . . the sturdy, rugged, daring lumber[men] of the region." Their average age was twenty-three, but twenty-eight of them, including Anderson, were still in their teens. Sixteen were only eighteen years old, ten just nineteen, and Martin Adams and Monroe Matthews were the youngest of the lot at only fifteen. On the other hand, fourteen members of the company were over age thirty, half of them exceeding thirty-five years of age. John Cochems, a forty-four-year-old farmer and the company's senior member, was also a married man with a family. Most other company members were not married. In fact, seventy-four of them were still bachelors. John Cochems was also exceptional in that, at the height of five feet, eleven inches, he was one of the tallest men in the ranks. Three others—Frederick Borcherdt, Charles Davis, and Julius Jackson—were just as tall, and James Anderson measured in at a lanky five feet, ten and three-quarters inches. But the average height was five feet, six inches, with Patrick McCawley and Theodore Rudiger being the shortest, each at a diminutive five feet even. Most of the men were farmers, laborers, and lumbermen, although a good many of the younger volunteers, having just left school, listed no occupations. Joseph Allen was a sailor, Fred Borchert a store clerk, James Leonard taught school, Perry Stewart was a blacksmith, and Theodore Rudiger made whiskey. There was also a bank teller, a boatman, and a tin smith, along with some carpenters, teamsters, and fishermen. Furthermore, the company, like the community itself, reflected a good deal of ethnic diversity. Native-born Americans and Germans had the largest representations, and by the time the company left town, it consisted of forty-two "Americans" and thirty-four Germans, along with eight Irishmen, seven Bohemians, four French Canadians, four Englishmen, three Norwegians, two Scots, and a Dutchman. Also, there were six pairs of men with the same last names. Some, like Joseph and William Cox and Arnold and Thomas Wagener, were brothers. But whether related or not, most members of the company knew one another well. They had grown up and gone to school together, played and argued and worked with one another, courted one another's sisters, and lived together in the tight confines of the small and isolated village. Thus, even before they experienced the bonding effects of battle, there already existed among them some strong feeling of common identity and comradeship.[6]

Their reasons for joining up were not all clearly articulated, and many of the volunteers may have been only vaguely conscious of their own motivations. Most enlisted while the community was still swept up in a mood of intense patriotic fervor. In fact, nearly half had gone forward and volunteered during a particularly emotional meeting the night of April 20. For some, the high value placed on the Constitution and the Union, if only imperfectly understood, was a factor. "Shall the Government, inaugurated by the revered Washington, the honored Franklin, the illustrious Jefferson and Monroe . . . be broken up by the ruthless hands of traitors, and our glorious institutions, the terror of tyrants and the hope of the oppressed, be torn down?" asked Smith. The first volunteers answered with their actions and saw themselves as the defenders of the revolutionary legacy. That association may have been especially important to those who had been born outside the United States, for they may have seen enlistment as a means of dispelling any lingering doubts about their allegiance to their adopted country. Perhaps they believed that participation in the war would win for them full acceptance as first-class American citizens. They were encouraged to think so, and such recognition was implied in Smith's comments when he singled out the Germans for special praise, saying that the example of "the ardor of their patriotism" ought to "shame those of native birth."[7]

Even more fundamental than patriotism, and undoubtedly much more on the minds of the boys who eagerly volunteered, was the question of manliness. War always brings gender issues and insecurities to the surface, invariably draws sharp and oversimplified distinctions between the masculine and feminine spheres and qualities of life, and the call to arms, which is essentially an "invitation to maleness," employs a rhetoric that consistently describes maleness in terms of physical power and violence. In the late spring of 1861, in places like Manitowoc, that ideal of true maleness was contrasted not only with the softer, weaker, more timid and emotional qualities associated with womanishness but also with the hedonism, decadence, and debauchery so abhorrent to a stoic middle-class morality. Appeals to patriotism and moral decency were combined in ways that played upon the insecurities and anxieties of boys and young men who wished to avoid, even at the risk of their lives, having anyone think them effeminate. Many must have seen the chance to serve in the army as an opportunity to demonstrate to everyone, and most especially the women in their lives, their courage and virility and that, they must have hoped, would end all doubts, including self-doubts, about their masculinity.[8]

There must have also been a wish to simply escape the routines and responsibilities of life and labor in backwoods Wisconsin and to experience the high adventure the war appeared to promise. Then too there was the matter of money. In the spring of 1861, privates were being offered thirteen dollars a month, with five dollars extra if they had families, and, in addition to that, there were prospects of free land grants when the fighting was finished. That clearly influenced young Anderson's decision. His family was poor. His army pay would help support his parents and sisters, and whatever he could save he saw as a vitally important "grub stake" to be carefully invested in land and education so he might escape their poverty and instead rise in the world.

Whatever factors and feelings influenced them, the effects were immediate and the company filled up quickly. During the first week in May they all met in Klingholz Hall, on the south side near the courthouse, where, in the tradition of the colonial militia, they elected their company officers. Temple Clark, a thirty-four-year-old attorney from the north side of town, was their unanimous choice for captain. Clark had moved west from New York state in the mid-1850s and had settled in Manitowoc, where, almost immediately, he became a leader of the local Democratic party. Known simply as "Temp" to most people, he was a popular, good-looking young man with a thick dark beard and a reputation for being a

Figure 8. Temple Clark was the first captain of the "Manitowoc County Guards," which became Company A of the Fifth Wisconsin Volunteers. Clark was elected captain by the men in the ranks. (Courtesy of the U.S. Army Military History Institute)

fair-minded lawyer and politician. He was so well thought of that, in 1856, he was elected to the state senate. There was no question about his character or leadership ability, and besides that, he had once worked as a sutler's clerk at an army post and that made him the most experienced "military" man in the company.

Joseph Rankin, also a north-side Democrat, was elected first lieutenant. However, a personal disagreement developed between him and Clark, and Rankin soon after resigned. Horace Walker took his place. Peter Scherfins, a twenty-three-year-old south-side German, was named second lieutenant in what appears to have been an effort to provide some ethnic balance to the company's command.[9]

Company members from outside the village were given free room and board in private homes and local inns. Some were billeted at Rosa's Williams House Hotel. Also, many "prominent citizens, with commendable liberality raised a large sum to support the families of those who go to protect the country," reported Crowley. Preparing for war was an endeavor in which the whole community participated, and villagers approached it as if they were assembling an athletic team that would go off to compete on their behalf. Even though there was plenty of talk about blood and sacrifice, most of it was metaphorical. The boys too, in those late spring days, only played at soldiering. Without weapons or uniforms, they met and drilled each afternoon in a hilltop park north of the river. Large crowds of spectators gathered after work to watch them strut and wheel upon the grass. Everyone thought them a fine outfit, and on one occasion, after observing them drill, Jeremiah Crowley declared with obvious pride: "Our hardy sons of toil who are compelled to work in the shops, fields, and forests to gain a subsistence for themselves and their families will make the best of soldiers."[10]

While the company marched and drilled, the village women set about making a special flag. A committee was formed. A collection was taken up. Then, in mid-May a delegation of ladies traveled by steamboat to Chicago to purchase suitable materials. There they had no trouble finding red and blue silk, but after frantically searching the city for almost a week, they returned home without any white silk. When news of their plight became known in the village, as Anderson later recalled, "a young woman who expected soon to be a bride, brought out the white silk purchased for her bridal garment and laid it upon the altar of patriotism." It was that cloth that was sewn into the flag the women gave the company.[11]

Spring comes late to the lakeshore, and sometimes it seems as if the warmth will never return. But then, in late May, it is suddenly there. The winds off the lake change, the slant of light is different, and the leaves and lilacs finally break forth. So it was in the spring of 1861, and as the fresh green days lengthened and grew increasingly more pleasant, the boys began to take on more and more the appearance of soldiers.

Monday, June 17, was an especially fine, sun-drenched day. The company, as usual, was drilling in the park, and, at about four in the afternoon, a group of well-dressed women appeared and moved out across the grass toward the troops. Captain Clark, on seeing them, drew his men up smartly into two long rows, each facing the other, as several hundred people looked on.

Mrs. Gideon Collins, wife of the village president, stepped out from the group and presented the flag to Clark. The banner was impressive. It resembled the Union flag, having seven horizontal red stripes separated by white ones and a dark blue rectangle in the upper-left corner. Within that rectangle there was a circle of thirty-four white stars and inside the circle was a golden eagle with widespread wings. Among the horizontal stripes, above the fourth and fifth red ones, in gold lettering, were the words MANITOWOC COUNTY WISCONSIN VOLUNTEERS.

Once Captain Clark had the flag, Mrs. Collins delivered a stirring speech. She referred to the company as "a gallant band of . . . self-denying men" willing to "buckle on their armor" and "go forth to battle for the right." The flag, she told them, was "a gift of willing hearts," and she urged the brave boys to "stand by it" amidst the "smoke and din of battle," and then, when the conflict had been won, to turn homeward with it "laden with honor."[12]

When she concluded, observed Crowley, there were many people with tears in their eyes, especially after all members of the company pledged themselves to protect the flag with their lives. Once the ceremony was complete, the village band struck up a march and everyone there—the company, the women, and all the spectators—paraded out of the park, down the hill, across the river and back, with the flag flapping above them.[13]

All of that, from the sewing of the bride's wedding dress into the flag to the melodramatic metaphors of Mrs. Collins's speech, contributed to the sense of drama in which this otherwise unassuming little village had become immersed. It also was all part of the rites of passage through which the boys began to take on their new roles and identities. Through the words and symbols and ceremonies they were made to feel, made to seem, like young knights-errant about to venture forth on some heroic crusade in which they, like characters in some Sir Walter Scott tale, would battle evil and restore proper order and moral decency to a confused and corrupted world. Such chivalric illusions disguised the brutality of war, glorified the willingness of men to sacrifice themselves for what might only momentarily be thought a noble cause, and sentimentalized the mass destruction of human life for the sake of vague and emotional ideals. But the symbols and rituals contained and exerted great power, a power derived from deeply rooted and shared myths through which the people perceived the world. The flag was such a symbol. It possessed a power, representing as it did a highly idealized sense of community that was, at best, only imperfectly realized during normal times. It stood for what they wished they were, and it was to serve as a tangible bond between those who marched away and those who remained at home. Therefore, as the band played and the flag fluttered in the fresh spring breeze, everyone there felt powerful emotions rising up from some unconscious inner core, from some shared collective cultural vision, and they all began to see themselves in a different light.[14]

After that the company was more eager than ever for action. Since shortly after volunteering they had been growing increasingly worried that the war might end before they ever had a chance "to show their valor and skill," and Temple Clark had gone to Madison to used his political influence in an attempt to avert such an inglorious fate. According to Fitch, Captain Clark had implored

Figure 9. The *Comet* was the Goodrich Steamship Company's vessel that took the volunteers from Manitowoc off to war and sometimes home again. (Courtesy of Wisconsin Maritime Museum, Manitowoc)

the governor, "almost with tears in his eyes," to call the lads up to active duty. The call came soon enough, and within less than a week of the flag presentation, the Manitowoc County Guards were ordered to report to Camp Randall. There, they were told, they would make their final preparations for war.[15]

The company left Manitowoc amidst the deepening twilight of Sunday, June 23, and without a doubt it was the biggest, most dramatic event in the village's brief history. Rosa was, as usual, at work in the hotel. She saw the boys as they passed by on their way from Dusold's Hall to the north pier. "I sat before the open window as they were marching to the boat, preceded by a band of music, [and] I thought of the friends and loved ones they left behind [and] I felt sadder than usual [for] a few minutes after they were passed," she wrote. That was just after six o'clock. About half an hour later the company began boarding the Goodrich Company's steamship *Comet.* "The scene on the pier just before the boat shoved off would have melted a heart of stone," Anderson wrote in his journal. "The people of the County were assembled by the thousands and the shore of old Lake Michigan, for a long distance, was a dense mass of human beings." For most, it was a time mixed with both sadness and pride. "Wives wept over husbands, mothers blessed their sons and [while] weeping told them to do their duty to their God and Country, sisters hung over brothers as though they could not let them go, [and] fathers and brothers, though far less demonstrative in their grief, felt deeply the sad passing; . . . [and] it was to many the last farewell," Anderson observed.[16]

Among those on the pier bidding goodbye to friends was a girl who worked for Rosa and who, Rosa said, was "desperately in love with Ezekiel Emerson," a thirty-year-old store clerk who also had worked at the Williams House Hotel. At first, he had resisted the call, and he did not join the company until the middle of May. When his sweetheart learned "he had enlisted, she wept night and day," noted Rosa. On the evening of Emerson's departure, Rosa let the girl off early so she could go to the ship to see him off. Later that evening, according to Rosa, when the girl returned to the hotel, she tearfully declared: "I went to the pier. He was already on the boat. He noticed me. I went to him. He pressed my hands and kissed my cheeks and now I am contented."[17]

As the lines were cast off and the huge side wheels of the *Comet* began to turn and thrash the cold dark waters, there was, recalled Anderson, "a great shout, which echoed and repeated from the pier to the bluff." It was an unforgettable sound that carried across the surface of the water through the fading light. "Good Bye: God Bless you boys! Good luck to you! mingled with the German, Aude! Aude! Auf Wiedersehn! Leberwohl! We were all somewhat saddened by the parting scene through which we had passed."[18]

The sorrows of the moment soon gave way, however, to spirited singing as their ship moved out into the lake and turned slowly southward with the village slipping away behind them into the shadows.

> Oh fare-you-well, my own Mary-Ann
> And its fare-you-well for a while,
> For the ship is ready and the wind blows free
> And I am bound for sea, Mary-Ann

Their voices rose above the sound of the engine, and the *Comet*
pushed on beneath its plume of black smoke past Silver Creek and
around South Point.[19]

The boys were in high spirits and became even more so when
they pulled into Sheboygan. There "quite a little crowd" had gathered to cheer them on their way. After a brief stop, they floated on
through cool darkness, reaching Milwaukee around 3:30 in the
morning. When their ship pulled up beside the pier and gasped to
a stop, they were still wide awake, playing musical instruments and
singing. Once off the boat they quickly left the waterfront area,
marching through the still dark streets to the Cross Keys Hotel,
where they were fed breakfast. From there they moved on to the
railroad station and at nine o'clock boarded a westbound train for
Madison. That trip, probably the first train ride for many, was a
jubilant excursion. "We were cheered all along our route at every
station that we passed," Anderson wrote home. They reached Camp
Randall by three that afternoon, and although it had been less than
twenty-four hours since their departure from the Manitowoc pier,
home must already have seemed a far away place.[20]

By the time they entered camp the afternoon of June 24, other
volunteers were arriving from all over Wisconsin, from the lumber
camps and sawmill towns of the north, the lead mining region of
the southwest, and from the grain farms, shops, and factories of
the southeastern corner of the state. Madison was then a modest-
sized city of dirt streets with a population of about seven thousand.
Most of its inhabitants lived around and on the hill, where the
white-domed capitol building stood, and along the isthmus between Lakes Mendota and Monona. Before the war was finished,
more than seventy thousand soldiers would march through those
streets, mustering in and undergoing their initial military training
at Camp Randall, which was located about a mile and a half west

of town. It covered the grassy, slightly rolling ten-acre area that had been the Wisconsin Agricultural Society's fairground. Governor Alexander W. Randall, after whom the camp was named, had taken charge of the area and quickly transformed its sheds, barns, and buildings into barracks and its machinery exhibition building into a giant mess hall. However, by the time Anderson and the company from Manitowoc had arrived, all the buildings were full, and so they were housed in large, cone-shaped Sibley tents clustered about the fields. Also, by then there was no longer sufficient bedding for everyone. Most soldiers had been issued old quilts donated by local women, but by late June there were no more of those available. Captain Clark appealed to the people back home to send blankets, and they were swift and generous in response. Furthermore, there were not nearly enough uniforms. All the tailors in Madison had suspended their other work to concentrate on the production of uniforms for the rapidly growing army of volunteers, but even then many new arrivals had to wait before even being able to put on the appearance of being soldiers.[21]

The food was mass produced at a cost of thirty-seven cents a day per man, but Anderson found it better than acceptable. At least in the beginning he thought so. "No pies or cakes or any such fancy fixings but good substantial food and plenty of it," he noted with obvious satisfaction in a letter home. Most of that "good substantial food" consisted of bread, beef, and coffee served up in tin plates and cups in the converted machinery building mess hall.[22]

Between meals they mostly marched, and the Manitowoc boys were good at that. In fact, they were impressive enough to catch the attention of a reporter from the *Madison Journal,* who described them as being "the strong, hardy men from the lumbering districts." At any rate, they soon developed a good opinion of themselves, and John Leykom, a member of the company who was the same age as Anderson, boastfully wrote home: "The Manitowoc Boys are the largest and hardiest on the camp grounds . . . [and] the best drilled company on the grounds." That was an opinion undoubtedly shared by Anderson, but he was somewhat more modest in expressing it, stating simply in one of his letters: "It would not look well for me to say that we are the best company on the grounds but I am willing to take my oath that we are not the worst." The folks at home could easily read through such transparent understatement to understand that the boys were doing them proud at Camp Randall. The boys felt even better about themselves once the uniforms were finally issued. They were dark gray in color and each tunic had a single row of brass buttons down the front. In distributing them the quartermaster made no attempt at matching sizes with soldiers, but the boys themselves traded around for appropriate fits. Before long Anderson was writing home telling people just how dashing they all looked. He was especially pleased with his own appearance and promised to have his picture taken and sent home as soon as he was paid.[23]

By then the Manitowoc County Guards had become Company A of the Fifth Wisconsin Volunteer Infantry Regiment. They were put together with two companies from Milwaukee along with companies from Beaver Dam, Janesville, Waukesha, Berlin, Richland County, and two others known as the North Star Rifles and the Pinery Rifles from the Lake Winnebago and Red Cedar River Valley regions. All were under the command of Colonel Amasa Cobb of Mineral Point, who had resigned his position as speaker of the Wisconsin Assembly to lead the regiment.

Drilling and marching, marching and drilling occupied almost all their time. "We drill about 6 or 8 hours per day," noted Anderson in his journal. At times that might have seemed excessive, but it was indispensable to the process of turning civilians into soldiers and assimilating autonomous individuals into cohesive fighting units. In all of that, Captain Clark, who soon gained a reputation for being a "strict disciplinarian," made every effort to "perfect them in the knowledge of their duties," and, in time, people were coming out from Madison in the evenings to watch them march in full-dress parades to the sounds of fifes and drums.[24]

For a while, Anderson and his comrades seemed to enjoy it all, especially when complimented on how well they marched and how good they looked. For many it was an adventure just being away from home. Living in tents and singing around campfires at night was also fun, at least for a while. But in time the novelty wore thin and the boys began to feel increasingly irritated with more and more of the aspects of army life. They soon grew to hate the thunderous boom of the cannon that awakened them every morning at five o'clock. The drilling, day after day, eventually became monotonous, as did the "good substantial food." As the days merged indistinguishably into one another, "nothing happened to disrupt the monotony of camp life," observed Anderson. At least that was so, he said, "till the fourth of July when . . . the people of Madison were getting up a grand Celebration." All regiments in camp were asked to march in the massive parade planned for that day. But although that promised to be a break from their regular routine, neither Anderson nor the other members of the company seemed thrilled by the opportunity, and the night before that Independence Day he wrote home that the next morning they would begin parading "all over Madison for the benefit of all the clodhoppers."[25]

For the soldiers, the "grand Celebration" was less than grand. The day was unbearably hot, and they tramped and marched, without a break, from nine in the morning until well after two in the afternoon. There had been no rain for weeks, and the dust from the town's dirt streets, kicked up by the pounding and scuffling of hundreds of boots, became overwhelming. "We were marched . . . amid clouds of dust that rose so thick," said Anderson, "that we could not see our hands before us and [it] choked us so we could not get [our] breath and we were not served with anything, not even a cup of cold water." He also noted in his journal that "many fell insensible from exhaustion." John Lykom also reported to the home folks about the many soldiers who, having become sick and exhausted from all the heat, dust, and thirst, had passed out, but he also indicated that all the members of Company A had held up well. Not one of them had collapsed, he said.[26]

But the hardships and indignities of the day did not end at the conclusion of the parade. After that, complained Anderson, "we were marched back to camp like a drove of prize cattle from the fair." Arriving there parched and hungry, they were shocked to discover that their supper would consist entirely of cold, unpalatable "hard bread and stinking beef." They were furious, and for most it was the last straw. The soldiers "commenced throwing the stuff around in all directions," exclaimed Anderson. Just a few days before that they had been served "chunks of strong meat" and there had been a good deal of grumbling about the declining quality of the food. Now they would tolerate no more. "Groans, Hisses, and yells rang through the buildings [and] plates were smashed and whole companies arose and marched from the tables and out of camp," reported Anderson. "Their rage," he said, "knew no bounds," and even "the buildings would soon have been razed to the ground had not Maj. [Charles] Larrabee got up and made us a speech saying he would see that justice was done us."[27]

Major Larrabee, who was from Horicon and had served a term in Congress until 1860, must have been persuasive at least with the Manitowoc boys, for, although they too were enraged by the food and the whole disappointing day, they retired to their tents and did not participate in the riot. There they were gathered together and informed by Captain Clark that he too would intervene on their behalf and that if the food did not improve substantially and immediately, they would all quit the place and return home.[28] Clearly, they were still green troops with something to learn about dust and marching and bad food.

After the Independence Day food riot more troubles befell the camp. As conditions became more crowded, sanitation problems became more severe. Camp Randall was still a makeshift military post and most of the officers were amateurs, appointed more on account of their popularity and political connections than for whatever practical knowledge they might possess about military matters. Most knew very little about the management of large encampments. As the heat of summer increased and the volume of garbage and sewage grew, the threat of epidemics escalated. By the middle of July, Dr. Alfred Castleman, the Fifth Regiment's chief surgeon, noted in his journal with considerable alarm that "measles had broken out in camp, and one-third of the soldiers were suffering from disease of some kind."[29]

Once again, however, the Manitowoc boys held up well. None of them, other than young Bill Cox, came down sick, and even in his case there were some suspicions about just what his ailment was. Cox was just eighteen years old, and most of his comrades were convinced that he was suffering from nothing more severe than a bad case of homesickness. All the rest of them were well and Anderson boasted that they had, in fact, acquired "the Reputation of being the Hardiest company on the Grounds."[30]

People in Madison felt sorry for the soldiers. They wanted to make up for the fiasco the Fourth of July had turned into and so proceeded to plan a "grand dinner" and party for the whole camp. In preparation for that, one member of the company informed Sewall Smith, "the boys . . . trimmed their tents and those of their officers with bushes, and swept the streets in anticipation of the visit." They also arranged white stones in front of the captain's tent to read CAPTAIN CLARK—GOD BLESS HIM. On the day of the "big feed"—Thursday, July 18—a large crowd of perhaps as many as six thousand people walked out from Madison with bands playing, banners waving, and "wagons loaded with substantials." There was a superabundance of good things to eat. Of course, there were speeches. Governor Randall made one and then presented the Fifth and Sixth regiments with their blue-and-gold Wisconsin state flags. After that there was still plenty of time left for singing and talking to the young ladies from town.[31]

Life seemed to pick up after that, and during the third week of July a sense of expectation began to grow throughout the camp. The boys of Company A began to anticipate their imminent departure for the front. They were extremely eager to leave, and their excitement grew especially intense on July 22 when news arrived concerning what, at first, was reported to be a great Federal victory along the banks of Bull Run Creek, in northern Virginia. "Cheer upon cheer rose from the Reg[imen]t and all was in the best of spirits," remarked Anderson. But the celebration proved premature. The good news was soon eclipsed by the shocking details of what had, in fact, been a humiliating defeat. Nevertheless, that disappointment was ameliorated the same day when another telegram arrived ordering the Fifth Wisconsin to report to Washington as soon as possible. They were ecstatic. They would rush to the rescue of the Union cause, so they thought.[32]

That next day they received their first pay, and on Wednesday, July 24, just a little after dawn, they struck their tents and packed their gear. It was a little after one o'clock in the afternoon when they moved out, marching to awaiting railroad cars just a short distance outside the camp. It was an overcast day. There was mist and light rain. But the tracks were lined on either side by hundreds of people from Madison as well as the members of the Sixth Wisconsin, all of whom had turned out to see them off. The crowd cheered as they boarded the train and began to rumble southeastward across the green and rolling Wisconsin countryside.[33]

Along the way, they stopped at Janesville. A large crowd awaited them there with baskets and boxes of good food. After that they sped on to Chicago, arriving there at dusk. Because they had to proceed to another station and board another train, they marched some distance through the streets. People were packed all along both sides of their route. In addition to those on the streets, Anderson observed that "the balconies were crowded with Ladies who waved Flags and handkerchiefs and the Men clapped their hands and cheered like madmen." After Chicago they passed on into the night and then on through a succession of days and nights, towns and villages and cities, through southern Michigan, through Toledo, then Cleveland, and into Pennsylvania. "Our journey through Ohio was a perfect triumph [and] at every little station the people would come on board the cars with baskets of Biscuits, Cakes and cans of hot coffee," noted Anderson with obvious delight. On they went to Pittsburgh, and then through the Appalachian Mountains, finally coming to rest, on July 27, at an army camp at Harrisburg. The boys remained in high spirits the whole way. "The trip throughout," wrote one, "was more like a pleasant excursion than a train of soldiers." But at the Harrisburg camp they found conditions much worse than at Camp Randall, and in disgust Dr. Castleman complained that "the stench of the camp was intolerable and the sickness of the troops rapidly increased."[34]

It was their good fortune to remain there only two days. On July 29, a jolt of excitement surged through the regiment when they were ordered to move out the next day to engage enemy forces at Harpers Ferry. "So great was the excitement," remarked Castleman, "that very few laid down for rest during the night." They were almost euphoric over the prospects of seeing action—violent action—and were so eager to be on their way that they had the tents down and rolled up by 3:00 A.M. They were at the train tracks before dawn, but when the sun rose nothing happened. They waited. Still nothing happened. In fact, it was well into the middle of what turned into a terribly hot afternoon before they even sighted a train making its way slowly toward them through the distorting heat haze that shimmered above the tracks. When it finally paused, hissing out great bursts of steam, they were loaded onto open flat cars and hauled across the Susquehanna River, where, to their astonishment, the train again ground to a halt and they were unloaded for no apparent purpose. There they were marched around without going anywhere until nearly nightfall and then, as dusk closed in, were ordered back on the flat cars and the train puffed off toward York, Pennsylvania, in a cloud of smoke, soot, and cinders. During the day, which Dr. Castleman described as the hottest he had ever endured, there had been a resurgent outbreak of measles among the boys, and that night their conditions became even worse when it turned unseasonably cold. Then it began to rain. Many soldiers, especially the sick ones, shivered almost convulsively as they rushed on through the frigid damp darkness without shelter of any kind. "The suffering men who had been all day washed with their own perspiration, were compelled to sit all night in the rain," lamented Castleman.[35]

They raced on through York without even slowing down, rushing southward and arriving in Baltimore during the morning of August 1. There they were hurriedly marched through the streets to the Washington depot, where they remained for the rest of the day. Finally, after a great deal more stalling and waiting, they were moved out to another camp just north of the city on McKim Hill. It had been another long, hard day for the boys, and Castleman complained in his journal: "The regiment did not get settled till midnight, and many were so exhausted that they threw themselves on the ground, with their clothes still wet from the previous night's rain."[36]

Once they were again dry, rested, and fed there was a chance to look around Baltimore. Anderson was impressed and called it "the handsomest city" he had ever seen, finding its many red brick buildings and shady tree-lined streets especially admirable. But as fine and dignified as things appeared on the surface, Anderson sensed something sinister in the mood of the place and felt, for the first time, that he had entered enemy territory. The day before their own arrival, an angry prosecessionist mob had attacked a New York regiment while it marched in the streets. Anderson himself had witnessed a violent altercation between a local Unionist and another man who took exception with the Unionist's complimentary remarks about the Wisconsin troops. The fight ended when the Northern sympathizer drew his revolver in self-defense and shot the secessionist, killing him instantly. Anderson told his father that the secessionists, of whom he suspected there were many, had better not try to tangle with anyone in his regiment for, although they had not yet been issued weapons by the army, many of the boys had revolvers and bowie knives that they would not hesitate to use if pushed to it. He also informed his folks that he had purchased, for just five dollars, "as handsome a Sharps Revolver as you could wish to see." Although it was secondhand, he knew it worked well and he kept it loaded at all times. Also, he declared, he was "fully determined to use it so as to kill" if the need ever arose.[37]

The talk was tough, but it was still just talk. Their brief stay in Baltimore passed without incident, and on August 7, about ten o'clock at night, they were back on the train heading for Washington, D.C., where they would become part of "the vast city of camps" that sprawled in the parks and fields within and around the embattled capital.[38]

CHAPTER 3

Marching Along and Waiting Around

The army is gathering from near and from far;
The trumpet is sounding the call for the war;
McClellan's our leader, he's gallant and strong;
We'll gird on our armor and be marching along.
—William B. Brandbury, "Marching Along"

SOON AFTER his arrival in Washington, D.C., James Anderson took a tour of the city and acquired a deeper awareness of what it was they had come there to preserve. He visited the Patent Office, an imposing classical-columned building used primarily as an art gallery and museum, and there saw George Washington's uniform and sword. With something of a sense of awe he called them "sacred relics of a great and good man," and wondered just how low some of Washington's "descendants must have degenerated to attempt the overthrow of those principles he labored so long and earnestly to support." From there he walked to the Capitol, where he was allowed into the Senate Chamber. He was impressed by the many paintings and statues as well as the grounds themselves, which he described as being "handsomely laid off and decorated with all sorts of rare flowers and trees." Eventually, he strolled over to the White House and there "got a squint of Old Abe as he sat at a window enjoying the cool breezes that would occasionally float by." Before he finished his tour and returned to his regiment, Anderson took the opportunity to climb to the top of the still-open, unfinished dome of the Capitol from which he looked out on the army camps sprawling across the city. He wrote to his family that "as far as the eye can stretch, rows of white tents could be seen denoting the vast military strength of the nation." He must have felt both insignificant and important by mere association with that immense power. A short time later he wrote home reflecting on the magnitude of the developments in which he was participating: "I will be greatly mistaken if the next 3 weeks do not compass events great in history"—events, he felt certain, that would affect the whole nation for ages to come.[1]

In the hot, humid summer of 1861, Washington was still very much, as one historian put it, a "sprawling and unfulfilled embodiment of a vision of national grandeur." It was an uncomfortable, unfinished, and unhealthy outpost of politicians and government clerks who worked in isolation from the country they attempted to govern. Henry Adams called it a "rude colony" scattered among the trees, swamps, and half-finished Greek temples far up the still nearly wild reaches of the Potomac River, and although there were almost sixty-three thousand people living there at the beginning of the war, it remained a primitive place where pigs rooted in the garbage-strewn gutters of unpaved streets. It was one of the few national capitals to which some European diplomats refused to bring their families. More an untidy collection of hotels, boarding-houses, mansions, shanties, and government buildings than an organized and orderly community, Washington was a place of foul smells, putrid waters, outdoor privies, and the mud, dust, flies, and mosquitos of long, sweaty southern summers. A great many government facilities remained under construction. The Capitol itself was surrounded by scaffolding and piles of stone, and a construction crane poked out through the open top of what would eventually become the dome. The Washington Monument was still only a huge chalky stub, less than one-third completed.[2]

The ugly and untidy qualities of the city were exaggerated by the arrival of the army. Thousands of soldiers poured in as workmen rapidly added warehouses, mule barns, supply buildings, barracks,

Figure 10. James Leonard, a school teacher from the village of Branch in Manitowoc County, was also a member of Company A, Fifth Wisconsin Volunteers. (Courtesy of The State Historical Society of Wisconsin, WHi [X3] 46552)

blacksmith shops, armories, and hospitals to the already existing labyrinth of brick and board structures. The military seemed to take over everything. Soldiers camped in the streets, parks, and vacant lots, and their officers commandeered buildings for offices and quarters. Even the grounds near the Washington Monument were taken over for the construction of a gigantic and grotesque slaughterhouse in which tens of thousands of animals were butchered to feed the expanding army. A near suffocating stench arose from it and blew over the city.

Nevertheless, Washington was a place of great psychological and symbolic significance. James Leonard, also of Company A, experienced much the same heightened sense of historical consciousness while there and, like Anderson, was profoundly impressed with the growing size and apparent power of the army in which he was a soldier. In a letter to his friend Mary Sheldon, he wrote that it was "almost impossible for [even] the greatest coward to be anything but a brave man" in the presence of the city and that mighty armed force. He also told Sheldon of the pride he felt on account of his own part in such a noble cause, a cause, he declared, on which "not only depends to a great extent . . . the happiness . . . of us that live at present, but the future generations throughout the world."[3]

Such feelings were magnified by the charismatic General George B. McClellan, to whom President Lincoln had entrusted the task of transforming the raw recruits and provincial militias into an effective national fighting force. In those early days of the struggle, McClellan was often compared to the young Napoleon, not only because of his diminutive stature but also because he seemed to share so much of the Corsican's brilliance and boldness. When he arrived in the capital that July, he appeared to everyone, with the possible exception of old General Winfield Scott, to be "the very embodiment of the spirit that would win the war." In contrast to Scott, who at age seventy-five was still the official commander of the army, McClellan was young—only thirty-four—dashing, dark, and boiling over with a youthful impatience to get on with crushing the rebellion. He was a majestic figure on horseback, riding with his hand thrust into the unbuttoned slit of his dark blue tunic, his sword dangling at his side, and appearing to possess all the natural greatness and romantic flair of the young Bonaparte. McClellan became an instant hero, and people expected him soon to become the military messiah who would save the nation from self-destruction and lead it into a new golden age. There was talk of him running for president and even suggestions that he be appointed military dictator until the crisis had passed. His own vanity convinced him that he was an unusual man with a special destiny, and in the months following his triumphal entrance upon the national scene he wrote his wife numerous times describing his growing sense of historic importance. "By some strange operation of magic I seem to have become the power of the land," he told her. "I feel that God has placed a great power in my hands." He soon came to have little respect for anyone's ability but his own and, in fact, arrogantly regarded even President Lincoln to be an "idiot" and General Scott a senile old obstacle standing in the way of victory. He was convinced that he, and he alone, could win the war. "The people call upon me to save the country," because, he told Mrs. McClellan, "no one else could save the country."[4]

McClellan's heroic image and his delusions of Napoleonic grandeur reinforced the romantic illusions of war the boys carried with them from home. The young general's supreme self-confidence seemed, indeed, to infuse the Army of the Potomac with a belief in its own invincibility. He took great pleasure in exerting such influence. "You have no idea how the men brighten up now when I go among them," he told his wife. As one historian has pointed out, "McClellan enjoyed the knightly trappings of command more than most, especially the deference directed to him in the pageantry of large reviews." Moved, then, in part by his own colossal ego and the pressing need to integrate thousands of still relatively untrained volunteers into a unified and machinelike force, McClellan himself began to drill the troops day after day, directing their mass motions into spectacular and stirring rituals of power and precision.[5]

It was theater on the grandest scale, and for their parts the members of Company A were issued blue Federal uniforms. That was during the first week of September, and after that Dr. Castleman was especially impressed with their performances. In his journal he described in detail some of the army's dramatic dress parades, and on one such early autumn occasion wrote: "There are about one hundred thousand men in battle array . . . on an immense plain, in squares and columns, marching and counter-marching, charging and retreating," all while drums beat cadence, bugles sounded, and clouds of smoke rose and drifted across the scene from flashing rows of thundering cannons. The pageantry filled the men with an inspiring sense of their own collective power and the greatness of their leader.[6]

Such feelings were enhanced by the deep loyalty and affection most soldiers felt for President Lincoln. He was often on the reviewing stand during their parades and frequently visited the boys in their camps. In early September, Anderson excitedly told his family about one such visit. "He is a fine man," he wrote, "he shook hands with the boys who crowded around him in large numbers and among them was your worthy son." James Leonard also reported on the same visit to Mary Sheldon, telling her that he had personally shaken hands and chatted with the president, and declared: "He was as free with us poor soldier boys as though he was one of us." Similar comments about President Lincoln's personal interest in the lot of the ordinary soldiers were made by Evan Jones, an Englishman from Milwaukee who served in Company B. He pointed out how pleased they always were to see the president, especially when he mingled with them: "We look upon Abraham Lincoln as upon our common father; we knew that he was true to us, and to the cause for which we were then in arms."[7]

These images, of Lincoln as a caring father and McClellan as a heroic warrior leader, made a significant impact on the impressionable boys, and early that fall Leonard summed up the sentiments of many: "With such men in supreme command as McClellan . . . and such a man, at the head of the government to guide the whole, as President Lincoln, I think that none have any reason to doubt as to the result."[8]

There seemed few doubts in the minds of most members of Company A as they broke camp on Kalorama Heights around midnight of September 3, and headed westward into the darkness. Although they had no notion of where they were heading, they felt sure that they were at last on their way to do battle with the Confederates. As they commenced marching, the regimental bands began to play, but soon after the long column got underway, the music stopped and "there was no noise but the dull and heavy tramp of four thousand men, and the occasional clatter of the wheels of the provision wagons and ambulances upon the loose stones of the road," wrote one of Anderson's comrades. They marched on through Georgetown, then on to Chain Bridge. There a sentry told them that troops and heavy guns and wagons had been crossing over all night in what looked to him to be a massive invasion of northern Virginia. The regiment passed over and trudged on until about an hour before dawn. Then, wrote Anderson, "we came to a halt, marched into a field, and lay down on our arms till daybreak with the rain pouring upon us." Eventually, as the gray light increased, they rose from the soaked ground and set about digging trenches and chopping trees.[9]

That day, for the first time, James was put on picket duty. They were in Fairfax County, Virginia, and therefore had to be on their guard. He was sent out some distance from the work details and was to act as a forward lookout to warn of approaching enemy forces. He remained alone at his post all afternoon and throughout the night, as well as for the duration of the following day. No sleeping was permitted. A man could be shot for sleeping on picket duty and that lesson was dramatically driven home to them all just a few days later when a young private from one of the Vermont regiments was sentenced to death for that very offense. "The poor fellow marched out to die with great composure, his face was pale but otherwise he appeared quite resigned," wrote Anderson. But the incident did not turn out as originally expected, because, continued James: "His sentence was read to him and troops drawn up in line to witness the execution when his reprieve was read to him, [and] it looked like passing from death to life to see his countenance change." Not all such lapses of vigilance would have such happy endings.[10]

When Anderson returned from his uneventful watch, he was surprised to see how much had been accomplished on the construction of what was then being called Camp Advance. He also found out that scouting parties were regularly being sent out to keep an eye on the movements of Confederate forces and learned that some scouts were getting "so close to the Grand Army of the Rebels" that they could hear, and even see, what was going on within their camp. "Our scouts are continually having a brush with them," he reported home. Then, on September 10, members of the Fifth Wisconsin saw some of the enemy close up when one such reconnaissance party returned to camp with three Confederate prisoners, along with two horses and two "contrabands," as confiscated slaves were then called. After that, prisoners, as well as "quite a few negroes," were brought in routinely. Also on September 10, President and Mrs. Lincoln visited Camp Advance, and one member of the company proudly reported home: "I shook hands with Abe. He was glad to see us western boys." Later that afternoon the boys were paid for the first time since leaving Wisconsin.[11]

Work on camp fortifications continued through the next week in spite of a constant downpour. The heavy rains made life particularly miserable because the regiment had yet to be issued tents. That was not attended to until September 15. That day Anderson wrote with exasperated relief in his journal: "Received our tents today and pitched them. Ever since we came here we have been without shelter of any kind." Their discomforts were also increased by the presence of marauding enemy bands. Fires from burning buildings and haystacks torched by the Confederates could be seen, and reports from patrols indicated that powerful Southern forces were fast moving toward their position. Those reports appeared to be confirmed when Anderson and some of his buddies captured a Confederate spy who, they said, had "important papers on his person"; and then, on September 24, approaching enemy forces were actually sighted. In response, Company A and some other units of the Fifth Wisconsin were sent out to lure the Rebels back toward Camp Advance, where, under conditions advantageous to the Union troops, they could be engaged in a full-scale battle.[12]

That turned into an exciting and dangerous assignment. As the Wisconsin troops moved forward, Southern artillery batteries opened up on them. Anderson and his comrades hugged the ground as their own cannons answered back. "Their shells came humming over our heads in fine style bursting a short distance from [us] . . . throwing the dirt around us in a lively manner," James joyfully reported home. He also indicated that their own batteries blasted back, some shells hitting Confederate positions, "making them fly in all directions and stretching not a few of them on the ground." It was his first real taste of combat and it all seemed such great fun. Under fire! Doing battle with the enemy at last! And no one in the company was killed or even hurt. Their only disappointment came when the Rebels backed off, thus depriving them of an even grander encounter, and that, in turn, led Anderson to scornfully conclude that the Southerners were "an awful cowardly set" who remained huddled behind "their entrenchments not daring to come out." After waiting a few hours, but failing to entice the enemy into their trap, the Union boys gave up the game and returned to camp.[13]

Just four days later they were out again and on the move, heading deeper into enemy territory. It was a fearful journey, and Anderson wrote: "It was dark when we started and soon [it] increased to a pitchy blackness; such a night I never wish to pass through again." They were not told where they were going, nor did they know what dangers might await them in the shadows of that unfamiliar countryside. By dawn they were again soaked to the skin, this time from wandering about in swamps, and during the morning those discomforts were made worse when temperatures turned bitter cold. By then they were near Falls Church.[14]

About half a mile outside that settlement some of the Company A boys moved in and surrounded a house and captured three Confederate soldiers. While they were so occupied, the main Union force of about twelve thousand soldiers caught up to them and then, to their disappointment, the Fifth Wisconsin was ordered back to camp. About that same time, said Anderson, "a terrible mistake was made." Some of the outfits, still unsure of where they were going or where the enemy was, became confused, and in sudden panic some soldiers in one of their columns—Anderson said it was the First California—fired into the Cameron Dragoons, a rear guard troop of Union cavalry, who, in turn, charged upon their attackers "with fearful effect." "All was confusion and some 40 or 50 was killed and wounded in the melee," wrote Anderson. None of the Manitowoc soldiers were involved—they were "mercifully protected by providence," said Anderson—but they returned to camp with their enthusiasm for battle somewhat diminished.[15] Two days later they abandoned Camp Advance and went into winter quarters in what the army called Camp Griffin, between Prospect Hill and Levinsville, still within Fairfax County, Virginia.

It was a very wet autumn. The boys remained occupied with the drudgery of fort construction, and as October wore on the weather and work caused morale to sag. Anderson wrote home in a dismal mood complaining about their conditions: "We have seen the hardest times the last week that we have seen so far. We would have to [be] out and chop hard all day and then have to be down in the line of battle all night under heavy rain. Besides all this our rations did not reach us regular so that we would be hungry, wet, and tired all at the same time." Furthermore, while out cutting and hauling timber they were sometimes fired upon by well-concealed Southern snipers.[16]

Although Anderson often felt miserable that autumn, he sometimes boasted about how well he was holding up compared to some other members of the company. For example, he thought himself a much better soldier than William Davison. Davison, another of the teenage volunteers from Manitowoc, came to be regarded as a whiner who not only complained about virtually everything but also tried to wiggle his way out of the army by pretending to be sick. Anderson saw through his act: "That Davison boy is not coming home, his principle Disease is laziness and as he does not find a soldier's life such a nice easy life as he supposed." Certain that young Davison was simply trying to fool the doctors into granting him a medical discharge, Anderson was delighted when the medical staff kicked him out of the infirmary and sent him packing back to the soggy, cold camp to do his duty.[17]

On October 14, however, the mood of the entire company changed dramatically when they clashed violently with Confederate forces. That confrontation, although irrelevant to the major developments of the war and therefore never given an official designation, may well have been called the Battle of the Cow Herd. The scene was set on October 13, when Anderson sighted "a drove of fine fat cattle" wandering about loose not far from camp. He reported it to regimental command and the next morning Company A was given the assignment of going out and driving the cows back to Camp Griffin. At first, it was regarded as just another routine task, the kind the army usually gave to rural troops, but as they approached the animals, contentedly grazing in an open field, the Manitowoc boys were startled when enemy soldiers suddenly opened fire on them. "We . . . found the Rebels in force" occupying a nearby hill and farm house, wrote Anderson, who estimated there must have been between one and two hundred of them holding what he judged to be an unassailable position. Captain Clark, who had been out front leading the way, halted his men, and they all quickly took cover in the woods along the fringe of the field. They hit the ground and there quietly but anxiously watched and waited for three or four hours. Eventually, growing exasperated with the inactivity, about ten members of the company volunteered to venture out in a bold attempt to stampede the cattle back into the forest. Anderson was among them. He and Joe Biehlie, who was just eighteen, crept carefully along a rail fence until they "got between the cattle and the Rebels," at which point they leapt out and startled the herd, which took off running furiously toward the trees. Anderson and Biehlie immediately came under heavy enemy fire, but their comrades, still on their bellies in the underbrush, returned fire so that all the boys still in the field were able to retreat to cover. Everyone got safely back into the woods. Then, once the shot stopped flying and the noise died down, thirteen of the cows were rounded up and driven into camp. That afternoon, with what must have been a bolstered sense of self-confidence, Clark and company returned to their battlefield, and after another "brisk skirmish" among the milkweeds and cow pies, they took possession of five more cows and "a fine horse." It was indeed exciting, but it was not all over until the next morning when they again set out, this time to confront the Rebels themselves. Staying clear of the woods, they boldly dashed across the open field to the base of the hill, and there, after another "sharp skirmish of about half an hour [they] drove the enemy clear off." They then ascended the hill and, in a destructive celebration of their victory, set fire to the farm house, hay stack, and granary located there.[18]

Through it all, wrote one of the participants, the boys had shown "perfect coolness," "never hesitating in their forward movement and always taking good aim when firing." They felt they had courageously met and beaten the enemy and in their encounter, claimed Anderson, had killed or at least crippled two or three of them. But more important than that, even though some had "a pretty close shave of it," none had flinched or run away in the face of danger and death. James informed the home folk that he, himself, had been among those who had bravely carried on in spite of nearly coming to a sudden and violent end. "A bullet passed so close to my ear, that it stung me but did not break the skin," he told them. Upon returning to camp, General Winfield Scott Hancock, who was their commander, praised them, calling them "natural skirmishers."[19]

It had been a small action, which, aside from putting some fresh meat on some soldiers' tin plates, had no particular influence on the direction of the war. Yet for the greenhorns from Wisconsin, it was an important step toward becoming soldiers. They were proud of what they had done and how they had done it, and as a result felt more sure of their ability to withstand the heat and pressure of the struggles still to come. They had been so eager to be courageous, so impatient to prove their manhood, that with the capture of the cows and the burning of the farmhouse, they, although still somewhat naïvely, began to assume that they were beginning to measure up. And in fact, they were.

Anderson seemed especially eager to have the hometown people know what they had done and how they had changed, and therefore sent letters north in which he declared: "Manitowoc may well be proud of the first company that she sent to battle for her honor for they have raised her name as high as that of any county in the state." He also sensed that a great battle would soon be fought in northern Virginia, one that would probably decide the outcome of the whole war. "If I should happen to be there," he wrote, "I trust I may not flinch. I have stood fire several times already and have not acted in any way cowardly and may God forbid that I [ever] should."[20]

Although those early skirmishes prepared Anderson and the others for the battles ahead, their easy and painless successes encouraged them to underestimate their enemies and to overestimate their own ability to bring the war to a swift and decisive conclusion. Such notions were reflected, for example, in a letter one member of the company sent to the *Manitowoc Herald* that fall, in which he brashly predicted that the Confederate forces would be "played out in a month," and then almost impudently announced: "You may look for me at home [by] Christmas, for a turkey leg."[21]

The boys were not home for Christmas. In fact, by the onset of winter their struggle had barely begun, and they were incapable of even imagining the trials still to be endured. In the meantime, as they settled into Camp Griffin and prepared to sit out the season, their attentions were absorbed by the day-to-day things they could understand. For weeks on end there was the tedious routine of picket and sentry duty and the monotonous repetition of the drilling to occupy their days. And when hard rains fell and the mud became deep and greasy, there was not even the drilling. Before long, Dr. Castleman grew exasperated with the inactivity and with the army's passive observance "from a safe distance" of enemy forces in the area. They should be fighting, he felt, not idly sitting around, and at one point he sarcastically scrawled in his journal: "[I] wonder if we may not soon expect a consignment of petticoats?"[22]

It seemed, then, to rain all the time. In November, Anderson received a letter from home describing the first blizzard to hit the lakeshore that winter. Immediately he wrote back telling his folks that not a single flake had fallen on Virginia, but instead, "cold chilling rains" had almost unceasingly poured down upon them.

James Leonard also complained about the miserable conditions: "Our tents are getting rather worse for wear, they leak very bad now when it rains, which is very often," he told Mary Sheldon. Then, in December, the rains stopped and conditions at least temporarily improved. It turned unusually warm, even for the upper South. "While you are enjoying so much snow and ice . . . we go around in our shirt-sleeves all day and it is only on guard at night that there is any use for overcoats," gloated Anderson in a letter home. But the balmy temperatures did not last. In early January it began to freeze hard at night, and snow fell, blowing around and through the tent flaps and drifting into ridges throughout the camp. But the cold snap was also brief and soon the rains resumed. The campgrounds were transformed into a quagmire. One member of the regiment complained that the sun was seldom seen anymore and then, in disgust, declared: "There is nothing here to write about but mud. Everything is covered with mud. Men and horses, soldiers and teamsters, tents and wagons, food and raiment are all covered with mud. Horses sink to their knees and the wagons up to their hubs." The boys were trapped inside by the mud, and as the rain continued its unrelenting drumming upon the tents' taut canvas walls, they fought back against the increasingly gloomy mood with whatever sense of humor they could still summon up.[23]

During that first winter of the war, Anderson and the other members of Company A were not the only soldiers from Manitowoc County to endure the frustrations and discontents of camp life. Shortly after their leaving home another infantry company had been formed at the initiative of George Waldo. Waldo was a young attorney originally from Prattsburg, New York, who, according to one villager, was "much respected for his agreeable and gentlemanly qualities." As soon as President Lincoln had called for volunteers, young George had gone off to Milwaukee, where he joined a company that soon after went on to participate in the embarrassing encounter at Manassas Junction that July. Then, in September, after his brief initial term of enlistment expired, Waldo returned to Manitowoc and recruited a whole new company, which elected him its captain. They too drilled in the north-side park, and then left, when their orders arrived, on board the *Comet*. A large number of villagers also turned out to see them off when they departed Manitowoc on November 3. But rather than going to Camp Randall for their training, Waldo and his troops reported to Camp Wood, just outside Fond du Lac.[24]

Almost from the moment they arrived there, and then on throughout December, it poured rain. One member of the company, writing to Charles Fitch of the *Manitowoc Herald,* described the camp as "a low, wet place" and suggested it should be renamed "Camp Mud Hole." Indeed, the water and mud were so deep it was impossible to drill or even walk around, he said, adding, "If it rains much longer, Abe will be obliged to furnish us canoes in order to get around camp." Everyone and everything was soaked. But then, suddenly, in January temperatures plummeted, sometimes going as low as twenty-eight degrees below zero. And the snow began to fall deep and heavy upon the ground. To everyone's surprise it did not last. In early February winter simply vanished and the rainstorms returned. By the end of that month, James Newton, another member of the company, informed his parents that "water stood ankle deep all over the camp."[25]

That early November, as Waldo and his company were just leaving for Camp Wood and Anderson and Company A settled in for the winter at Camp Griffin, eighteen-year-old private Paleman Smalley was slogging through the sodden countryside of Maryland's eastern shore with the Fourth Wisconsin Volunteers. He too was from Manitowoc. His father, E. L. Smalley, who had migrated west from New York state, ran an iron foundry there, near the lake on the north side of the river. Before moving up the lake to Manitowoc, the Smalleys had lived in Sheboygan. That was where Paleman had finished school, and when the war broke out he returned there to serve with his school chums in what became Company C of the Fourth Regiment.[26]

They left Baltimore by steamship around sunset, November 7, crossed Chesapeake Bay, and then churned southward along the jagged shoreline for more than half the bay's length, finally landing at Whitehaven near the mouth of the Wicomico River just after dawn the next day. Throughout the night the Wisconsin boys had slept, or at least lay wrapped in their blankets outside on the ship's windy upper deck, and when they landed in the morning they were fed a fast, unappetizing breakfast of bread and cold, uncooked pork. About the breakfast, Smalley remarked: "It wasn't very palatable but a hungry stomach ain't very fastidious." After that, they were sent marching off to hunt down Rebel forces rumored to be somewhere in Westchester County. They headed southward at a quick pace making for the village of Princess Anne. By the time they arrived they had been marching all day without a break, from early morning until seven o'clock at night, and as their journey had lengthened, Smalley said he had found the "weight of the knapsack and the labor of the march . . . very fatiguing." At Princess Anne the worn-out soldiers simply threw themselves down and "slept in their blankets on the damp ground." But well before sunup their rest was disturbed by a hard rainstorm. The downpour continued throughout the dull overcast day, but rather than seeking shelter, the troops pushed on, believing the Confederates they were after to be close at hand. All day and into the night they marched, soaked through, chilled to the bone, heading eastward with expectations of overtaking their enemies at any time. When they reached the Pocomoke River, they were ordered to ford it, but by then some of the boys could go no farther. Smalley reported that there he "saw many poor fellows fall from sheer exhaustion into the water." Some never got up again. On the other side of the river, those still on their feet finally took refuge in a barn, where they ate some cold food, rested a few hours, and then, before daybreak, set out once more in hot pursuit of the phantom Rebel forces they were told were encamped somewhere near Jenkin's Bridge.[27]

By November 14, they reached Snow Hill but still without so much as sighting the elusive Confederates. The Rebels, if they even had been in Maryland's eastern counties, had simply vanished from that part of the state. So with unflagging determination, the Fourth Wisconsin crossed over into Virginia and proceeded to march down the entire length of the peninsula while the cold rains of winter poured down upon them. Eventually they came to the southern tip

Figure 11. Leopold Kellner, Rosa's younger brother, volunteered for military service at age sixteen in the summer of 1861. (Courtesy of Lynda Dvorachek.)

of Northampton County and could go no farther. Still no Confederates were found. "Our career of conquest is ended. We have had a bloodless victory," Smalley wrote self-mockingly at that point.[28]

After that, they returned again by ship to Baltimore, where they sat out the remainder of the winter in a makeshift community of flimsy tents. "The tents," complained Smalley, "sway and flap as the fierce gusts of wind rush over and through them." On New Year's night he wrote home in low spirits describing what had become of them: "Here, with blankets thrown around us, we sit . . . some reading, some writing, some sleeping—all mutually miserable."[29]

While Smalley and his comrades sat and brooded in Baltimore about the enemies who got away and tried as best they could to contend with the heavy bout of homesickness brought on by the holidays, Rosa Kellner's younger brother, Leopold, battled an unpleasant succession of misfortunes in yet another camp back in Wisconsin. Although barely sixteen, Leopold had volunteered for military service toward the end of that summer. He did so against Rosa's wishes and advice, and when he left town on September 13, she wrote in her journal: "O God I thought my heart would break, so young, so beautiful, so talented exposed to all the hardships of the soldiers life [and] perhaps often brought in contact with wicked rough men." Although sad to see him go and fearful of what might befall him, Rosa envied the opportunities his maleness offered him, and once more declared: "If I was a boy I would go with him and . . . try to rid the world of traitors."[30]

After arriving in camp nothing seemed to go right for young Leopold. From time to time Rosa learned something of his situation when members of his company returned to town and drifted into the hotel. Sometimes they brought notes from him, and on rare occasions Leopold sent a letter to his sister. Such a letter arrived in early December and, in some considerable detail, Leopold described the chain of personal calamities that had made his life increasingly miserable since leaving home. First, he said, he had come down with a "fever" that grew so severe he had to be hospitalized. When that cleared up he was sent back to his barracks. However, there was no stove in the building and it was so cold and damp that he soon became sick again. He told Rosa he had developed "a bad cough & cold which seemed settled on his lungs." Unable to sleep due to coughing and severe chest pains, he once again returned to the hospital. Then, the very next day he broke out with measles. He was miserable and unable to eat, but in time that too passed. However, that bout of suffering was soon succeeded by another, and poor unfortunate Leopold wrote his younger brother John, informing him that "one of his ears aches badly," due to having "a sore inside [it] and matter running out all the time."

When Leopold was again well enough to return to his quarters, he was deeply disturbed and disappointed by what he discovered. During his absence, a book and blanket Rosa had sent him, along with his pens, paper, envelopes, and "a good many little things," had been stolen by other members of his company. "Poor child, whilst he was sick the brave and manly Americans steal their sick comrade's things . . . O how fervently I wish he would return [home]," wrote an indignant Rosa in her journal on December 13.

Within two months, her wish was fulfilled. Leopold was given a medical discharge and sent home. On February 14, Rosa exclaimed in her journal: "Happy joyous glorious day, our brother, our absent soldier boy, has returned home and nothing shall part us more. O it was joy, it was heavenly bliss to hold his hand, to feel his warm kiss. No more gloomy visions of battle fields."

Their happy reunion had come as a complete surprise to her. Soon after it occurred Rosa went into the hotel kitchen, and there one of her employees, a girl named Margaret, asked her, "O Miss Rosa what made you turn so white and the tears spring to your eyes when you saw your brother?" "It was all joy," she responded, wondering whether young Margaret "had never wept for joy."

There was no doubt about Rosa's happiness and relief, but perhaps her effusive outpouring of sentiment on that occasion was also an expression of some powerful and conflicting feelings generated within her by her own ambivalence about the war. On the one hand, she was a militant supporter of Lincoln and the Republican party and she clearly considered the conflict a just war waged for the most noble of causes. Consistent with that, she scorned any local men who tried to evade military service, and she frequently talked tough about the fighting and what should be done to the Southerners, and repeatedly wished she were a man so she could become a soldier and thereby take a personal part in the war. On the other hand, whenever the war ceased to be an abstract development, whenever it touched close to home and involved, or even threatened to involve, members of her family or other men about whom she cared, Rosa expressed strong reservations about how the war was being conducted and how it was becoming a source of evil rather than a force for good. That was revealed in her reactions to Leopold's situation, and again, later on, when her older brother Michael was drafted. In Michael's case, she fervently hoped he could purchase a substitute, but worried that the growing shortage of able-bodied local men would drive the price of substitutes beyond Michael's financial reach. Neither reaction, however—her support for the war or her simultaneous reluctance to have the men she cared for personally involved in it—was insincere or untypical of views held in the village. Perhaps Rosa was not even conscious of her own inconsistencies, which, all the same, must have produced a powerful, often painful, conflict within her.[31]

James Anderson, too, acquired some ambivalent feelings about the war that winter as he coped, as best he could, with the monotony and irritations of camp life in northern Virginia. At Camp Griffin he shared a crowded tent with Bill Crocker, Bill and Joe Cox, and Bill Turpin, and for weeks on end they sat idle, without purpose, within their tent, less than a hundred miles from the Confederate capital of Richmond. They did not venture out, nor did the enemy draw near, and it was as if the war had simply been suspended. Sometimes it seemed that there never had been a war or never would be a war again.

In the meantime, while they waited for things to change, they grumbled about food, complained about weather, rolled and smoked harsh cigarettes, picked lice from their hair and clothing, and grew ever more annoyed with the petty trivialities of army life. When it was too cold or too wet or too windy to go outside, they sprawled upon their musty bedrolls in the damp dimness of the

tent and fantasized about girls and home and warm spring days
and what they might do once their time in the army was done.

Ruminations about the future were especially common on pay
days. Anderson almost always sent most of the money straight home
with recommendations for what was to be done with it. In October
he had told his sisters that the cash he was sending ought to be
used to buy a few good, but inexpensive, acres of land just outside
the village, where they could establish "a nice homestead" on which
they "might all live happily after the war is ended." Another time
he told his father that he wanted some of the money saved so that
he could continue his education when he got home: "My inclina-
tion for study is the same as ever and that as soon as I am discharged
from this service I will take up the study of Law . . . so I can earn
a livelihood by it and work my way up to a position in society."[32]

During that fall and winter, however, most of the money he
earned went to cover the costs of medicine and treatment for his
seriously ailing mother. Shortly after James had left for Camp
Randall, Rosa Kellner paid Mrs. Anderson a visit. Rosa and the
Andersons were members of the local Presbyterian church, but Mrs.
Anderson had not been to services in months, and when Rosa called
on her, she was surprised with both the deteriorating condition of
her health and also her attitude about that condition. "How pale
and meager she looks . . . [and for] 14 weeks she has been laying
on a bed of sickness and suffering, and yet how calm and resigned,
almost happy, she looked," remarked Rosa. In discussing the serious
state of her health, Mrs. Anderson told Rosa she considered her
condition to be "the Lord's will," and that she was fully prepared
to accept whatever befell her.[33]

James was not so fatalistic. Rather than simply acquiescing or
trusting his mother's physical well-being completely to the super-
natural, he fought back with his money in the hope that medical
science might assist in restoring her failing health. When he learned,
for example, that Dr. D. J. Easton was recommending "another
operation" for his mother, James was determined that she should
have it. He would come up with the required money somehow, he
told his father. Easton, who was in fact a tailor by trade and who

had never had any formal medical training, performed the surgery, and James was most grateful for his services. Understandably worried, he was therefore "very happy to read that she had gone safely through it," he told his father. He praised Dr. Easton, saying that he had "certainly acted a most gentlemanly part" and with considerable "kindness on more than one occasion," and indicated that the news of the operation's success gave him great relief. "It took a heavy weight of trouble from my mind," he said. A couple months later he wrote from Camp Advance instructing his sister Jean: "Take good care of Mother till I come back." "I will send all the money I can home," he promised. Occasionally, Anderson offered some of his own suggestions for his mother's recovery. "I think if mother could only exercise *a little, if it was ever so little,* it would strengthen her back after laying so long in bed," he recommended in mid-September. At first, no matter what she did or what was done for her, her recovery was disappointingly slow, but, then, just after Christmas, Anderson became much more optimistic when he received a new picture of his mother and was astonished by her greatly improved appearance: "I got your likeness last night and you do not know how much good it done me. . . . It looked like home to see the likeness of my dear mother."[34]

During that same time, whenever Anderson thought of home he invariably thought of his sweetheart Addie Carpenter. Addie was from the northern part of the county but lived in Manitowoc with the Eldree Abbott family, who employed her as a servant. She was also good friends with James's two sisters, Harriet and Jean, who were both still in their early teens.

At the time of his departure, James and Addie had apparently exchanged vows of love and loyalty. As soon as he arrived at Camp Randall he wrote his sisters asking them to give Addie his love, and promised he would write her directly as soon as he was settled. "Do not forget to kiss Addie for me," he wrote a few weeks later, and then again, toward the end of July, he requested that a picture of his dear Addie be sent him as soon as possible. After he arrived in Washington, he had his own picture taken and sent to her and shortly after that a small portrait of Addie reached him. He was nearly overjoyed and exclaimed in a letter to Jean: "Addie looks as handsome and fat as ever." In early autumn, when the regiment moved over the Potomac and into enemy territory, James put her picture, along with those of family members and his New Testament, in the pocket of his tunic for fear he might lose them if he ever had to throw his knapsack away.[35]

His affection for Addie remained intense throughout that summer and fall, but apparently her feelings for him must have begun to wane soon after he left Manitowoc. In late summer Anderson began to wonder why she did not write more frequently and at greater length, for while he sent her long, loving letters three and four times a month, she responded only occasionally and then only briefly. Those short notes, he complained, were almost impersonal. His feelings were hurt, although he did not want to admit it. In a letter to Jean, with that hurt only thinly covered by a mildly humorous tone of male bravado, he addressed matters by saying: "Tell her that if she does not write me [soon] I will have to cut her acquaintance and fall in love with some of the Southern Beauties." If the message was passed on, which it probably was, it failed to have the effect James sought. In early September he once again wrote Jean. "I think she has forgotten me altogether as I have not received a letter from her for nearly a month," he lamented. He then declared that he would not write Addie again until he heard from her directly. He wanted an explanation. He wanted her to keep her promises. But that was not to be. By December the situation had grown nearly intolerable for him. "Tell her," he sarcastically instructed his family, "that if she is sick of her bargain I shall not hang myself nor commit suicide nor go to the grave with a broken heart." But James continued to brood. Then, about a week before Christmas, he became angry when he heard reports that Addie had left the Abbotts and had moved back north to her mother's place where she intended to marry another man. He asked his sisters if there was any truth to the stories. "Who is this beau she has got which makes her forget me?" he demanded. By then he felt deceived and betrayed, and soon after the beginning of the new year he decisively severed what remained of his ties with Addie

Carpenter. "I wrote rather a hard letter to Addie and told her to return my head picture to you and burn my letters," he informed Jean on January 12.[36]

Very little seemed to be turning out as Anderson had expected, and as the time in camp dragged on, he became increasingly depressed. He put on weight, getting up to 162 pounds, and that, he assured his family, was not from feasting on rich food. The fare was plain and monotonous at best. "We have hard crackers for breakfast, hard crackers for dinner, and for supper we have hard crackers," complained James Leonard to Mary Sheldon. That, of course, only added to that winter of discontent in which even Christmas, which the boys had so eagerly anticipated, was a disappointment. Anderson spent the day alone, sitting in the rain-drenched woods on picket duty. It was his twentieth birthday as well, but there was nothing special about the day on either account. The long-awaited Christmas packages from home did not arrive. The boys must have felt forgotten and left with little in life worth celebrating.[37]

New Year's Day was a little better, however. James, in fact, called it a "a gala day," on which some of the officers organized games—foot races, wrestling, catching greased pigs, and climbing greased poles—for which prizes were awarded to the winners. "Much amusement was caused by the efforts," he told his family while bragging a bit about how well the boys of the Fifth had done in the competitions. They had won a first place in running and a second in wrestling. Then, just a few days later, they were celebrating again when their Christmas parcels finally arrived. "In the evening we had a little sort of merrymaking in our tents and although there was more company than room we got along firstrate," he informed the people back home, explaining that they had seventeen men crowded into their own ten-foot-square tent, where they "sang songs and cracked jokes" until finally ordered to quiet down.[38]

After that the singing and cheering stopped and life returned to "the same dull routine." "We have laid still here till we have grown into old fogyism—gone to seed," protested Dr. Castleman in mid-February. By then, however, it was not just the idleness that bothered him, for he was becoming increasingly concerned about the excessive drinking in camp, and particularly about the "drunken orgies of officers." "It is with deep regret that I notice the rapid increase in drunkenness in the army," he wrote. Eventually, efforts were made to resolve the problem, and Anderson instructed his family not to send him "any spirits of any kind" because they would most likely be confiscated by government agents. Packages were searched and tents inspected, but all efforts proved futile.[39]

As the men tried to fight off boredom by rolling dice and playing cards, gambling also became a problem. "I am sorry to say," wrote Anderson, "that a great deal of gambling exists in the company." Leonard also complained to Mary Sheldon about excesses in that regard, indicating that the soldiers bet on everything and that within the company itself "the boys spent . . . most of their leisure time in gambling." In an attempt to discourage such activities, an example was made of Sergeant Sam Clark of Company A, who was demoted to the rank of private, and then, still unreformed, was court-martialed.[40]

Sickness was also added to the troubles of camp life that winter. Anderson blamed that too on the idleness and told his sisters: "A great deal of sickness is owing to the want of excitement as there is nothing for us to do but drill and go on guard." He may have been at least partially correct, because the prolonged periods of confinement to the tents created conditions within them that were both disgusting and unhealthy. Dr. Castleman observed: "So foul are the tents that if a soldier . . . remains three days in his quarters, he is sent to the hospital in a condition approximating ship fever. The seeds of disease are sown in the regiment, which, in despite of the greatest care, will not fail to yield a rich harvest of sickness all winter." In December there was smallpox, succeeded by epidemics of measles, dysentery, and a host of other illnesses. While many took sick and scores were sent to the hospital, Charles Rath was the only member of Company A to die of disease that winter. Again, the Manitowoc boys seemed unusually healthy, but Anderson informed his sisters that death was common among the tents of other sections of Camp Griffin. "Almost every day we are called upon to follow some comrade to the soldier's grave," he told them. "It is very sad," he continued, "to see a funeral party marching slowly to the mournful wail of the fife or the dismal tap of the muffled drum and think of some poor fellow laying buried in the field." There were many such somber processions in Camp Griffin before spring finally arrived, and until then most of the boys must have waited and wondered if they too would soon end their days beneath the cold dirt of northern Virginia.[41]

They were all under great strain, and in time unit cohesion began to give way. In a letter home in late January, Anderson mentioned, without elaboration, that Sergeant Jack Glover had been "reduced to the ranks for insubordination." Soon after that, in a very long letter sent to the *Manitowoc Pilot,* Captain Clark explained that he had also been forced to demote Sergeant Henry Roehr to the rank of private because of his stubborn refusal to obey a direct order. Clark called Roehr's insubordination "mutiny" and said that it had been made much worse by the fact that his act of disobedience had been committed in front of the entire company. However, as disturbing as those incidents were, the most serious signs of internal strain became apparent on the occasion of Second Lieutenant Peter Scherfins's resignation. Scherfins was the young German from the south side of town and the only officer in the company who was not a native-born American. However, his performance as an officer proved disappointing. Anderson was candid in his assessment: "We all liked Lieutenant Scherfins firstrate but he was very thickheaded and it was very mortifying to be in his command at times and I for one am glad that he is gone." Clark also said that he had been inundated with complaints concerning Scherfins's "want of knowledge," and had, with great reluctance, come to the conclusion that the whole company was being adversely affected by his incompetence. Clark had, therefore, asked him to resign.

Although Clark felt fully justified in taking that action, he was defensive about the ethnic sensitivities that had been irritated by it. "I have endeavored to act towards the members of my company as if there was one nationality . . . [and] I never entertained a prejudice against any one on account of birth place," he asserted in the letter he sent to the *Pilot.* He also made it clear that he deeply resented the accusations that he was a bigot who persecuted some soldiers simply because they were German. On that, fellow Democrat Jeremiah Crowley jumped to his defense, declaring, "Capt. Clark has many friends among our German citizens."[42]

No matter what was said, the Scherfins incident opened wounds within the company and at home. It also stirred up a disagreeable controversy over the issue of Scherfins's replacement. Clark wanted to promote Sergeant Wilson Goodwin, but First Lieutenant Horace Walker, who did not always get along with Clark and who had his own personal following among the men, was a strong advocate for Martin Adams, even though Adams was only a private and still just sixteen years old. Most men in the ranks were clearly unenthusiastic about Adams, but, on the other hand, they were decidedly hostile toward Goodwin. On the issue of Goodwin's promotion, Anderson bluntly stated: "The men do not like him and if he is appointed I should not wonder if the company would protest against it and try to have him thrown out." In the end Clark had his way and Goodwin was promoted, and although there were no reports of open rebellion in response, there was likely a great deal of private grumbling and discontentment.[43]

Through it all the hard rains continued to fall, and when they stopped and the ground froze hard, the boys drilled. Otherwise, they sat and waited for the spring to come, for the sun to shine once more, and for the war to begin again.

CHAPTER 4

Spring Offensives

But many there stood still
To face the stark blank sky beyond the ridge,
Knowing their feet had come to the end of the world.
—Wilfred Owen, "Spring Offensive"

*T*HE SPRING OF 1862 arrived in northern Virginia wet and stormy and much earlier than spring ever did along the Lake Michigan shores of Wisconsin. In early March, as the warm light lengthened and the countryside around Camp Griffin grew green, the boys became increasingly eager for action while at the same time feeling even more lonesome for home. The approach of spring was always a special time in Manitowoc. There, when the days and nights alternated between thawing and freezing and the clear cold maple sap began to rise and run, a renewed sense of optimism returned with the March winds. As the ice in the river began to break up and geese were again heard honking their way uplake, the village emerged once more from the long season of frozen inactivity and people gathered in cooking huts in the bush, crowding around long steaming pans of simmering sap that the steady fires slowly turned into amber syrup and then to golden sugar. They joked and sang and celebrated their own survival of another northern winter as well as the impending rejuvenation of the land. It was an almost magical time, and as the season changed around Camp Griffin, James Leonard recalled and reflected upon all of that: "It would be first rate sugar weather were it in Wisconsin [and] . . . I should like very much to be home for a few days during the sugar season and share in the pleasures."[1]

But neither Leonard nor Anderson nor any of the other boys of Company A would be home that spring, and for them there could be only the memories of that season and its pleasures. For them home would become even more distant in the months ahead, a place some would never see again, and even for those fortunate enough to survive the spring offensive, it could never be quite the same again.

Even at home the early spring sunshine cast some sad shadows. March opened with a crack of lightning in the night, which struck a tall frame house on the north side of town. The dwelling burnt to the ground in a matter of minutes. Everyone inside was asleep when the bolt hit, but neighbors managed to rescue the children, and Carl Luling and his wife escaped in their scorched nightclothes. J. O. Smith's three-year-old son was not so fortunate. While playing in the sugar bush, he stumbled and fell into a boiling pan of sap and was so severely scalded that he died in terrible pain a few days later. Rosa Kellner's oldest sister, Barbara, also died that spring. For weeks Rosa had stood helplessly by the bedside watching Barbara waste away with tuberculosis. It was the same sickness that, just the summer before, had killed her much beloved brother-in-law, Samuel Williams. She still grieved for him, and when Barbara finally passed silently into death Rosa descended into a deep melancholy. "There is unspeakable heavy sorrow in my heart," she wrote. "If I could [only] weep it would ease my heart." But poor Rosa could neither weep nor escape the morbid images of Barbara's pale white face and frail body, which continued to haunt her memories and dreams. "O why must we part, My Sister, my heart is breaking?" she sorrowfully asked.[2]

The mood within the company was also mixed that early spring. On the one hand, the soldiers too seemed revitalized by the sun, and rather than lingering, looking backward, they prepared themselves for the campaign that was soon to come. "The signs of the times at present seem to indicate that this army here is to fight sooner or later the battle that is to decide the war," James Leonard informed Mary Sheldon on March 9. Just a few weeks before that Anderson had come to expect that such a battle would occur sooner, rather than later, and told his family: "It begins to look now as though there would be an end of the war soon, the Rebel cause . . . will soon receive its just desserts in Virginia when we advance." There was a great deal of anticipation associated with that, for the boys believed the spring offensive would not only allow them to escape the boredom of camp life but also bring an end to the war. They were also excited about the possibility of returning home soon. "Give my respect to all the girls and tell them we will soon be home to see them," Anderson told his family in mid-March. But for all their high hopes and expectations, there remained a strong undercurrent of caution, even foreboding, about impending events. "I sometimes feel satisfied that the war will be ended and the volunteers return home by next harvest time while at other times it looks gloomy and I think if we get home by next Spring we will be doing well," confessed Leonard. They had all been soldiers long enough to understand the unpredictable nature of war, and to recognize that even the best laid plans all too often falter and fail. "In time of war," wrote Leonard, "all signs fail and nothing is certain that is not fully in the grasp, [and] a man can scarcely believe his own eyes." They were still somewhat fearful about being part of a situation "where a man could not depend on anything."[3]

However, as the weather continued to warm, all signs pointed toward the beginning of large events. In preparation the boys had been issued new breech-loading Austrian rifles to replace what Anderson described as their "old Harpers Ferry Muskets," which they had been carrying since leaving Baltimore the summer before. James was most impressed with the new rifles, referring to his own as "a terrible weapon" that could be fired "with great precision and at a good distance." By early March he was eager to put it to good use.[4]

Finally, after frustrating delays caused by torrential storms, the order to move out was given at two o'clock in the morning, March 10, and when the Fifth Wisconsin departed Camp Griffin, Dr. Castleman proclaimed in his journal with great relief: "Well, the Army of the Potomac is at last in motion . . . [and] the Van Winkleish sleep

Figure 12. Dr. Alfred L. Castleman was a regimental surgeon for the Fifth Wisconsin Volunteers. (Courtesy of The State Historical Society of Wisconsin, WHi [X3] 1740)

apparently broken." Their immediate destination was Manassas Junction, where they felt sure, as one of them put it, "the day of retribution" would occur and they would "sweep every particle of rebellion from the land." At Manassas Junction, said Anderson, they would frighten the Rebels from "their rat holes" and soundly thrash them in the "first great battle" of the season.[5]

Not all went as planned and predicted. The weather remained stormy, the roads were bad, and just the marching became a strenuous ordeal. "Rain, rain, mud, mud!" complained Castleman, who also observed: "The men have suffered much and many have fallen out of the ranks."[6] Along the way the good doctor came upon just such a man—a mere boy, really—who was lagging far behind the rest of the regiment. He was, said the sympathetic Castleman, "a poor weakly little fellow," half-drowned in the downpour, who had in a near desperate attempt to catch up "unpacked his knapsack and thrown away his clothes." Taking pity on him, Castleman dismounted and helped the lad retrieve the soaked contents of his pack, which the doctor himself then carried until the march halted for the night. Although pleased with his own efforts, he was harshly reprimanded by the regimental command. Soldiers of the Army of the Potomac were expected to keep up and to bear their own burdens.[7]

As they approached Centerville, it was discovered that Joseph E. Johnston's army, which had been encamped in that area earlier, had blown up the bridge spanning Bull Run Creek and vanished into the countryside somewhere to the south. "No enemy here to fight or to watch. What shall we do?" asked Dr. Castleman. What they did was to make camp at Flint Hill, where they remained for three stormy days, sleeping for the first time in their new "dog tents," which, according to Castleman's evaluation, were "in time of rain, . . . good for nothing." Then, on Sunday, March 16, they packed up and began heading back toward Alexandria, marching, said Anderson, "through a drenching rain with knapsacks and two days rations to carry." Dr. Castleman rode ahead, stopping briefly at Fairfax Court House, where he looked back to see the army coming up the road toward him. It was an awesome sight. By then the rain had stopped. The sun shone and the whole spectacle, he declared, was "grand beyond description" as the ranks and rows of soldiers were "pouring steadily forward" for as far as he could see: "The three roads presented a long blue line rendered more striking by the glare of the bayonets, which at a short distance look like a solid body of glittering steel over the blue bulk below." It must have seemed a vision of armed invincibility.[8]

By the time they reached Alexandria, an immense force had already been assembled there along the south bank of the Potomac River—more than one hundred thousand soldiers, nearly twenty-five thousand horses and mules, hundreds of wagons, artillery guns, and ambulances, and tons and barge-loads of equipment and supplies. Three hundred and one ships, both steam and sail, as well as eighty-eight barges were gathered to carry that army southward in a grand armada. Castleman called that great gathering at Alexandria "a solemn and imposing pageant." Infantry regiments and cavalry troops swarmed over the hillsides, river banks, and flood plain. Flags flapped like flocks of wild birds in the brisk March wind, drums pounded, bugles blared, and horse teams tugged and strained to haul their loads to the piers. Men, thousands of them, boarded boats to begin their descent of the broad Potomac.[9]

The Manitowoc boys departed during the late afternoon of March 22. There was, wrote Anderson, loud "cheering as each boat shoved off with her load of human beings," and then, as their steamboat moved out and swung into the current, the boys felt a special sense of excitement. But after traveling only about five miles downstream, they abruptly dropped anchor for the night. The next morning their journey resumed in earnest. They proceeded down the Potomac and out onto Chesapeake Bay, turning southward and churning ever closer to the war. As they moved over the water it seemed as if they almost drifted back in time, back toward the origins of the nation, back toward the heroic age of the Revolution. They passed by Mount Vernon, where, wrote Anderson, he was deeply moved "to know the father of his country dwelt there while living and . . . reposed there in the slumber of death." Eventually they would go to Yorktown, where the first British Empire ended with the surrender of Lord Cornwallis to that earlier army of plowmen and mechanics; then on to Williamsburg, the colonial capital of the Old Dominion; and then up the James River Valley, where America had, at its very beginning, sunk roots deep into the rich soil of the New World. They would pass through them all, waging new battles on the same ground where Powhatan and John Smith, Nathaniel Bacon and George Washington had once struggled to push the course of human events in new directions.[10]

Their voyage from Alexandria took only about thirty hours, and then they passed through Hampton Roads and landed at Fort Monroe. From there they commenced a slow ascent of the swampy and forested Peninsula wedged between the York and James rivers. Upon disembarking from their ship they marched through the deserted streets of Hampton, which had been abandoned by its own inhabitants and partially destroyed by retreating Rebel forces. "It must have been a splendid place judging from the appearance of the ruins," remarked Anderson. Castleman, who called it a "once beautiful, but now desolate little city," also expressed some sympathy for the people who had once lived there but who had suddenly become "scattered and hunted, exiled and homeless." The regiment passed through without incident, and during their first night in that part of Virginia they camped near Newport News. The next day they made their way up the James River Valley and were shocked, even somewhat disgusted, by the scenes of destruction left behind by their fleeing enemies. "It was perfectly awful," declared Anderson, "to see the manner in which they have deserted the country here; splendid mansions all in ruin by fire, barns with implements of agriculture in them burned, and the dead carcasses of cattle in all directions shot by them." Before long the boys were moving along the very "same road on which Lord Cornwallis marched to Yorktown," James informed his family, while also reporting that the entire army was in the highest spirits because their invasion of the Confederacy was proving to be almost a springtime excursion. Even the chronically complaining Dr. Castleman rejoiced: "The weather is beautiful, roads good, troops in fine condition, [and] warm weather coming on." It was like some grand picnic, and when they paused to rest along the river, some of the boys stripped off naked and went swimming, others hunted for and feasted upon fresh oysters and clams scooped up along the banks at low tide, and most simply lazed about in the sundrenched grass, dressed only in their shirts and pants and without the least concern about making war. At one point along the way, Joe Cox, one of Anderson's tent mates, found a discarded Confederate knapsack full of still warm, freshly baked biscuits, with butter, bacon, and some bottles of whiskey. Although they did not eat the food for fear it might be poisoned, they were not nearly so cautious about the whiskey.[11]

Unfortunately, the fine weather and easy days did not last. In due time, the rains resumed with a vengeance. Furthermore, after April 4, as they drew ever closer to Yorktown, their almost effortless progress was impeded by skirmishes with enemy patrols. Upon reaching the old city, and while most of the army made camp there, the Fifth Wisconsin was sent on about another three miles to Warwick Court House, where the regiment "lay down in the mud and rain for the night." The night was not, however, completely uneventful, for during the darkness Captain Clark and some of the boys raided a nearby farm and came away with thirty chickens and some ham. That made for some fun and an excellent breakfast.[12]

Three days later, on April 7, they were sent out on what proved to be an unusually demanding march. "The rain poured in torrents," complained Castleman, who became upset when the men were forced to keep on marching in the wet and the mud from early morning until well after ten at night. The situation was made worse by hunger. "The men are almost starved, having been for two days entirely without rations and lie tonight in pools of water," protested the enraged doctor. But that was not all that angered him. The men in the ranks, he observed, not only slogged and slipped along in the mud carrying their own considerable burdens, but were also required to carry the tents and heavy packs of their officers, who rode above it all in wagons and on horseback. Castleman was most upset by the grossly undemocratic character of those arrangements and wondered why "in the organization of an army under a republican government, was such a distance between officers and men contemplated?"[13]

Next day the soldiers neared their breaking point. "There is almost a mutiny this morning. No rations and unless there should be better things before night, I should not be surprised at any violence," noted Castleman in his journal. But by sunset the crisis had passed. "A few boxes of hard bread have partially calmed the angry storm," he observed, while also mentioning that other promises had been made concerning bread, beef, and coffee for the day after that.[14]

Anderson also complained about conditions but seemed to take an almost perverse pride in his own capacity to endure the hardships. In a letter home from Yorktown he informed his family: "I have seen some very hard sights since we advanced on this place and have suffered a good deal from exposure and hunger, but have come through it all right and lively."[15]

Martin Galvin was not so lucky. Galvin, a thirty-seven-year-old Irish immigrant, was a neighbor of the Andersons back in Manitowoc and had joined the company just two days after James. During winter camp he had taken sick and was sent back to an army hospital in Georgetown, where he remained while the rest of his comrades went off into Virginia that spring. On April 14, from his camp near Yorktown, Anderson wrote home: "I am very sorry to inform you that Martin Galvin is no more." Anderson and Galvin, despite their age and ethnic differences, had been friends, and James felt an especially deep sympathy for Ann Galvin, Martin's widow, and their two children—nine-year-old Ann Marie, and John, who was then just seven. "His widow and family have one consolation in knowing he was well cared for and the place where he now sleeps is marked so that it can be found at any time," wrote James, who also said that since coming to Virginia he had "seen more than one poor fellow buried where he fell . . . with nothing but the martial cloaks around them and nothing save a little mound of fresh earth to mark where they lie."[16]

Anderson learned of Galvin's death just two days before participating in a hard assault on the well-fortified enemy position near Lee's Mill, along the Warwick River. In that attack, he said, he found himself confused and nearly lost "in the midst of a terrible scene." Thunderous artillery barrages were first unleashed from both sides. For a while the Wisconsin boys lay low until ordered

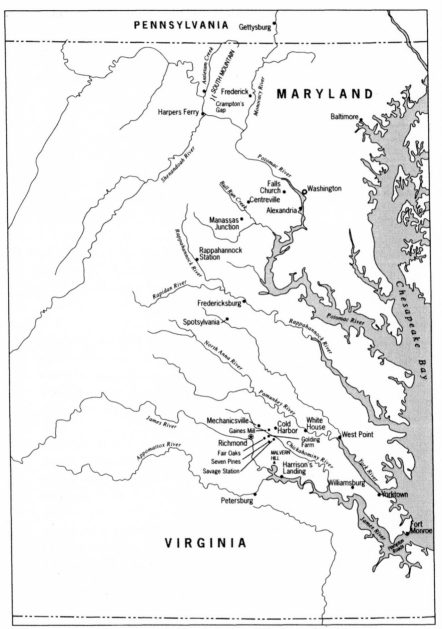

Figure 13. Virginia and Maryland, showing the regions and locations where James Anderson and the Fifth Wisconsin Volunteers were engaged in the violent conflicts of the Civil War. (Map by Paula Robbins)

to leave the woods and assault the enemy's earthworks, which Castleman described as being "thrown into great ridges, a quarter of a mile long, mounted with cannon, bristling with bayonets, and covered with men." It was their first serious armed engagement, and it ended with their orderly withdrawal.[17]

After that, fighting was not resumed for another twelve days, although the artillery shelling persisted, especially during the nights. That kept the boys anxiously awake much of the time, and along with the prolonged periods of hunger and fatigue, made them lightheaded and consequently less cautious than usual about the dangers around them. In time it was almost as if they had been drugged, for when the fighting began again, Castleman observed: "I am astonished at our own men's indifference to danger, and their apparent insensibility to the suffering of their comrades. During the fight our whole regiment were lying on the ground, laughing, talking, whittling, and cracking jokes as unconcerned as if they were preparing for a frolic."[18]

Nevertheless, during what stretched out into the month-long siege of Yorktown, the only casualty suffered by Company A occurred when a careless comrade accidentally wounded John Leykom in the cheek with a bayonet. However, that same April far to the west, in the valley of the Tennessee River, the war claimed its first combat victim from Manitowoc.

Early in the morning of March 8, just two days before Anderson and the Fifth Wisconsin were to leave winter quarters at Camp Griffin, George Waldo and his company departed from Camp Wood in Wisconsin and traveled by train to Chicago. Like others before them, they were cheered along their way by large crowds. From there they went on to Alton, Illinois, where they boarded a steamboat that carried them down the snow-swollen Mississippi to St. Louis. After a restful two-week delay at Camp Benton, they again took to the water as part of a large army, under the command of Ulysses S. Grant, on its way to strike at the western flank of the Confederacy. Slowly they ascended the Tennessee River, and on March 28 Captain Waldo and his troops were landed at Savannah, Tennessee, while most of the other soldiers proceeded on another

nine miles to Pittsburg Landing from where they were to move
against Albert Sidney Johnston's powerful army concentrated in
Corinth, Mississippi. Back at Savannah, the Manitowoc boys made
camp and for the next ten days simply sat and relaxed in the warmth
of the Tennessee spring.

Their lazy wait for something to happen ended shortly after
sunrise, Sunday, April 6, when the thunderous roar of war echoed
down the river valley toward them. It came from the area between
Pittsburg Landing and Shiloh Church, where Johnston's troops had
fallen "like an Alpine avalanche" upon the unprepared Union camps.
The Northerners had dug no trenches nor erected any earthworks,
and many of the boys were still wrapped in blankets when the attack
hit. They paid a heavy price for their generals' lapse in vigilance.

It was not until dusk that Waldo and his company were ordered
to move to the support of their comrades upriver. Again they took
to the boats, moving over the water through a starless darkness and
reaching the landing about midnight. Before arriving, however, it
began to rain, and by the time they were climbing up the river's
steep west bank, the shower had become a fierce thunderstorm that
raged and blew throughout the night. Upon reaching the flat
ground above the river, they carefully picked their way through the
exhausted soldiers sprawled sleeping on the wet ground among a
maze of wagons, ambulances, caissons, and artillery pieces. Many
of the dead and wounded from the day's battle were still scattered
about in blood-tinted pools and puddles. When the Manitowoc
soldiers finally came to a halt, they simply stood quietly for the rest
of the night, their rubber-coated groundsheets stretched out over
their heads, and anxiously awaited the dawn.

By early morning the storm had stopped and Waldo's company
moved up and into position two miles south of the landing along
the main road to Corinth. There they prepared for the brutal
conflict they all knew would soon break upon them. It began shortly
after seven, and throughout the first half of the day units clashed
and collided as the tide of battle ebbed and flowed in a deadly
rhythm of attacks and counterattacks. It was during one such
attack—while charging up a slope toward a well-defended New

Orleans battery—that George Waldo was hit. He was leading his troops, setting the kind of courageous example expected of young captains, when he was struck by a musket ball in the chest, just above the heart, crumpling him to the ground. He died almost immediately. He was just twenty-seven years old, and John Reed, another Manitowoc soldier who had followed him into the fight, said of Captain Waldo that "there was no flinch about him . . . that bloody day."[19]

News of his death reached Manitowoc on April 17. It came as a shock. Jeremiah Crowley noted that all flags were immediately lowered to half-staff and "a deep gloom prevailed throughout the town." Waldo's death was their first experience with the lethal violence of the war they had all so eagerly entered. He was the first local soldier to be cut down in battle, and that, along with the fact that he was an officer from an important north-side family, gave his death a special significance and distinguished it from those of Martin Galvin and Charles Rath, two ordinary soldiers who had quietly and undramatically expired from sickness in army hospitals far removed from the front. Both Galvin and Rath had been buried in military cemeteries near Washington, but when news of Waldo's death arrived, a collection was taken up and the Episcopal rector, George Engles, was sent south by the villagers to bring his body home.

On Saturday, April 27, the *Comet*, which not so long before had carried him off to war, landed at the north pier with the metal casket containing the captain's last remains. From that moment, the whole community engaged in an elaborate ritual through which it seemed to both mourn and celebrate the loss. In life Waldo had been regarded as one of their very best. "All who knew him loved him, for he was possessed of a soul of true nobility," wrote Sewall Smith. He had embodied the Puritan values so well, so fully, that it seemed a sorrowful twist of fate that he should meet his end so early in what appeared to have been such a promising life. But in their sadness there was also a pride, made evident in the many near-boastful expressions concerning the fact that he had died upon the battlefield. He had demonstrated courage, had set a proper

manly example, and Rosa Kellner undoubtedly reflected the sentiments of the whole community when she wrote: "He died the death
of a hero, of a patriot, died for liberty and his country." Thus,
although his death may have raised questions in the minds of some
about the realities of war, it became the stuff from which the
community fashioned new myths.

The funeral took place on Sunday, April 28, 1862, and for Manitowoc it was a spectacular event. People flooded into town from
throughout the surrounding countryside. In late morning, as a funeral knell sounded throughout the otherwise quiet village, Waldo's
flag-draped coffin was solemnly moved by horse-drawn hearse from
the Masonic Hall, where it had lain in state the day and night
before, to St. James Episcopal Church, where the Reverend Engles
preached a stirring sermon about fallen heroes and supreme sacri-
fices. Such a "great throng" crowded into the church that Rosa,
who arrived late after working in the hotel, was unable to get inside.
She stood in the street for a while trying to hear, but when she
could not, she decided to set off for the cemetery, which was located
on a high sandy hill above the river. She had not reached there
before being overtaken by a large procession of Masons, lawyers,
civic officials, and relatives, all escorting the captain's body to its
final resting place. More than two thousand people lined the way.
Many wept. "People from [both] the country and the town attended
and everyone admitted that such a large concourse never assembled
in Manitowoc before," observed Crowley. The numbers were impressive, but "there was sad solemn music too," and that, confessed
Rosa, "made me feel very sad." But for most it was such sweet
sorrow. That was certainly so for Sewall Smith, who seemed especially moved by the sights and sounds of the spectacle and descrip-
tively reported in his newspaper: "The wailing notes of the death
march; the hollow sound of the muffled drums; the slow measured
tread of the procession; and the subdued sympathetic looks of those
present all combined to make the pageant mournfully sublime."
Then, when the crowd surged forward into the cemetery, pressing
toward the open grave, Rosa once more found herself relegated to
the fringes of the event. It was from there she observed the dramatic

Figure 14. Map of the United States, showing the routes of the wartime travels of George Waldo, Paleman Smalley, and Mead Holmes, soldiers from Manitowoc who participated in three different theaters of the Civil War. (Map by Paula Robbins)

closing scene, feeling especially sympathetic for the "young lady dressed in black who wept bitterly" by the side of the grave as the coffin was slowly lowered into the shadows.[20]

Anderson read about Waldo's funeral in the newspapers sent by his father. He also read the reports about the exploits of the young captain and his company at Shiloh. All that was covered in considerable detail, and it made James decidedly jealous. In contrast to all the attention paid to those other hometown boys, little was said about Company A. As a consequence, Anderson felt forgotten and unappreciated by the people in Manitowoc, which likewise led him to regard Waldo and those other local volunteers to be his rivals. In a sharply worded letter to his family he derided their efforts at Shiloh by declaring that they had merely "traveled a few miles in mud and water to get into a fight and then found [it] more than their match." He also informed his parents and sisters that he and the others of his company bitterly resented the implications plainly made in those newspaper reports that, when compared to Waldo's outfit, "no Wisconsin Regiment can compete with them in fighting, marching, or anything else." Anderson angrily shot back: "Our Boys have by continual skirmishing got so used to the enemy's fire that we think nothing of what the 14th boys would call a sharp fight."[21] War for James was clearly still a contest for attention and approval. Many hard and ugly lessons were soon to be driven home to him and the others, however, as the Peninsula campaign unfolded and they beheld as never before the horrors of combat.

On the fourth of May, after an unprofitable month-long siege of Yorktown, McClellan ordered his troops to storm the city. So they did. But they soon discovered that Joseph Johnston and his army had once again already slipped away, moving farther up the Peninsula toward Williamsburg. After declaring their occupation of the abandoned city a great victory—"our success is brilliant," was the message McClellan wired to Secretary of War Stanton—the "American Napoleon" ordered his soldiers to set off in hot pursuit of the retreating enemy.[22]

For some time before that, Captain Clark had been under considerable pressure, and his reputation had suffered from malicious gossip and some damning accusations. In February, for example, Anderson felt compelled to rise to Clark's defense, and bluntly informed the people back home that there was absolutely no truth to the rumors that the captain had sold supplies that should have been distributed among the soldiers. There was also the fallout from the Scherfins incident, and Anderson took Clark's side in that as well, especially after Scherfins himself wrote a whiny, self-serving letter home, which Crowley published in the *Pilot* during early April. Scherfins had called Clark a thief and liar and accused him of "obtaining fraudulently from the Quartermaster" money that rightfully belonged to the rank and file of the company. Furthermore, he asserted, Clark had only managed to evade a court martial due to "influences used by family connections with superior officers." Finally, Scherfins, who tried to represent himself as the champion of the ordinary soldiers, claimed that his own unjust fall had been engineered by Clark, who wished to discredit him and drive him out of the army because he knew too much about the captain's sordid activities. He concluded by declaring that Clark was "detested by the [whole] Company, with the exception of a few pliant tools."[23]

Such accusations, along with some persistent dissension within the company, eroded Clark's authority and, even during the early stages of the Peninsula campaign, Anderson heard rumors about the captain's intentions to resign his command. James had always admired and supported Clark, despite some partisan political differences, and was therefore disturbed by the gossip. He was not only concerned about the possibility of losing an officer he considered a capable leader but also worried about his own self-interests. "It will be hard on me," he told his family, "as I do not like Lieut[enant Horace] Walker, who will probably be Capt[ain]." In time, both the rumors and Anderson's concerns proved well founded. Clark did resign and Walker took his place.[24]

The truth about Temple Clark's alleged activities remains unclear, but when he left Company A that April he did so voluntarily and was immediately made a captain in Waldo's old outfit, the Fourteenth Wisconsin Volunteers. Toward the end of that month Clark was severely wounded in the Battle of Corinth, in northern Mississippi, and was shipped off to an army hospital in Illinois. While recuperating there he was promoted to the rank of major, and still later, after recovering from his wounds, was transferred to the adjutant general's office in Washington. Meanwhile, back in Company A some members seemed extremely pleased with the changes that had occurred, and one wrote to the *Tribune*, stating: "Since Captain Walker has had command of the company things progress more satisfactorily and the boys are well satisfied with him and the other commissioned officers."[25]

It was Horace Walker who led the boys on the morning of May 5, 1862, in their bloody clashes with Confederate forces at Williamsburg. The fighting there was against the Rebel's rear guard commanded by James Longstreet. It was particularly ferocious, and the Fifth Wisconsin was in the thick of the struggle from the very start. With the Wisconsin troops in the vanguard, units of the Army of the Potomac plowed through deep mud until they reached the banks of Queen's Creek, on the other side of which lay the enemy army, concealed behind a series of long earthen mounds. Union artillery opened fire. "Our shells made terrible work in it; there was not a single tree within reach of our guns which was not torn to pieces," reported Thomas Wagener, another of the Manitowoc members of Company A. After the shelling had softened up the defenses, the regiment quickly crossed the creek and seized the first line of earthworks and rifle pits. Then the second. But as they drew nearer to the town, Rebel resistance stiffened, and just outside Williamsburg they were greeted, said Castleman, by "a roar of cannon and the shrieks of shot and shell." At one point, they were almost outflanked and forced to fall back. Part of their army panicked, with soldiers "whooping, hollering, running from the field as if chased by a thousand devils," Castleman observed. In that confusion, Thomas Wagener was almost lost. He was already on the brink of exhaustion from days of marching in mud, rain, and rising heat, as well as from the exertion of the battle itself: "I was too weak to fire much, in fact I dropped down several times, and was obliged to leave my knapsack on the field for lack of strength to carry it." On the other hand, his younger brother, Arnold, was especially impressive that day. Thomas reported home with considerable pride that Arnold had "acted during the whole engagement as if he was made of ice, and at one time, when his gun miss fire[d], he sat coolly down in the open field, amidst the shower of bullets, and fixed it." After that, the younger Wagener determinedly rose from the ground and gunned down several rapidly advancing Southerners. At about that same time, Castleman, who was watching the battle from a short distance away, saw a shell hit and explode in the area occupied by Company A, and then saw Captain Walker as he "whirled in the air and disappeared among the rails and rubbish." The doctor, who naturally assumed that Walker was dead, was utterly amazed when the young captain emerged from the debris to rally his troops and lead them in a determined counter-attack. As that was happening, General Winfield Scott Hancock waved his sword in the air and shouted to them: "G[od] d[am]n it boys, just give them a cheer with your fire." Then, wrote Thomas Wagener, "the whole regiment gave a glad harrah and ran in at a rapid pace at the foe. This was too much for them; they took to their heels."[26]

After that Hancock dubbed them the "Bloody Fifth." He was full of praise for them and they were full of pride in themselves. "Our boys fought like devils and have earned a name for themselves and their state," Anderson exuberantly informed his folks. "I do not think there was another regiment on the field fought so desperate as ours [and] even our best generals stood and looked on amazed at our bravery." Dr. Castleman credited them with saving the whole army. Even General McClellan, who arrived on the scene after the fighting was finished, recognized their important contribution, and in a short speech complimented them on their "bravery and discipline," declaring: "Through you we won the day."[27]

They were, of course, pleased with such recognition, but gaining it had been costly. Jacob Cochems, David Eddy, and David Woodcock had all lost their lives in the Battle of Queen's Creek, and Captain Walker, along with Gottlieb Herman and Joseph Allen, were wounded. These were the company's first combat casualties. Woodcock, a thirty-one-year-old laborer who had migrated to

Manitowoc from New Brunswick, was shot through the right side
and "died in about an hour," Anderson reported. George Engles,
the Episcopal rector's son, was another member of the company
who saw Woodcock go down, and he informed the readers of the
Manitowoc Herald that while in severe pain, Woodcock had kept
reloading and firing his rifle into the advancing enemy forces.
Furthermore, wrote Engles, "he told the boys not to come to his
assistance—that he had to die, and they could not save him." In
the end, David Woodcock did "die as the brave only can," concluded Engles. There were no such details about the death of Private
Eddy, but it was reported that he had been shot in the head. Thomas
Wagener saw Jacob Cochems die, and indicated that he had met
his death when a cannon ball struck him directly in the chest while
they were all charging toward Williamsburg. It "blew him fully ten
feet backwards, killing him instantly," wrote Wagener, who carried
his friend's broken body back to camp when the fighting was
through and observed that "not a single expression of pain was
marked on his face."[28]

While in the Williamsburg fight, Anderson and Sergeant Willard
Rickaby experienced an especially close encounter with the enemy.
Both were taken prisoner by a troop of Georgia cavalry. They had
been caught by complete surprise, and "the first thing I knew,"
wrote James, "I had 3 or 4 around me with drawn sabers demanding
my Rifle." Then, in an apparent attempt to make the situation
perfectly clear to Anderson, one of the Confederates took out his
revolver, cocked it and held it to within about an inch of James's
face. He sternly repeated the order. Anderson and Rickaby surrendered their weapons without further hesitation and were led off in
the direction of Richmond. They must have gone with considerable
concern, undoubtedly having heard tales about the inhumane treatment of Union prisoners as well as about the atrocious conditions
in which captives were imprisoned. However, while "passing close
to some fine thickets and not being closely watched, we darted into
them and were freed," rejoiced James in his journal. It was a daring
move, and their lives remained in danger until they were safely back
in camp. Anderson was the first to return. Captain Walker saw him

come in without his rifle and dressed him down harshly, refusing to believe his story until Rickaby was there to corroborate his claims.[29]

The confrontation at Williamsburg, although hard-fought and bloody, was not a decisive victory for Union forces, for, while Longstreet delayed McClellan's advance, inflicting twenty-two hundred casualties on his army, Johnston and the bulk of what was soon to be known as the Army of Northern Virginia, slipped away and pulled back toward Richmond. Having discovered that, and after only a brief pause, the Northern troops again broke camp, and on May 9 set off for what most of them anticipated would be the final act of the war. Those assumptions were reinforced by what they observed along the way. As they marched they found "the road lined with fragments of wagons, gun carriages, and baggage of the retreating army showing great haste," and they surmised the Rebels to be in a state of fearful disarray. Also, all the farm houses along their route had hung out white flags, and the advancing army was greeted by scores of slaves, all of whom looked upon them as their liberators. By all appearances the Confederacy was crumbling and collapsing even as they pressed on toward its capital. Furthermore, the news from within Richmond indicated that conditions there were in a sorry state. Anderson for one was convinced that final victory was little more than a matter of marching, and felt even more certain of that when, while on picket duty, he took captive a young Irish corporal serving in one of the Georgia regiments: "He told the same story as other prisoners about being fed on half rations and represented Richmond as being in a peck of trouble." Around that same time, another member of the company, identified only as "C. A.," informed the readers of the *Manitowoc Tribune:* "We are now within twenty-five miles of that city [Richmond], and I expect the next letter I send you will be mailed from that point." He, like the others, assumed that by then the seat of the rebellion would be back under Federal authority.[30]

On the surface, everything seemed to be running in their favor as they moved on through what Dr. Castleman described as "the most beautiful country on earth." The bright blue days were in full bloom, spring flowers swaying in fields and on green hillsides, and the whole scene was breathtaking enough to inspire Anderson to exclaim that it was "as lovely a country as you would wish to see."[31]

But not all was well. In spite of the high optimism and pleasing scenery, many of the soldiers were nearing the point of exhaustion from marching under sixty-pound packs while subsisting for long periods on little but hard biscuits and salt meat. Many also burned with fever brought on by drinking bad water. For most even daily doses of quinine and whiskey brought little relief.

At White House Landing, on the Pamunkey River, General McClellan established his new headquarters while most of the army went on into the valley of the Chickahominy River, closer yet to Richmond. There Dr. Castleman went to work in what was being called Liberty Hall Hospital. More a collection point for sick, wounded, and dying men than anything actually resembling a hospital, it was a foul place where swarms of bluebottle and black flies buzzed, where some men were crowded into an old farm house while many more were left "lying about in stables, alive with vermin," or in chicken sheds where the stench was overpowering. The greatest number by far, however, had no shelter at all and simply lay in their agony on the bare ground, fully exposed to the hard rains and the scorching southern sun, without blankets, groundsheets, or even straw scattered beneath them. Until Castleman's arrival, there had been no one there to tend to even their most basic needs and they had therefore suffered terribly "for want of the commonest attention," he said. "The dead and dying are lying together . . . and the living are dying for want of the necessities of life, which, in great abundance, are in sight" but under guard, he angrily protested. The stiff, pale dead men were a grotesque sight to look upon, but the horrors among the wounded were even more disturbing, for as Castleman observed, they "had been neglected till their wounded limbs or bodies had become a living mass of maggots." "Limbs were dropping off from rottenness, and yet these poor men were alive," he anguished. There were hundreds, perhaps thousands, of them, most of whom had no hope of survival, and their numbers continued to mount throughout late May and on into June as the fighting was resumed. Ole Olson, who James called "the monarch," and George Henrick, a twenty-seven-year-old farmer also from Manitowoc County, both died of sickness at the Liberty Hall Hospital and were quickly buried in the hot, damp soil of the Chickahominy Valley.[32]

On May 24, Company A made camp north of the Chickahominy near Gaines' Mill. They dug rifle pits and remained on constant alert for fear the enemy might suddenly strike at them. By month's end Anderson indicated that they were "completely worn out" and that the regimental sick list was growing at an alarming rate. Even most of the men still up and on duty, he said, "looked like living skeletons." But they held on as best they could, believing the end of their ordeal was at hand. "I think we will be in Richmond in less than a week from now as they [the army engineers] have commenced throwing bridges across the Chickahominy at different points," Anderson wrote his family on May 25.[33]

While they anxiously waited near Gaines' Mill, a letter from home arrived for Anderson. Enclosed were a few pressed violets. They grew wild in Wisconsin during the warm days of early May, and those fragile purple flowers, so lovingly sent, were small fragments of the serenity he had left behind and to which he hoped to soon return. He kept some, pressing them among the letters in his pack, and shared the rest with friends in the company.[34]

As Anderson and the Fifth Wisconsin waited, Paleman Smalley and the Fourth Wisconsin were caught up in their own spring offensive. They had departed Baltimore by ship during the first week in March with no notion of where they were heading. All they knew was that they were going south and that soon they were likely to see action. They stopped briefly at Newport News but then quickly boarded another ship—the *Constitution*—in which they continued on down the Atlantic coast. It was, said Smalley, "a somewhat perilous voyage," during which they were caught in a severe storm off Cape Hatteras and were thrashed about by high winds and waves until they reached and rounded the tip of Florida and glided out into the calmer waters of the Gulf of Mexico. On March 13 they landed on Ship Island, which Smalley described as "long, low, flat, sandy," and there made camp on its treeless west end. It was there, just off the coast of Mississippi, that David Glasgow Farragut assembled a fleet with which to attack southern Louisiana and to then enter and ascend the Mississippi River.

They remained on Ship Island for a little more than a month, and in that time an epidemic of typhoid fever broke out and spread throughout the camp. While it raged, reducing both the size and strength of the army, Farragut and General Ben Butler continued to lay plans for their invasion of the lower South. When that planning was completed, and just before the ships again set forth, the officers culled through the army and, noted Smalley, "all soldiers who were unable to sustain the greatest privations" were discharged and sent north to military hospitals. Fifty from his own regiment were let go, including Robert Robinson from western Manitowoc County. At the same time, Smalley sardonically observed that a surprisingly large number of officers who had, he said, "zealously served their country for a year and drawn therefore some $1200 . . . discover a peculiar inability to proceed and a decided inclination to get out." Indeed many resigned and went home.

Young Smalley was among those who boarded the *Great Republic* on April 17 and steamed off toward the mouth of the Mississippi. Conditions on board were far from ideal, and about that one member of the Fourth Wisconsin wrote: "Three thousand of us [were] stowed thickly on her deck, with few or any arrangements for comfort or subsistence." Smalley, too, was appalled by the "filth and confinement and sickness" and reported that "the men were actually covered with vermin."

Once they reached the delta, the *Great Republic* was towed upstream as far as Fort St. Phillip, but could go no farther, having too deep a draft to make it over the sandbars. "Ever since" arriving there, wrote a member of the regiment, "we have been rolling and pitching at anchor in one of the filthiest ships I ever set foot upon and emitting a stench from all parts of it that would knock a man down at eighty yards as surely as a Minnie ball." He also derisively suggested that if the *Great Republic* could somehow be moored within gunshot of New Orleans, the city would gladly surrender within twenty-four hours simply because of the stink.

Meanwhile, the vessels in Farragut's fleet that were able to make it upriver bombarded New Orleans. On the last day of April 1862, the city surrendered to Union forces. When Butler's troops went ashore they found it full of burning buildings, blazing cotton bales, and demoralized citizens. Soon after that, Smalley and his comrades were transferred to the *Colorado* in which they moved on to participate in the fall of Baton Rouge. Then, in late June, they pushed on upstream against the mud-ladened current all the way to Vicksburg, Mississippi, which stood defiantly upon a two-hundred-foot bluff on the east side of the river, its guns surveilling the channel.

On June 29, four days after arriving there, Smalley, in a still somewhat humorous state of mind, wrote home concerning their campaign against Vicksburg: "The siege of it has commenced in earnest. The Yankee General has put down his foot, and the city must fall, for what ever withstood earnest Yankee perseverance? Southern chivalry, most certainly never!" But Vicksburg did not fall. A great many Northern soldiers once again took sick as a consequence of drinking directly from the river, which caused lethal outbreaks of typhoid and dysentery. Smalley reported that out of the 1,040 members of his regiment only about 300 were still fit for duty. "And of these," he added, "not one half could march under the hot sun for ten miles without complete exhaustion." By the end of June the Fourth Wisconsin was in truly dire condition. "Its spirit was completely broken," lamented Smalley, who then sadly observed that "the dead, dreary shuffle of spirit-broken men tortured the ear at every step." "Bent forms, melancholy-looking faces, and the scraping feet show that there is pressure greater than the horrors of battle, which can crush a man," he concluded in his distressing report home.

Their attempt to take Vicksburg was a failure, and when in the hot summer sun the water level of the river began to drop, it was decided to pull out before the larger ships were caught and stranded on the exposed mud. "Thank God!" Smalley declared, "soldiering, like everything else, must come to an end! May it be soon!" For many on that expedition it had tragically ended all too soon in the heat and agony of that early southern summer.[35]

Back in Virginia, the situation for the Army of the Potomac also took a decided turn for the worse by the beginning of June. It had been an exceptionally wet winter and spring, and the night of May 30 was filled with the rumbling and rain of yet another powerful thunderstorm. The Chickahominy, usually a slow and shallow stream that time of year, rose and flooded, sweeping away most of the Union army's pontoon bridges. Before that, McClellan, in positioning his forces, had divided the army, putting one-half of his soldiers north of the river and the remainder clustered in several places to the south of the Chickahominy. The flooding and consequent destruction of the bridges, of course, separated his forces even more. Then, in the midafternoon of May 31, a Confederate force led by Longstreet hit Union troops near Seven Pines, south of the river. The fighting was fierce, much at close quarters in heavy forest, thick mud, and nearly knee-deep water where wounded men could drown, and the casualty counts were very high in what turned out to be a battle with no clear winner. They fought throughout the remainder of the day. "During the night," wrote Anderson, "Old Bull Dog Sumner [General Edwin Sumner] crossed with his [Second] Corps and at dawn the contest was resumed with great fury." By the time it was over, the Union troops had managed to push the Confederates back as far as Fair Oaks.[36]

The Fifth Wisconsin, still in camp north of the Chickahominy, did not participate in the battle, but Anderson described in a letter home some of what he heard and saw of it. "The booming of cannon and the continual roll of musketry is perfectly awful and . . . no less than 5000 were detailed last night to bring in the wounded," he wrote. To that he added: "It is said to have been the bloodiest fight on the continent."[37]

Union forces suffered about five thousand casualties at Fair Oaks. And even though the Southerners lost a thousand more than that, McClellan seemed to lose his nerve. Rather than retaking the initiative and moving on to attack Richmond, he ordered his forces to dig in where they were. In fact, following Fair Oaks both armies shelled each other for more than three noisy but otherwise uneventful weeks. During the evening of June 12, Anderson wrote home describing their state of affairs: "Every night the rebels throw shot over into our camp and even now as I write I hear shells scream and bust in the woods on our left." As the explosions went off, he hit the ground, waited for the dirt to settle, and then got up and resumed writing. The next day, James Leonard, just to pass the time and satisfy his curiosity, walked over to the site of Battle of Fair Oaks. He was stunned by what he found. "Trees, Fences, Bushes, and every thing around is literally torn to pieces with Bullets and Shell [and] the signs of the terrible slaughter were yet to be seen on the ground and the fields were filled with the graves of both Union and Scesh Soldiers," he informed Sheldon.[38]

The brutal business was begun again on Thursday, June 26, 1862, when Major General Ambrose P. Hill struck the Union camp near Mechanicsville, north of the Chickahominy. That was the opening blow of a series of ferocious Confederate assaults that, planned and put in motion by Johnston's replacement, Robert E. Lee, pounded and pushed back the Army of the Potomac at Gaines' Mill, Savage Station, White Oak Swamp, and Malvern Hill in what became known as the Seven Days' campaign. Through it all, Anderson told his family, the Southerners fought like fanatics, "rushing on desperately as they were frenzied by the whiskey and [gun]powder with which they were supplied." Those onslaughts, in turn, sent Union forces into agonizing retreat, and as a consequence, concluded one historian, "the hope that the war could be something less than a revolutionary struggle died somewhere between Mechanicsville and Malvern Hill."[39]

At first, however, the Northerners thought they had won. On Beaver Dam Creek, close to Mechanicsville, Fitz John Porter's boys bloodied the Confederates badly, inflicting close to fifteen hundred casualties. "There was great rejoicing in camp tonight [and] McClellan sent orders around that we had met the enemy and they were defeated," noted Anderson in his journal that evening. But although "bands were playing and the troops cheered lustily," Anderson and his comrades thought the celebration somewhat premature: "Our

Reg[imen]t was silent as the grave. We had been deceived so much that we all said, 'Wait and See.'"[40]

The Wisconsin boys were right. The enemy had not been defeated, and the very next day the Southerners struck hard against Porter's forces near Gaines' Mill. The weather was sultry, the fighting intense, and this time the soldiers of Company A and the whole Wisconsin Fifth, having been moved to the area of Goldens Farm, were very much involved in the conflict. The battle went on throughout the day and into the night. "The fight was continued long after dark and was one of the most splendid sights I ever witnessed," wrote Anderson. "But the illusion was dispelled by a musket ball which struck me in the leg just above the knee making a painful but not dangerous wound." It was his left leg, and it made retreating, once that became necessary, difficult for him. In the same battle Captain Walker was hit in the arm, his second wound in less than a month. Morris Mullin, John Thureau, and William Turpin were also injured by enemy fire, but only Thureau's injury was serious.[41]

After much effort, the Rebels were finally driven back, but early the next morning, at about four o'clock, the boys were rousted out of their bedrolls and quickly drawn up into battle formation. They remained at the alert until dawn, and were then ordered to fall back once again to Gaines' Mill. They were somewhat bewildered by that move because they had been expecting to push on to Richmond. They grumbled and then followed orders. Throughout that whole day, "which opened bright and beautiful," wrote Evan Jones, there was "an ominous stillness in the air so well understood by veterans, and we knew that fighting would soon commence." The anticipated attack finally came around sunset. It was terrible. It came as a deafening storm of smoke, lead, and cold steel. Some soldiers faced it still armed with old-fashioned muskets that, Jones complained, "became so hot after firing about twenty rounds, that those who fought with them were obliged to stop" in order to allow them to cool. But in spite of such handicaps, they fought on, and eventually the enemy was again thrown back.[42] The next day, McClellan gave up the advance on the Confederate capital. Rather than completing the spring offensive, the Army of the Potomac began a general withdrawal, fighting by day and retreating by night until the soldiers stood with their backs to the James River and nowhere left to run.

At Savage Station, before pulling out, Union soldiers destroyed an immense quantity of their own supplies and munitions to prevent the Rebels from getting possession of them. "Boxes of Splendid Rifles were ruthlessly smashed to pieces on the rails, cars and locomotives blown up, shells and cartridges thrown into pools and wells, while we . . . waded knee deep in coffee and sugar," observed Anderson in near disbelief. Captain Walker also reported that everything and anything that could not be easily carried was deliberately ruined. Everything, that is, except for the hospital tents. They were set up and left to provide shade for the sick and wounded soldiers who also were left behind. Thomas Olcott and Joseph Beth were company members who were sick, and John Thureau was wounded and unable to march. They stayed at Savage Station, where they were taken prisoner by the Confederates. That Independence Day, in a Richmond prison, Thureau died of his wounds.[43]

The destruction of supplies was completed during the morning of June 29, and then the troops waited tensely throughout the oppressively hot, fly-filled afternoon for another enemy assault. They waited in vain, or so it first appeared, and around supper time the army finally pulled out. The Manitowoc boys, who were part of the rear guard, had marched only about two miles, however, before they heard heavy gunfire behind them. They swung about, rushed back to Savage Station, and took up a position along the rail line, where the Rebels crashed upon them in three successive waves before finally being driven back. Then the regiment rushed off into the night and was swallowed up in the hot, humid darkness. They did not stop or even look back until three o'clock, at which time they collapsed into the sleep of exhaustion. "We threw ourselves down by the side of the road and slept till dawn when we was again aroused and marched to join the rest of the Brigade from which we had been cut off," noted Anderson in his journal. They caught up with the others at White Oak Swamp.[44]

There, too, the Confederates crept up and opened fire with a flash of artillery directed on their wagon train. That, said Anderson, created "a scene of great confusion." Evan Jones indicated that the teamsters panicked and "some of them mounted their mules and galloped off, leaving the wagons to their own fate; and more would have followed the example but for the armed guard which compelled them to do their duty."[45]

The boys of the Fifth took cover in a nearby pine forest and remained there until ordered to reemerge and confront the enemy. Once again, it was an extremely hot day. "Men were dropping down from sunstroke and exhaustion like hops," declared Jones. Anderson was among them. "My wounded leg had been troubling me and fatigue over-powered me and I fell insensible in the road," he later explained. He was revived when comrades poured water from their canteens on his head, but remained too weak and disoriented to join in the fight. When the attackers were eventually driven off, and as night descended, the Wisconsin soldiers once more took flight. Anderson was unable to keep up and was indeed fortunate to have escaped at all. "Some of the stragglers," he recounted, "caught some mules that had been stampeded by the panic and hitched them up to an empty wagon and about 20 of us proceeded in that way." "Had it not been for this," he added, "I should certainly have fallen into the hands of the enemy."[46]

In making its escape, the regiment once again became separated from the main army. Because of the darkness they did not realize this until well into the middle of the night, and once they did, they halted, turned about, and fretfully retraced their route all the way back to White Oak Swamp, before again setting out to cover another nearly eighteen dark miles before rejoining the others. It was a night, recalled Castleman, "full of terrible anxiety and danger." He worried—they all worried—about enemy soldiers lurking in the darkness of the dense pine forest as they walked through that unfamiliar region. They contended with the phantoms of their own imaginations, perhaps more terrifying in some ways than real flesh-and-blood enemies. They could have been cut down, declared the doctor, "without the chance of a chivalrous fight," and that, he charged, would have been "murder of the worst sort." Besides the fears, it was "one of the hardest marches" they had ever endured, said Anderson. During the night most of the soldiers cast aside packs and bedrolls in desperate last-ditch efforts to keep up. James also told his father that he, too, had left everything behind on the trail, everything except his rifle, letters, family pictures, and New Testament. In the morning, when they finally caught up with the main Union force, they quietly fell into line and marched off to Malvern Hill.[47]

It was there that the last terrible clash of the campaign took place. But before that battle commenced Anderson and his regiment were moved off, through still another storm, toward the James River. The next day, July 1, they climbed to the top of a high hill and there became spectators to "some of the most terrible fighting ever known in the history of the world," where McClellan's "Grand Army scattered like a flock of sheep, everyone going his own way."[48]

Castleman also reported on Malvern Hill. From what he witnessed, he was convinced that not "since the invention of gunpowder," had "so bloody . . . or so obstinately contested" a battle ever been fought. Although something of an exaggerated claim, it must have seemed justified from his vantage point. Wave upon wave of Confederates charged up the long, steep slope, one following another into the storm of whining shot and shell. Dirt and shrapnel flew everywhere through the humid, smoke-filled summer air, and the constant thundering of Union batteries, which leapt and thudded along the ridge, was deafening. Once again, remarked Castleman, huge trees were "uprooted and torn to shreds," the splinters spraying out in all directions. The artillery fire, however, was especially cruel to the attacking Southern infantry. "Down it mows their charging ranks, until they lie in heaps and rows, from behind which our men fight as securely as if in rifle pits," wrote the sickened doctor. In time, it all seemed to him like something from the darkest depths of hell, like some malevolent force loosed upon the world and moving across the broken ground littered with countless corpses. The Union soldiers fought on, engulfed in sights and sounds so overwhelming and surreal that "the combatants seemed infatuated with excitement and the very terror of the scene lashed them into a love of the conflict," declared Castleman.[49]

The Southerners finally fell back, and as the firing ceased and the shadows of twilight lengthened, the cries of wounded men and injured animals could be heard for the first time. Around midnight the exhausted Union survivors set out for Harrison's Landing. As they did so the skies opened up and rain crashed down in torrents. The roads were soon turned to "deep and sticky sheets of mud." For the soldiers, most of whom had not slept or eaten in days, the retreat demanded more strength and stubbornness than many could summon. "The men, at every step, sank nearly to their knees in mud," wrote Castleman, who, by then, was himself approaching a state of complete demoralization. He observed many who could not keep up and who "dropped by the wayside and were left." "Some," he wrote, "died from exposure, some dragged themselves into camp, and many were captured by the enemy." Those who could still walk and who hunched their shoulders and pushed on became, said Evan Jones, a procession of "men famished for food, men lame and bleeding, men with ghostly eyes looking out between bloody bandages," collectively "the grim, gaunt, bloody picture of war in its most terrible features." When they finally reached Harrison's Landing they were fully spent, and there, while most collapsed to the soaked earth, some remained propped against their rifles and slept where they stood. That night "the wind blew damp and chilly" off the James River.[50]

On the morning of July 2, it was apparent that the brash self-confidence so evident among the soldiers in March, at the time of their landing at Fort Monroe, was all but gone. Now the Army of the Potomac shivered in the mud along the river flats awaiting the final crack of doom. It was as if they had been driven to the very edge of the world, and when the sounds of the approaching enemy were again heard near midday, they must have believed they would soon to be massacred where they lay.

But that was not their fate. Anderson and most of his comrades were still in the land of the living for the eighty-sixth anniversary of American independence. That day, in Manitowoc, Sewall Smith told his readers that "the brave boys" of Company A had been "treading in the footsteps of the men of the Revolution." So they had, but to the boys themselves it appeared that their situation had become even more miserable and far more desperate than it had ever been for the soldiers of Valley Forge. The Army of the Potomac was both beaten and disillusioned. Their spring offensive had collapsed and they had become, said one of them, a sorry pack of "careworn, weary Northmen in the night of hunger and defeat."[51]

CHAPTER 5

Autumn Storms

We had done nothing more than endure. We had survived,
and that was our only victory.
                              —Philip Caputo, *A Rumor of War*

NEVER SINCE the retreat of Napoleon from Moscow has there
been so disgraceful a failure as the Peninsula Campaign,"
wrote a disgusted Dr. Alfred Castleman in his journal. By midsummer of 1862 he was fed up: "In the year that we have been in
the field our fine army has been frittered away without having
accomplished anything." He asserted, "Without a change in leaders
our cause must be abandoned." The leader for whom he had the
least respect was General McClellan. "I fear McClellan is a failure,"
he concluded, and that was an opinion shared by a growing number
of men in the regiment. But there was no change in leaders, not
then, not for some months to come, and during that time the mood
of the men became still more dark and cynical as the disasters and
dashed hopes of spring and summer were compounded by an
equally demoralizing autumn campaign. Along the way many more
young men were used up. Their lives seemed to become like mere
commodities, too often misspent and squandered as the costs ex-
acted by the war became much higher and harder to pay than any
of them had ever bargained for.[1]

It was mid-August before the Army of the Potomac was evacuated from the muddy river flats at Harrison's Landing. The survivors
of the Peninsula campaign retraced almost the same route by which

they had come, making their way back through Williamsburg and Yorktown, back to Hampton and Fort Monroe, from where they were again carried north by steamboat to Alexandria. They arrived there on August 24.

In the weeks between Malvern Hill and the final evacuation of the James River Valley major changes occurred in the general military situation in the East. McClellan was demoted, Henry Halleck was brought in from Mississippi and made general in chief, and, at the same time, a second large Union army was assembled in northern Virginia and placed under the command of John Pope. On the other side of the struggle, once it was clear that McClellan was indeed leaving the Peninsula, Lee made countermoves that shifted the focus away from Richmond toward Washington, D.C. Thomas "Stonewall" Jackson and his corps were first sent northwest to Gordonsville and Cedar Mountain and then up the Rappahannock Valley. Pope had sufficient force to handle that new development, but on August 26, Jackson swung sharply to the east at Salem and in less than two days marched his twenty-four thousand men more than fifty miles along the railroad tracks, through Thoroughfare Gap, all the way to Manassas. There they fell upon the huge Federal supply depot, consuming and carrying off all they could and destroying what remained before vanishing into the countryside.

General Pope, who had misjudged matters, moved to regain control of events, and Halleck ordered McClellan, then in camp near Alexandria, to hasten to Pope's support. By the time Pope again located the elusive Confederates it was August 29, and they were well positioned along a wooded ridge about two miles west of the old Bull Run battlefield, north of the Warrenton Pike. Eager for a fast and stunning victory, Pope opened the attack before his army was ready, before reinforcements could arrive, and well before he had a clear understanding of what needed to be done. What followed was a succession of wrong guesses and fatal mistakes, and although Union troops fought with brave determination, their efforts were poorly organized and their advances repeatedly thrown back. On the second day, when James Longstreet and his army of thirty thousand joined Jackson in the battle, Pope and his men were decisively defeated.

McClellan and his army never arrived in time to help. Sulking with hurt feelings and resenting his subordinate role to men he considered his inferiors, McClellan was at first unresponsive to Halleck's orders to assist Pope. Anderson noted in his diary that the entire Army of the Potomac remained idle in camp for five full days before finally taking to the road on the morning of August 29. By then Pope had already begun the battle. Even after they were on the move, McClellan's forces proceeded at a truly leisurely pace, covering less than seven miles and stopping at noon to make camp "within hearing of the cannonade at Manassas." They moved no faster the next day. "We resumed our march but were in no great hurry as we rested about every half hour," noted Anderson, who also indicated that it was already dusk by the time they reached Centerville. There they rested again before going on to the battlefield. But by then, he observed, "we were too late to be of any use as our forces were completely whipped and retreating in disorder."[2]

Pope, soon to be exiled to the Indian wars of Minnesota, blamed much of his humiliating loss on McClellan, and President Lincoln was convinced that McClellan had sabotaged Pope's chances for victory in a venal attempt to advance his own ambitions. Nevertheless, with no one of proven ability to replace him and being well aware of the continued power of McClellan's cult of personality, Lincoln dared not dismiss him. Instead, McClellan was given command of the defense of Washington and allowed to absorb what was left of Pope's forces into the Army of the Potomac.

After returning to Alexandria on the second of September, Anderson and his comrades were soon again on the move, camping in one place or another, crossing at Long Bridge, passing through Georgetown and Washington, then traveling by train to Tenally-town and Rockville, Maryland, all without much apparent sense of purpose. While they were thus in motion, off to the west, upstream on the Potomac, General Lee and his Army of Northern Virginia were crossing over into Maryland. In response, McClellan quickly gathered a large army at Rockville, and on Monday, September 8, the Fifth Wisconsin was on the march again, heading northwest as part of a massive force, all being sent to stop and destroy the Southerners, who by then were already in Frederick.

The Wisconsin boys tramped on to Barnesville, Buckeystown, and Jefferson, but along the way, as had been the case so many times before, some soldiers were "forced beyond their powers to endure" and they collapsed and were left behind by the roadside. At Jefferson, however, they had their spirits raised by the reception given them by the local citizens. Anderson wrote home that they "were greeted with the greatest enthusiasm [as] flags floated from nearly every window and ladies waved their handkerchiefs from every balcony." "I must say," he declared, "this aroused our Patriotism which was becoming dormant." Indeed, the entire mood and demeanor of the regiment seemed to undergo a transformation as it moved on through the Maryland countryside. Castleman noticed and commented: "It is surprising what change has taken place in the feelings and appearance of the men. The sallowness of face has given place to flush, the grumbling of dissatisfaction to joyous hilarity, [and] the camp at night, even after our long marches, resounds with mirth and music." By the middle of September, the shame associated with their earlier failures in Virginia had begun to fade and they began regaining some of their old confidence and sense of adventure. They began to hope and even believe that they were on their way to the war's final battle, and came to see the Maryland expedition as a second chance to redeem their reputations and deal "the rebel monster its death blow." They marched, observed Castleman, with "the cool determination of veterans," declaring to one another in the ranks: "Let us now come together and settle this war. . . . Let us destroy them, close the strife, and return to our homes."[3]

By the beginning of their second week on the road even the scenery seemed to contribute to their improving spirits. They were then in the mountains, it was cool and clear after the sun went down, and one night, while crossing over Catoctin Mountain, the whole landscape took on an almost magical appearance. "As we climbed the mountainside the moon rose beautifully, lighting up hill and valley, and shrub and tree. 'Twas all beautiful!" exclaimed Castleman.[4]

The very next night—September 14—they met with substantial resistance for the first time, at Crampton's Gap through South Mountain. There, said Anderson, "we found the enemy in force," and after a hard fight, "carried the pass, driving [out] the enemy with great slaughter." In that encounter Anderson and his comrades played only a supporting role, but even that added to the excitement and contributed to their renewed confidence, and they were more eager than ever to triumph. They passed through the Gap and into Pleasant Valley, moving toward Harpers Ferry with the intention of rescuing the besieged Union garrison there. Before they could reach their destination, however, the Federal commander, Colonel D. S. Miles, decided to give up what for him had become a hopeless struggle. "We started for Harpers Ferry but as the cannonading ceased we halted, our generals rightly judging the cause of the silence," noted Anderson in his journal on Monday, September 15.[5]

They made camp near Brownsville amidst the gently rolling Maryland countryside divided into patterns by the zigzag lines of split-rail fences. Anderson was put out on picket duty for two days and nights, and then, very early in the morning of September 17, after his regiment had already departed, he was brought in and sent rushing north up the Hagerstown Pike to Sharpsburg and beyond for still another mile to where huge opposing forces were gathering near Antietam Creek. "I joined the Regiment on the field where it lay in the front line of battle under heavy artillery fire," wrote Anderson. The field to which he referred was a forty-acre cornfield on the Miller farm, north of the simple whitewashed Dunker church and between the East Woods and West Woods. It had been a dull and drizzly fall morning, but as Anderson arrived on the scene, the sky cleared. As the sun broke through, their general, Winfield Scott Hancock, made a brief but stirring speech that he concluded by declaring: "Men, this will probably be the last battle of the war, if we win. Do your duty, as you have done at Williamsburg and elsewhere, and I ask no more." That was an encouraging thought—the idea of ending the war right there and then—and it made the soldiers want to do their duty and fight hard that day, during which, Evan Jones sadly observed, "the best blood in America discolored the banks of Antietam Creek."[6]

As eager as they were to contribute to the winning of the battle, the members of Anderson's regiment were given only a limited chance to participate. "We were ordered by Hancock to charge the enemy in our front, but Gen[eral] McClellan countermanded the order," wrote James, explaining why they had not played a more prominent role. Hancock himself described how they initially had led the advance in support of Sumner's right flank, crossing over the creek just below the upper bridge and rushing out into the cornfield where they were "fiercely engaged and hard pressed by the enemy." The Fifth Wisconsin and Sixth Maine led the way, but once in the field, and as a result of orders from above, they were repositioned between two of their own artillery batteries. They were to stay put and guard the guns. In front of them, across the field, was the West Woods, from which the Confederates soon emerged, setting up their own artillery with which they began shelling Union positions. That pinned the Wisconsin troops down, but from where they crouched they could observe much of the terrible bloodletting. "I shall never forget the horrible sights I witnessed where we lay in the cornfield," Anderson later told his family. When the battle was over "the wounded and dead were strewn thick as autumn leaves after a storm."[7]

At one point they were briefly engaged when the Twenty-first Georgia attempted to climb over the rail fence around the field. With their packs and weapons weighing them down, the Confederates had considerable difficulty clearing the obstacle, and in the congestion that developed, especially at one corner of the fence, they became "a confused struggling mass" into which the Northerners fired volley after lethal volley. "The catastrophe which overtook them was appalling," wrote Anderson. "The fallen soldiers were piled upon each other in a huge heap at the corner of the fence," while still others hung grotesquely over the weathered and blood-stained rails. The image of the officer who led the assault was deeply impressed upon Anderson's mind: "Their colonel, an old white headed man of powerful frame, lay a little in front of them with his face turned up to the sky, his toothless jaws firmly set together and an expression of grim determination upon his countenance which death only seemed to render more visible." James, just twenty years of age, had acquired a sad respect for the brave men he had had a hand in killing.[8]

The entire field, above and below Sharpsburg, became a place of death—a huge outdoor abattoir for the butchering of men and horses. "The dead in rows—in piles—in heaps—the dead of the brute and of the human race mingled in mass. Here lies a boy of fifteen years, hugged in the death embrace of the veteran of fifty— the greasy blouse of the common soldier here pressed the starred shoulders of the Brigadier," observed a horrified and nauseated Dr. Castleman. As usual, the scenes among the wounded were the worst. Thousands—tens of thousands—of mangled men littered the ground. Castleman was able to reach and help only a few. Most had fallen beyond his reach, between the lines, and there, said Anderson, they "tossed helplessly in the burning, broiling sun groaning, screaming, and calling vainly for help."[9]

That night, soon after midnight, Company A was sent forward. The boys carefully picked their way among the corpses and after advancing some distance, five of them, including Anderson, were sent even farther ahead. In the darkness they mounted a ridge on top of which, he declared, "it seemed as though Death had held high carnival." They paused there momentarily and then eagerly turned back.[10]

More men—nearly twice as many, in fact—went down dead and wounded during that single mid-September day at Sharpsburg than all the Americans who fell during the War of 1812, the Mexican-American War, and the war with Spain yet to come. Twenty-three thousand casualties lay upon the fields, in the woods, and along the creek banks, where it seemed, as one Wisconsin soldier put it, there had been "a great tumbling together of all heaven and earth."[11]

The next day an eerie hush prevailed over the scene, and when the darkness again descended, Lee and his army slipped southward, back over the Potomac and into northern Virginia, leaving behind their unburied dead and uncared-for wounded. Union forces had won at Antietam, but it was a victory made hollow by the enemy's escape. Because Lee had been allowed to retreat, the war would not be ended there, and the Northern soldiers knew only too well that the brutal struggle they had so much wished to conclude could grind on indefinitely. They blamed McClellan for that. In his own oddly myopic view, the general called the battle a great victory and boast-fully informed Washington: "Maryland is entirely freed from the presence of the enemy, who have been driven across the Potomac." But more accurately, he had foolishly permitted Lee's army to survive to fight again, thereby squandering the Northern lives that had been spent there. The soldiers who buried the dead and bandaged the wounded seemed to understand that much better than he, and Castleman noted that after that, the hostility and disdain the men felt toward McClellan was "no longer expressed in muttered disaffec-tion." They could no longer stoically suppress their disappointment or contain their rage. "He can be nothing short of an imbecile, a coward, or a traitor," declared the good doctor.[12]

While death held sway among those cornfields and woodlots of Maryland, it also haunted the thoughts and dreams of Rosa Kellner back in Manitowoc. Since the death of her older sister, Barbara, Rosa swung erratically between a deep love of life and a dark morose wish for her own death. She had vivid and terrifying dreams about the deaths of her other sisters, her brothers, and herself. She dreamed of being buried alive, in images so disturbingly real that she became fearful of falling asleep. She also expressed some strong desires to be reunited with Barbara and "to go to that place where the good dwell." Her preoccupation with death became especially intense that summer when an unusually large number of villagers took sick and died of tuberculosis. News from the front undoubt-edly contributed to the deepening of her dark moods. Her dejection reached an especially dismal depth when she heard rumors about the death of her dear friend, Charles Butler, having been killed in battle. Even before his departure for the war, Rosa had disturbing dreams about Butler's violent demise, and in the late summer of 1862 those premonitions seemed to be coming true. She brooded

about the possibility of her dreams reflecting some prophetic powers, which further complicated and intensified the grief she suffered
over the loss. Rosa had felt both affection and admiration for Butler:
"He was a brave, intelligent man . . . and a skilled millwright . . .
in all the strength and vigor of manhood." She took the news of
his death very hard. It came on top of so much else and made
coping with her many trials even more daunting.[13]

That September her tribulations took on a frightening new
dimension when shocking news of an impending Indian attack
reached the lakeshore community. Suddenly, everyone, both in
town and throughout the surrounding region, was terrified over the
prospects of being brutally massacred by painted, rampaging savages
from out of the west. That August the hunger and inhumane
conditions brought on by the near-criminal neglect of the Federal
government had provoked the Santee Sioux of Minnesota into
violent rebellion. They raided frontier farms and near the end of
the month made a devastating attack on New Ulm, Minnesota,
which they left in rubble and flames. Several white settlers were
killed and many more taken captive. That set off a wave of hysteria
that rushed across the entire region from the Dakotas to the shores
of Lake Michigan.

During the evening of September 2, 1862, that hysteria finally
reached Manitowoc. Rosa heard a great commotion in the streets
about nine o'clock, and on stepping outside the Williams House
Hotel to see what was happening, she discovered a large mob of
people "hurrying hither & thither [and] the drums were calling
men together." There were refugees from the countryside—hundreds of them—pouring into town. "One wagon after another
comes containing Farmers & their families [and] they say that ten
families have been murdered by the indiens [*sic*]," exclaimed Rosa.
Some people coming in warned that there were at least four hundred bloodthirsty, nearly naked savages heading eastward at great
speed, spreading their reign of terror throughout the countryside.
Others claimed there were as many as fifteen hundred, but whatever
the estimated numbers, the fear those rumors incited was of sufficient magnitude to cause widespread panic. Ox carts rumbled into

town and over the Eighth Street bridge all night, and hundreds of people hid themselves within the protective brick walls of the courthouse. At one point some horsemen came galloping in, shouting at the top of their lungs that the Indians were already within four miles of Manitowoc, and another man, who sought a room at Rosa's inn, told her that "the green bay road was covered with Indiens." In only a short while the Williams House was crowded to overflowing with women and children whose husbands and fathers remained in the streets, organizing into armed companies and marching up and down in preparation for battle. Church bells clanged hour after hour in the darkness, so that no one went unwarned, and people continued to pour into town "hurrying up to the court house with each one a bundle on their backs probably thinking the indiens were not far off." Men were posted outside the courthouse with loaded guns, while inside women boiled large cauldrons of water and pitch to pour down on the savages if they ever attempted to storm that bastion. Other men gathered at Laverenz's blacksmith shop, just around the corner from Rosa's place, and melted lead into bullets and musket balls, and still others patrolled the south bank of the river armed, in some cases with only pitchforks and axes. Rosa herself suddenly wished she owned a gun of some kind, but because she did not, she proceeded to gather the hotel's carving knives, meat cleavers, and toasting forks, and to accumulate a large pile of stones, which, she said, she intended "to hurl at them as they passed by," if they managed to cross over into her part of town.

The fearful commotion continued on through the night and into the next day. That morning Rosa's brother Michael rode into town. He had been skeptical and initially ignored the warnings, deciding to remain on his farm. During the night, however, people had continually run up to his house, pounded on his door, and shouted, "the indiens, the indiens, pack up, pack up, fly, fly!" Finally, just before dawn, he later informed his sister, "about two hundred men arrived and told him that every road was crowded with Savages." At that, he ended his holdout and headed for town with everybody else.[14]

No Indians, painted or otherwise, ever appeared. But a full four days passed before the panic subsided. Only then did the people jammed into the courthouse, Klingholz Hall, and the Williams House Hotel begin somewhat sheepishly to return home. Fear had been at the heart of it—all kinds of fear of things both real and imagined, and much of it could be neither admitted nor articulated. By the second autumn of the Civil War, even for the people in Manitowoc County, the world had become a more menacing place, but unlike the soldiers, who faced present dangers and real enemies, the civilians had to contend with phantoms and with their own vague and haunting insecurities. That had been so until news of the Indian uprising spread throughout the state and reached the lakeshore, and then, even among people whose personal experiences with natives should have informed them otherwise, those dark, disturbing feelings emerged and took on a form and focus. Myths and images as old as Europe's encounter with America rose up and took control, bringing a perverse clarity into the emotional confusion and persuading the people, at least for a while, that bloodthirsty savages were the embodiment of their phantoms. Such myths and images suddenly made their fears so understandable, so acceptable, and their hostility seem so justified, and even after the panic had passed, racism persisted as a means for venting the community's emotional pressures.[15]

Soon after the Battle of Antietam, President Lincoln issued his Emancipation Proclamation, by which, starting the first day of the new year, he intended to liberate all slaves still in bondage within Confederate-controlled territory. Many Northerners hailed that as a good beginning to the ending of an ancient evil, but there were others who saw it as a threat to their way of life. Both views were expressed in Manitowoc, but among certain groups, and particularly among unskilled immigrant workers, fear of the policy's implications reached near-panic proportions that fall and early winter. Many such people were convinced that the abolition of slavery would result in a massive flood of cheap, unskilled, and easily exploitable black labor. As a consequence, they believed, wages would be diluted, opportunities for white workers would be washed away, and all they had struggled to achieve would be lost.

Such concerns may have been justified to a degree, but economics was not the sole reason for opposition to emancipation. Bigotry was certainly a major ingredient in their reactions. It had been there, only slightly beneath the surface, for some time. In the autumn of 1862, the political developments associated with the war forced it out into the open, where it took on even more vicious qualities.

Even before the war, in 1857, the issue of granting to free black adult males the right to vote had been put to the Wisconsin electorate. The Republican party officially supported the idea; the Democrats did not. In the end, the voters rejected the proposition by a margin of 41,345 to 28,235, opposition being especially intense in the lakeshore counties.[16] In Manitowoc County, where an unusually small number of voters turned out, the Democrats beat the Republicans by a margin of 586 votes. In the village itself, their victory was a narrow one, only 40 votes.

The Saturday before people went to the polls, Charles Fitch, himself a staunch Democrat, told readers of his *Manitowoc Herald* that the election was an important one, for it would decide "whether the party of disunion and negro suffrage" would "hold dominion" over public affairs. After the voting was completed he reported with considerable relief that "the vote on negro suffrage does not vary much, so far as we have learned, from the strict party vote," adding that, "in some towns, the vote in favor [of black suffrage] was a little less than the Republican vote." It would appear that the community (at least its voting members) was almost evenly divided on the enfranchisement issue, and public comments made it clear that feelings on both sides were very strong.[17]

Many people in Manitowoc abhorred slavery, and they vigorously supported emancipation. In fact, Rosa's older sister, Frances, struck her own blow for black freedom and bravely did her part to sabotage the Fugitive Slave Law. On October 18, 1860, Fannie, as her family called her, went to town and ate dinner with Rosa at the hotel. Soon after she left, Rosa wrote in her journal: "Dear sister, the secret you have told me I will tell none. You are doing a noble action in sheltering the poor runaway slave. God will reward you." Rosa hated slavery. She saw it as being at the very root of much of the evil that had come to infect the country, and she believed the war to be a divine punishment the nation had brought on itself by its toleration and support of slavery. "The people of the United Sates have sinned against a just God by going to Africa, stealing human beings, and selling them into bondage," she declared. Furthermore, Rosa was convinced that the South's immoral rebellion was nothing more than a "frantic effort to keep the demon Slavery amongst them," and therefore, the good people of the North had a sacred duty to strike down the Rebels and liberate those poor enslaved people from their chains.[18]

James Anderson shared many of the same sentiments and convictions. Even as a student in Manitowoc he had opposed slavery, and that, at least in part, may have contributed to his strong support of the Republican party. Moreover, after he had viewed slavery firsthand, his opinions hardened and he never wavered in his condemnation of it. His first direct encounter occurred in Baltimore, in the early summer of 1861, and he immediately informed his family: "I am more of an anti-slave man than ever." "A Nigger here," he observed, "is thought less of than a Horse or Ox and any white man [can] knock him down and maltreat him without fear of the consequence." Upon conversing with some black men, Anderson became particularly upset over the injustice of their condition and the falsehoods used to justify it, for he discovered, as he told his family, that black people "could talk as intelligently about any subject as a majority of white men." After Baltimore, the farther south he traveled and the more acquainted he became with slavery, the stronger grew his opposition to the "peculiar institution." At one point during the Peninsula campaign, Anderson, who always appreciated the sight of a pretty lady, remarked about seeing some well-shaped, dark-eyed, light-skinned girls who were "as handsome . . . as one could wish to see." He was therefore shocked to learn that they were slaves. Although they had "hardly any trace of Negro blood about [them] . . . yet they were slaves and very likely the daughters of their owners," he declared. Such sins of the fathers, visited upon their defenseless and enslaved sons and daughters, were unforgivable.[19]

Figure 15. Jeremiah Crowley was the fiery editor of the *Manitowoc Pilot* and an intensely partisan leader of the Democratic party in Manitowoc County. (Courtesy of The Manitowoc County Historical Society)

But not everyone in Manitowoc was in agreement about slavery. Jeremiah Crowley, for one, characterized the Emancipation Proclamation as a "crazy act" that was "condemned by all classes of people except Abolitionists." He also made it abundantly clear that he was among those who strenuously objected to even the suggestion that "the niggers shall be made free." The threat of forced emancipation, he argued, would only prolong the war and "strengthen the determination of the rebels to fight to the very last." He also objected to the idea, he plainly pointed out, because the slaves were members of "a degraded race" and thus inferior to white people in every way. Furthermore, Crowley warned his readers, "the exodus of freed Blacks from the South has already become great and alarming," and it threatened to overwhelm the Northern labor market even as far up as Wisconsin. He was deeply offended at the very thought of thousands of "niggers" being shipped north by the Republican regime, at public expense, to take the places of "true and patriotic white men," who, at the same time, were being sent south to fight and, possibly, to die in the war. Millions of dollars were being misspent for the abolition of slavery while soldiers went unpaid and their families "suffered actual want." That simply was not fair, nor was it at all sensible, for in his opinion it would only create more problems and even greater costs by granting to those people a freedom they could never properly handle. "The public money is to be further wasted," he declared, "on the liberation of a class whom we shall also have to feed afterward." But in Crowley's mind the highest and hardest costs for emancipation were not financial, they were the expense of the human lives recklessly squandered, and he informed his readers in no uncertain terms that he bitterly opposed so many good white men "being butchered and their once happy homes made desolate to the end . . . that the nigger shall be made free."[20]

In early November, Crowley stirred up racial phobias even more by reporting that large gangs of black workers had already been sent to Beaver Dam, Wisconsin, to supplement the diminished labor supply there. Beaver Dam was only about a day's journey from Manitowoc, and therefore the racial situation many of his readers most feared appeared to be getting alarmingly close to home. "This is the beginning of the end," he predicted, warning his readers that they could soon expect an inundation of ignorant black workers to come pouring into their mills and shipyards and neighborhoods. "The Abolitionists would protect 'free labor' by swarming our farms and workshops with Southern negroes purchased with the money of the people," he derisively declared. But worse—much worse by far—Crowley later added, "the leading Abolitionists" advocated "a general mixture of their own blood with that of the negroes," which would result, he forewarned, in America eventually becoming a land inhabited by a weak and mongrel race.[21]

A considerable number of Manitowoc soldiers were also infected with Crowley's virulent strain of bigotry, and among the troops, said Paleman Smalley, "the eternal nigger question . . . was a source of much annoyance and ill feeling." One from the village, who identified himself simply as an "Old Soldier," stated that a large majority of men in his outfit—the Twenty-seventh Wisconsin—concurred with his own assessment that "if it had not been for the niggers the war would never have happened." Most of his comrades strenuously objected even to allowing the "niggers" into their camps. The "contrabands," he said, were all "supported and clothed at the expense of the government," and the soldiers were required to treat them kindly, which, he added, "goes down pretty hard" with the men, mostly because the runaway slaves showed no willingness to fight for their own cause or to work for their own keep. "They are offered opportunities to enlist, but they do not seem anxious [to do so] . . . and, in fact, we find they prefer to lay around [rather] than soldier it," he informed the home folks in Manitowoc.[22]

Another local soldier also wrote about the same subject, and Crowley printed his letter in the *Pilot* under the pseudonym "Manitowoc Boy." This anonymous correspondent, who was probably a member of Anderson's company, protested vehemently that the purpose of the war had been radically changed by emancipation. He asserted: "We are [now] fighting for the abolition of slavery

and not for the restoration of the old Union." Many soldiers,
including himself, felt betrayed by that and deeply resented being
required to put their lives in danger for the purpose of freeing the
"niggers." Besides that, he complained, the freed slaves did not
even appreciate what the white soldiers were doing for them, and
he found it insultingly ironic that the freedmen taken into their
camp "have got to be so important [that] they will scarcely speak
to a white man." He admitted that before going off to war he had
been somewhat sympathetic toward the plight of slaves, but the
more personal contact he had with them, the more his mind was
changed: "My opinion is that the negroes are a race of people to
be despised, and one can arrive at no other conclusion after being
among them a short time. I am convinced from what I have seen
that they are better off today as they are than if they had their
freedom." He suggested Lincoln's policy might be motivated by
the president's own sexual interests in black women, closing his
letter with the assertion that he would not be at all surprised to
learn that Lincoln was "getting a divorce from Mrs. L[incoln] and
wedding a [Negro] wench."[23]

On the home front, race remained largely an abstract phenom-
enon. At the time of the 1860 census there were only four people
of color residing in the village, and there were none anywhere else
in the county. James Gaton, identified as a forty-one-year-old mulatto barber, originally from New York state, lived on the north side
of town with his twenty-eight-year-old wife, Irilia, a "colored female" from Cuba, and their daughter Amanda, aged seven. Otherwise, there was only Absalom Wilson, an eleven-year-old mulatto
servant, who had been born in Canada and who worked for and
lived with the O. H. Platt family. It was much the same in most
communities throughout Wisconsin, for black people comprised
only two-tenths of 1 percent of the state's whole population—only
1,171 in 1860—and most were concentrated in the southeast corner,
in Milwaukee, Racine, and Rock counties. Although few in numbers, the prejudice against blacks was widespread, and particularly
intense among Irish and German immigrants. That was made evident in the fall of 1861, in Milwaukee, when a predominantly Irish

mob dragged Marshall Clark, a young black man, from the city jail and hanged him from a piledriver following an incident involving two white girls. The lynching of Marshall Clark was an act of terrorism that for a time resulted in a decline of the city's already modest black population.[24]

A year later, in Manitowoc, just a day before the Indian scare of that early September, some of the threats many whites associated with blacks seemed briefly realized. During the afternoon of September 1 the steamboat *Iowa* took refuge at the harbor's north pier to escape the high winds and waves that made the lake especially treacherous. On board was "a party of contrabands"—Crowley referred to them as a "gang of negro deck hands"—who came ashore in the early evening and went off to one of the village's many waterfront taverns. During their "spree," according to Sewall Smith, once they had "imbibed sufficient . . . to make them feel rich, courageous, and self-important," they began brandishing revolvers and bowie knives and proceeded to bully a number of white people. Crowley claimed they engaged in "insulting everybody they met, and [were] pushing ladies off the sidewalk." In due time, however, a group of upset whites gathered, and that "small crowd of determined men pitched into them, gave them a regular thrashing, and drove them [back] on board the Boat." Smith called them "darkies," and Crowley denounced them as "miserable wretches." The incident must have provided some strong reinforcement for racial stereotypes already deeply rooted in the minds of many villagers.[25]

Concerns about race, slavery, and ethnicity also played a significant role in the election campaign that fall. What would be decided in that election, Crowley told the villagers, was nothing less than the fate of freedom itself in Manitowoc County. The Republicans "day by day were tightening the cords of despotism" about the people of the region and nation, and through their ruthless abuses of power and their blatant displays of favoritism had demonstrated that they cared much "more about the Niggers than . . . about the Union."[26]

Fitch, the editor of the *Manitowoc Herald* and also a Democrat, although one of somewhat moderate views, felt that Crowley was out of line with some of his more crude and cutting accusations. He was also upset with Crowley's uneven support of the Democratic ticket. Fitch blasted him for his cynical attempts to manipulate ethnic sensitivities as well as his claim about the Irish holding the balance of power in the county and claiming that "all other nationalities must become subservient to them." "He cares nothing for principles," declared Fitch, who accused Crowley of using his newspaper to "stigmatize private character and to accomplish his ends by falsehood." As a "zealous defamer" he had destroyed the peace and harmony that had once prevailed within the county's Democratic party, asserted Fitch. "It is strange how so bad a man can accomplish so much."[27]

Crowley called Fitch's newspaper "a bastard sheet . . . which should be perused more in a bawdy-house than in decent society" and accused Fitch himself of being a traitor to the Democratic party and to the true cause of liberty. He had been "bought up by the black Republicans," Crowley charged, and had thereby "stuck his dirty nose into that no less dirty dish of the candidates of their worn-out and used-up party."[28]

Crowley reserved some of his most bitter ink for his blistering attacks on Henry Sibree, who was running as a Republican for county superintendent of schools. Sibree had been a Union Democrat but broke with the party over the issues of slavery and the war, and in 1862, at the age of thirty-eight, was a popular lawyer and justice of the peace in Kossuth Township, with a reputation of being a "man of wide reading and fine taste." He was a Scottish immigrant—he was James Anderson's uncle, in fact—and was well respected, especially by English-speaking Protestants and Bohemian settlers. Besides that, Sibree was enthusiastically endorsed by Sewall Smith in the *Tribune,* where he was described as being "a friend to education" and "well qualified by education and natural ability" for the office he was seeking. He therefore appeared to have a good chance of winning.[29]

But Crowley portrayed Henry Sibree as a fanatic, particularly on the race issue, asserting that he was an out-and-out abolitionist with even more radical beliefs and goals than the mainstream Republican party. Sibree, claimed Crowley, was completely "in favor of the equality of the negro and the white man" and if ever given power over the schools, "he would not hesitate to grant a black nigger buck or a nigger wench a certificate to teach school as quick, if not quicker, than he would grant one to our white boys and girls."[30]

Because of the family connection, Anderson took a special interest in that fall's political contest. Just before the election, he urged his father to send him whatever information he could, as soon as he could, concerning outcomes, and indicated that he hoped the local Republicans had "done their duty" in preparation for the voting. Meanwhile, Anderson did his own part to promote his uncle's cause among the members of Company A. A good many of the young soldiers strongly favored the Republican candidates, and Sibree in particular, but were unable to vote because of their ages. If they could only vote, Anderson felt sure, his "uncle Harry" would carry the day. As it was, eighteen members of the company intended to vote for him, and there would have been more, explained Anderson, if Jack Glover had not worked so hard to convince the Manitowoc soldiers that Sibree was "a *Damned Abolitionist* and one who thought niggers as good as a white man."[31]

Sibree was not elected. He did well in the village itself, where he beat his opponent, Joseph Thombs, by a healthy margin of 318 to 224 votes, and he also carried the townships of Kossuth, Cooperstown, Gibson, Eaton, and Liberty. But in the end he received only 40 percent of the county's total vote, and Thombs won convincingly by 668 votes. Henry Sibree's defeat was unusually devastating in the largely Irish tannery settlement of Two Creeks, where he failed to receive a single vote. He also did very poorly in Two Rivers and Maple Grove, both of which also had substantial Catholic and Irish populations. But besides Thombs's victory, and to Jeremiah Crowley's great delight, the Democrats also swept the entire county, winning every office up for election that year.[32]

Race and the fears it stirred up had a considerable influence on the voters, but the outcome of the election in Manitowoc County also reflected diminished confidence in Lincoln and his handling of the war. Most people had assumed the war would be short, decisive, and even exciting. By the autumn of 1862, however, following a series of embarrassing failures and setbacks, the end of the war seemed nowhere in sight and there was increasing disenchantment with Lincoln's leadership, as well as with the policies of the Republican party. As a result, people in northeastern Wisconsin turned E. L. Browne, their incumbent Republican congressman, out of office and replaced him with Ezra Wheeler, a Democrat they favored by 785 votes. Also, Democrats Joseph Vilas, E. K. Rand, and Ira Smith were elected to state senate, state assembly, and as county sheriff, respectively, and all by substantial margins over their Republican rivals.

In addition to that, there was a dramatic decline in the numbers of Manitowoc County men volunteering for military service. An internal debate pulled the community in contrary directions concerning the war. Those conflicting sentiments were reflected in a maudlin poem published in the *Pilot* late that summer by Lovina Classon. It may have been inspired by an actual conversation:

> Oh brother, must you leave me,
> Leave me here to mourn,
> Must you to the war go
> And will you never return?

The brother responded:

> Yes sister, I must leave you,
> My country's call obey,
> So do not weep, my sister dear,
> Nor try to me delay.[33]

By the time of that poem's publication, far fewer brothers were obeying their country's call. In an effort to restimulate patriotic fervor, a meeting was held in the village in late August. Those in attendance were told that "father Abraham" needed more good men. Judge David Taylor spoke about "the duty and necessity of enlistments," and Perry P. Smith made a powerful speech in which, according to the *Herald,* "every sentence was charged with bomb-shell explosiveness, and the harder he hit, the more he was applauded." But the response was not as great as the speakers and organizers had hoped for. Increasing numbers of villagers were, by then, becoming more and more convinced that the war was being dragged out mainly as a result of the incompetence of the military officers as well as the greed of war profiteers and power-hungry politicians. Even Rosa Kellner, a staunch pro-war Republican, was convinced that too many self-serving officers wanted the war to go on much longer than ought to be necessary, and she declared: "There are so many traitors among our commanders for the sake of gold [and] they prolong this terrible war and sacrifice so many human beings." By harvest time she also observed that the war had caused a serious manpower drain from the county, and that, in turn, was beginning to affect the local economy. Workers were becoming harder to find and much more expensive to hire, and among other things, that put the harvest in jeopardy. The effects were being felt on the Kellners' homestead. "Father said that so many men were gone to the war that he could not get all the hired help he wanted and that Johnny [her fifteen-year-old brother] had to work beyond his years and strength," noted Rosa while asking, "O this dreadful war, when will it end?" That was a question on the minds of many that autumn.[34]

Although Rosa had some strong misgivings about the handling of the war and worried about some of its repercussions on the home front, she could not agree with the antiwar movement, which was beginning to emerge with some strength in Manitowoc County. Nor was she sympathetic toward the local men who attempted to evade military service. That September, while waiting in a doctor's office, she observed with considerable disdain "about twenty [men] there who were anxious to pass for sick but not anxious to serve their country." For understandable reasons, Anderson shared her opinions about such fellows. He had grown increasingly upset with the unfair situation that had developed. For while he and the other volunteers did their duty at the risk of their lives and endured all manner of hardships, the slackers who remained securely at home were raking in big wages and high profits. About them, he commented to his father: "I only wish I could pick out certain ones there and say to them *you must go.*" Then he declared: "Oh those lubbers who have lain back till the 11th hour . . . I despise them! I could almost curse them!"[35]

While some Manitowoc boys avoided military service, others were feeling the full force of the storms. In October, for example, word reached the village from Corinth, Mississippi, that the local members of the Fourteenth Wisconsin (Company E had been Captain George Waldo's outfit) had clashed with the Confederates in a hard battle there. It had been "a grand row," Lieutenant Don Shove told his brother, T. C. Shove, who ran the south-side bank in Manitowoc. Temple Clark, who had left Company A during the Peninsula campaign, was also there for that fight and was severely wounded. A bullet grazed him on the back of the head, another struck him under the chin, and yet another hit him in the chest, entering just to the right of his breastbone and blowing out through the muscle and bone of his back. At first he was pronounced dead, but fortunately for him he regained consciousness just as a burial detail was about to throw him into a shallow grave. Clark was saved at the very last moment and sent north to an army hospital in Illinois.[36]

Morris Vandoozer, another member of the same company, was not so lucky. In a long letter printed by Fitch in the *Herald,* his comrade, Andrew Sloggy, described what befell Morris. According to his report, an enemy sniper spotted him and "Vandoozer was shot through the head while taking a chew of tobacco." Sloggy also mentioned that although Vandoozer's body was not buried for another three days, "he still had retained the tobacco in his fingers."[37]

The company's captain at the time was Levi Vaughn, a well-liked young officer from up the lake at Kewaunee. He too was a victim of the Battle of Corinth, and his death, said Sloggy, had "cast a gloom over the whole Regiment." Sloggy himself had been right there, right beside Vaughn, when he was hit and went down. He tried to lift him up and carry him out of danger; he struggled to pull him off the field but could not do it. The Rebels were rushing down upon them "like so many demons broke loose" and "nothing seemed to check their progress," he reported. Private Sloggy stayed with him as long as he could—as long as he dared—and Captain Vaughn finally insisted that he leave in order to save himself. Before fleeing, however, Sloggy attentively listened to the captain's last words. "Tell my wife and all my friends that I did my duty and died for my country," he requested. It was important, perhaps more important than anything left in life, for Vaughn to have the people back home know he had died well. There was still a remnant of romance left in the war, and dying with dignity, with one's emotions still under tight control, remained the mark of a good man. That season, many young men worried about their ability to do that, worried about how they would face death when their time came, and hoped they might be as controlled and courageous as Levi Vaughn had been.[38]

In that same battle at Corinth, Francis Engle and John Reed, who had been friends back in Manitowoc before the war, were both taken prisoner by the Confederates. Engle, whose brother George was in Anderson's company and whose father was the Episcopal priest who had buried Waldo, had been hit behind the left ear by a piece of lead. It penetrated his head, moved down along his jawbone, and lodged in his chin, causing him considerable pain. That weakened him during their long and fatiguing march across Mississippi. "The sun was very hot and I think I should have fainted, but for John's tying the handkerchief over my head," he later said. But young Engle became even more enervated from a lack of food during his first two days of captivity and, he noted, it was not till the third night that "there was some beef thrown in among us." Although there was very little of that, it was at least fresh rather than salted meat, and he remarked that he greatly enjoyed the taste.

The next day, they plodded on to Ripley, Mississippi. There they camped in the fairgrounds, were fed some cornbread and more fresh beef, and were marched off the next day to Holly Springs, where they were loaded on a train that carried them south to Jackson. By then Engle was reaching the point of exhaustion. His strength was gone, his spirits depressed. But Reed looked after him and saw to it that he had water to drink and a portion of whatever food there was. During the chilly autumn nights, when they were bedded down on the bare damp ground, Reed tried to make Engle as comfortable as circumstances would permit. "He . . . took off the only coat he had and gave it to me for a pillow and slept in his shirt sleeves," and when the "rebels brought in blankets for the wounded . . . he saw that I had one," Engle later informed his family. From Jackson they were sent to Vicksburg and imprisoned there in the county workhouse, which was surrounded by a forbidding twenty-foot-high brick wall. There, for the first time in their captivity, they were fed reasonably well. It was simple food—beef, corn meal, and molasses—but there was plenty of it and they got it with some regularity. However, their stay in Vicksburg was brief. They remained there only a week, and then a prisoner exchange was negotiated. Soon after that, Engle and Reed were on board the Federal steamboat *Dakota,* which carried them up the Mississippi River to Benton Barracks, just outside St. Louis. They had spent time there the previous spring before heading for Shiloh. Although it was good to be out of the Confederate prison, the trip up the river took eleven full days and during it, complained Engle, "we received worse treatment than we did in Rebeldom—worse than dogs."[39]

That autumn, Company K of the Twenty-first Wisconsin made its way through Kentucky and Tennessee with the Army of the Cumberland. That company, organized late that summer, contained eighty-eight recruits from Manitowoc County and was under the leadership of Captain Charles Walker—Horace Walker's older brother—who had been a county judge until entering the army. In early September they all left Manitowoc, and after a brief stop at Oshkosh, where they joined other companies from central Wisconsin, they departed the state for Cincinnati. After that, they seemed almost always on the move, never staying more than a few days in the same camp, always packing up and pushing on southwest to Louisville and then down to Perryville. Throughout the march they slept on the stony ground without tents or shelter of any kind. It was hard going through the hilly rough countryside of northern Kentucky. Some of the boys became exhausted, and many others— far too many, indicated Captain Walker—were "scattered along the route . . . sick in hospital."[40]

The company also suffered losses on October 8, on the Chaplin Hills, near Perryville, where the boys were introduced to the enemy for the first time. The regiment had been assigned to guard the Third Division's ammunition train and was therefore marching near the rear when the battle broke out. They were rushed forward about a mile, and Colonel John C. Starkweather of Milwaukee positioned them in a cornfield at the base of a hill from where two Union artillery batteries were operating. "We entered the fight about three o'clock in the afternoon, and were under fire until after sunset," wrote Captain Walker. The worst time, however, came during their first half-hour in the field. No sooner were they in position than they came under intense attack. "I then ordered the Twenty-first Wisconsin to fire and charge the front, but," wrote Starkweather, "being a new regiment, their colonel being wounded and their major killed at about the time such order was given, no field officer was left to carry the command into execution . . . [and] being sorely pressed by the brigade and battery in front, it retreated in some disorder and confusion." Their colonel, Benjamin Sweet of Chilton, was seriously wounded, Major Fred Schumacher was killed, and sixty-five other members of the regiment lost their lives that afternoon. Eighty more of them were wounded at Chaplin Hills. Three Manitowoc County soldiers in Walker's company were among the dead—Warren Mosher, John Sullivan, and William Wight—seven were wounded, and six taken prisoner. When the battle was over, one veteran told Walker that the gunfire at Chaplin Hills was "much more severe than at Shiloh, for the same length of time," and the captain himself confessed: "I hope it will not be necessary to see another battle. One such as we have passed through should suffice for a lifetime."[41]

Mead Holmes, Jr. was a member of that company. He was the twenty-year-old son of the town's Presbyterian pastor and was himself the superintendent of the church's sabbath school. He was very popular with the children he taught, as well as the adult parishioners, of whom Rosa was one. Rosa held young Holmes in high esteem and felt deep affection for him. Holmes and Anderson were also good friends. They were the same age, belonged to the same church, and had been classmates together, and when Anderson left with the army, Mead's mother wrote him regularly. While Anderson volunteered for service and went off to war, Holmes stayed behind to work as a clerk in John D. Markham's law office. Over time, however, as he grew more militant in his support of Lincoln and his policies, he must have also become increasingly uncomfortable about remaining in his safe situation while others were risking their lives in defense of the principles in which he so vehemently believed. Eventually, after what must have been some painful soul searching, Holmes decided to become a soldier, and when Charles Walker organized his company, he joined up. That was in August of 1862, and when Anderson heard the news he simply remarked: "So Mead has enlisted, well I am glad of it."[42]

On the Sunday prior to his departure, Holmes assembled the whole sabbath school together, announced that he would soon be going off to war, and briefly explained why he felt morally compelled to take up arms. "I think there was not a dry eye there or a heart that did not feel sorrow," wrote Rosa, who was present for the occasion. Holmes was moved by the show of affection his students made toward him and wept a little himself. In his speech he said: "I go to lay my life upon my Country's altar." After he bid them all goodbye, Rosa sadly remarked: "Perhaps we have seen his gentle, ever pleasant face for the last time."[43]

In letters to his parents, Holmes provided some vivid and detailed accounts of life in the Army of the Cumberland during its first fall campaign. In October he described the dry, desolate countryside of northern Kentucky, where there had been no rain in weeks and where the earth was like powder, which they kicked up in clouds when they marched. "Often we could not see the company ahead (only ten feet) and our faces [became] so begrimed with dust that we could not recognize each other," reported Holmes. To make matters even worse, they soon ran low of both food and water. "Water, water, water, was the cry," he said, and in due time, they became desperately thirsty. "We drink from mud holes where the swine are wallowing," he informed his parents, but went on to say that sometimes the situation became so bad that even that "thick and stagnant" swill had to be reserved exclusively for the sick and wounded.[44]

On October 8, 1862, when the Confederates hit his regiment with such devastating force in the cornfield near the Chaplin Hills, Holmes was out on what proved to be a successful search for water. He returned after the battle was over and was stunned by what he found. His shock became even more severe when that night, "while the moon shone full upon the scene," he was sent out to help retrieve the dead and wounded still scattered about the field. To his horror and disgust he discovered that most of the fallen men had already been robbed and stripped naked of their clothes and boots by the Confederates. The dead men were piled like cord wood in wagons and in the morning were hauled off and unceremoniously flung into a huge mass grave. "It seemed hard to throw men all together and heap earth upon them, but it is far better than to have them lie moldering in the sun," wrote Holmes. Although understandably disturbed about the very large number of Union dead, he was also troubled in discovering the unburied bodies of hundreds of Southern boys abandoned among the woods and fields of the area. "It was a fearful sight," he said, "their bloated and decaying bodies . . . torn by swine and crows—oh it is sad!" He also observed with some horror: "It is surprising how quick the dead become black." They lay there cold and still with open eyes, and one dead Rebel soldier in particular gave Mead an unusually eerie sense even among all the other grotesque sights there. "One had died leaning against a tree," he wrote, "and as we passed [he] stared at us with that wild, ghastly look that you could scarcely summon courage to meet." The corpse's gaze seemed to follow them wherever they moved, and that image disturbed Holmes for months to come.[45]

As October wore on it turned unusually cold for Kentucky. Water froze in the canteens at night, and by midmonth, complained

Holmes, the "wind was piercing" and the "snow flew thick and fast." Even that far along in their march, the soldiers still had no tents or overcoats. Some were even without blankets. But they tried to make the best of it. At night they huddled around huge fires, warming at least one side of themselves at a time. Life was made more miserable by a chronic shortage of food. In time, uniforms grew baggy, belts were tugged in another notch or two, and more men became sick and exhausted. Conditions got worse before they got better, but of all the hardships and discomforts Holmes clearly seemed most bothered by the uncleanliness of their situation. "We have had no change of clothing for a month, and are often obliged to go for days without bathing our faces. There is [only] one towel in the company, and no soap!" he complained. Before the end of the month, however, and in spite of the chilling temperatures, he managed to achieve at least some temporary relief. On October 23 he recorded: "After a slim breakfast, I went to the river and took a good bath; what a luxury! the first for a month." Things seemed to look up a little after that. The tents finally arrived, and there was a brief but glorious interlude of Indian summer. Holmes's twenty-first birthday, on October 29, came right in the midst of it. "Never was a day more glorious," he exclaimed. It was a day for memories and for putting life in perspective. "I thought of home, of each of you, of all our little picnics and birthday festivals in the groves," he told his parents. But the fine weather did not last; the warm days of Indian summer soon faded, as sleet and cold rains swept down out of the north over the Tennessee countryside. It was November.[46]

The region of the South into which they marched appeared even more desolate and depressing than the one they had left behind. It was a poor land of boulders and burned-out fields, sparsely settled by poor and backward people. At least that was Holmes's impression as he trudged on toward Nashville. Agriculture there was still in a very "rude state," and farm implements were of the "roughest kind," he observed. Furthermore, the people who worked that impoverished land lived in crude, crowded, log huts with dirt floors, stick-and-mud chimneys, and no windows. Most of the stereotypes that existed in Northern minds about the South and Southerners, and from which Northerners derived such a self-congratulatory sense of their own superiority, seemed confirmed by what young Holmes saw. He concluded that the causes of those wretched conditions could be traced to two primary sources: "The people here are ignorant in the extreme" and show "no enterprise, no genius." He attributed that to the virtual absence of schools in the region: "The glory of the North—our system of public schools—is not found there." But even more than that, he was convinced that slavery had a profoundly negative impact on the economic and social development of the whole region. About that, he wrote: "But for slavery, Middle Tennessee would be densely populated. This 'peculiar institution' curses whatever it touches. It is truly wonderful to see the difference between free and slave territory."[47]

Farther east, James Leonard was having similar thoughts about the character and quality of life in northern Virginia. He had just returned from a month-long leave in Wisconsin and must have drawn some comparison between conditions in each place. "The inhabitants in this neighborhood are awful hard up," he told Mary Sheldon. Of course, the war had contributed to that, and the war, he predicted, would make it a lot worse before it was over. "I am satisfied that they will suffer dreadfully this winter," he wrote. "Virginians will be all used up if the war lasts another year."[48]

In early November President Lincoln's patience with General McClellan's caution and messianic arrogance ran out, and he relieved him of his command of the Army of the Potomac. The would-be new Napoleon was replaced by Major General Ambrose E. Burnside. Both the army and the president expected something dramatic and decisive to happen as a result. However, for some weeks after the abrupt change in command, the Fifth Wisconsin and the boys of Company A continued to aimlessly march and camp. On November 18 they came to a complete stop about twelve miles upstream from the mouth of Aquia Creek. There they made camp on the south bank. Then they waited. "I have not seen a rebel or loaded my gun since I have been here," Leonard told Mary Sheldon a few weeks later, indicating that he and other members of the company were assuming they would all soon go into winter quarters, thereby ending, none too soon, what had been a disastrous campaign. Anderson said that he, too, had heard "some talk about going into winter quarters" but dismissed it as premature. He did so, in part, because he knew of the movements of large numbers of Union troops into the Rappahannock River Valley, to the area around Fredericksburg. Leonard was also aware of that but was not sure what would come of it. General Edwin Sumner's army was at Falmouth, just upriver and on the opposite bank from Fredericksburg, and Leonard informed Sheldon that Sumner had issued an ultimatum to the Fredericksburg city officials. He had, Leonard informed her on December 1, "demanded the surrender of that city ten days ago, giving them sixteen hours to remove the women, children, sick, and aged, at the expiration of which time he was to shell the town unless it was surrendered as demanded." The deadline had come and passed and nothing had happened. There was then more talk about winter camp.[49]

All predictions about winter camp proved wrong. Instead of suspending the war for the season, the Fifth Wisconsin broke camp at Aquia Creek on December 3 and marched southward to near Brooks Station, and then toward White Oak Church. The weather turned bitterly cold, and a heavy snowstorm left more than three inches of snow on the frozen ground. The night of the storm the boys took refuge in the woods, but after that, because conditions remained bad, they put up their tents and remained inside them until December 11, when, at four in the morning, they were awakened and told to get ready to move out. It was a clear, cold morning with a bright moon and no wind, and they were on the road well before dawn. They tramped through White Oak Church about daybreak, turned west, and set off at a quick pace for Fredericksburg, from where they had heard the booming sounds of siege guns since shortly after sunrise. "We arrived near the Rappahannock River where we lay all day [while] our Engineers were trying to lay pontoon bridges but were annoyed by the enemy's sharpshooters in the houses which were finally shelled," wrote Anderson. They got there about eleven o'clock and took up a position on the north bank of the river about two miles downstream from Fredericksburg. There was still snow on the ground but it was an otherwise beautiful day, and the Union artillery flashed and rumbled and smoked from the leafless woods along Stafford Heights.[50]

Fredericksburg was a community of about five thousand, strategically located on the Rappahannock River, midway between Washington and Richmond—each being about fifty miles to the north and south. Through the city and over its bridges (before being blown up) ran a number of important roads as well as the Richmond, Fredericksburg, Potomac Railroad line. Through late November and early December, large Federal armies had been gathering nearby, and on December 11, when Anderson and the Fifth Wisconsin arrived, there was a total of 120,000 Northern troops opposite the city on the Rappahannock's north bank. Sumner's Right Grand Division, along with Joseph Hooker's Central Grand Division, was in Falmouth, and William B. Franklin's Left Grand Division, of which the Fifth Wisconsin was a part, was downstream across from Deep Run. Deep Run was a substantial creek that cut through a deep tree-lined ravine before pouring into the river about a mile and a quarter south of the demolished railroad bridge at Fredericksburg. Anderson and the Manitowoc boys were part of the Left Grand Division's Sixth Corps commanded by General William F. "Baldy" Smith. Within that twenty-five-thousand-man corps they were under the more immediate leadership of Brigadier General Calvin E. Pratt, head of the First Brigade of Albion P. Howe's Second Division.

Throughout the afternoon and early evening of December 11, Northern gunners on the heights shelled the enemy while Northern engineers completed the construction of the pontoon bridges over the river. There were six such bridges in all—two up near the north end of Fredericksburg, between where the canal joined the river and the railroad bridge crossed it. There was another just below that railroad bridge, and three more downstream a little beyond Deep Run. Anderson's regiment was close to those three lower bridges, and around dusk, when work on them was through, two regiments from their division crossed over to guard the bridgeheads until morning. At the same time, the soldiers of the Fifth withdrew about a half mile into the woods for the night.

Across the Rappahannock from the Fifth, a flat treeless plain stretched out between Deep Run on the north to Massaponax Creek on the south, and rising from the river bank it extended back nearly two miles to a range of hills that ran almost parallel to the river. About three-quarters of a mile in from the river, and running north and south along the plain, was the Richmond Stage Road, and beyond that another five to six hundred yards, the Richmond, Fredericksburg, Potomac Railroad tracks. In between the two, until it turned at nearly a right angle to make its way to the Rappahannock, flowed the upper stretch of Deep Run. Confederate forces with artillery were concealed in the Deep Run ravine and on the ridge of hills, particularly on Prospect Hill down near Hamilton's Crossing, where Stonewall Jackson waited with infantry and artillery.

Early on the morning of December 12, the whole Sixth Corps moved out of the woods and down to the bridges, each soldier carrying plenty of ammunition and three days rations in his pack. There was heavy fog. Upstream, Fredericksburg was on fire and Dr. Castleman remarked: "The smoke of the burning city and the cannonading yesterday, have settled, casting a thick pall over the country, and we could not see more than a few rods around us." Although the smoke and fog combined to severely limit their visibility, it also hid them from the enemy and made it possible for them to cross the river virtually undetected. "Our Reg[imen]t leading the Division over the left bridge, we formed a line close to the river while the other troops were crossing," wrote Anderson in describing their initial move into enemy territory. Then, when all of Albion Howe's division was on the other side, it formed into three long lines parallel to the river and headed inland about four hundred yards. All the while, their movements remained concealed by the smoke and fog.[51]

They moved forward. Calvin Pratt's brigade took the lead, with the Fifth Vermont and the Fifth Wisconsin in front. "The whole force advanced on the enemy till we came to the road that ran through the field in which we were," wrote Anderson, who said that they then "crossed the road and formed into line of battle." That was the Richmond Stage Road. As they took up their position there, around ten o'clock, the fog began to lift and the smoke blew away. The sun broke through and Evan Jones was impressed with the grand display they all made, noting that, "forty thousand bayonets and sabers gleamed and glistened over the level plain." But soon after crossing the road they came under heavy attack. Confederate skirmishers arose out of the Deep Run ravine just ahead and came rushing toward them. The Union boys, with the Fifth Wisconsin still in the front line, held their ground for a while, but when the infantry attacks were followed by heavy cannon fire, they withdrew a short distance and took cover. "We again fell back across the road and lay behind a bank which was alongside [and] we lay there all day and night and the next morning was relieved by another reg[imen]t and put into the 2nd line of battle," Anderson wrote.[52]

It was just after daybreak that Saturday when they were moved back to the second line. Once again there was dense fog, and because of that it was not until after nine that they realized the Rebels had used the cover to move artillery right up in front of Pratt's brigade. Anderson and his comrades had just warmed themselves with drinks of fresh coffee and were wrapped in blankets, hoping to get some rest, when those guns opened fire. "I never in all my experience saw the rebel artillery fire so accurate as they did on this occasion," remarked James. They were subjected to a heavy pounding all day, and although they were protected by a small hill, three members of the regiment were wounded by flying shell fragments and one later died of those wounds. Along with the shelling there were renewed infantry attacks in the afternoon. Those attacks were driven back and broken up three times, due mainly to the efforts of the two Vermont regiments at the front of the skirmish line.[53]

About dusk, Anderson and the other members of his regiment were ordered out on picket duty. He told his family: "You may be sure this was not very pleasant news for men who had been lying in the mud shivering with cold for 3 days to hear, but it was no use to say no or swear about it so off we went in no very pleasant mood." They went out to within about fifty yards of the enemy's pickets, and remained there throughout the night. In the early evening and for a while after dark, they could see and hear battles raging to both the right and left of them. But the night passed uneventfully. After dawn, they could plainly see and communicate with the Confederate pickets opposite them. They were from Texas, and like the Wisconsin boys were not at all interested in dealing with any more danger or discomfort than was absolutely necessary. The boys on both sides got to talking and in a short time negotiated their own armistice and "agreed not to fire at each other unless either side advanced." "On the whole," wrote Anderson, "they were pretty good boys and kept the bargain of no firing sacredly and it was fulfilled equally by us." All of them were undoubtedly eager to live long enough to celebrate another Christmas and maybe even make it home again.[54]

On Sunday morning, December 14, the Fifth Wisconsin was relieved of picket duty and the boys gladly marched back to the rear, where they rested all day. Again there were artillery duels and skirmishes, but none of that seemed to disturb them. They rested through the next day as well, but then, about eight o'clock in the evening, just as they were bedding down, they were ordered to pack up and fall into line. They assumed they were going back to the front, and maybe into an attack on Southern forces near Deep Run, but those expectations were short-lived, for no sooner had they lined up when they were ordered to about-face, and, noted Anderson, "in a very short time we found ourselves again on the North bank of the Rappahannock."[55]

During most of their time on the Fredericksburg side of the river, they had been subjected to what General Pratt described as the "incessant fire from the enemy's batteries." He reported that even under such pressures and threats they had "displayed the utmost steadiness and the best of discipline during the whole affair," reacting to the shelling with "heroic indifference." The Manitowoc boys could take pride in that and relief in the fact that no one from their company had been killed or injured in that engagement. But although they had held steady, they had not won, and when they pulled back across the Rappahannock, they did so without having achieved a victory.[56]

That was true for the entire Union army at Fredericksburg. The battle there reached its peak on Saturday, December 13, when just after the fog lifted, Generals George Gordon Meade and John Gibbon of Franklin's Left Grand Division moved against Stonewall Jackson's forces dug in on Prospect Hill far to the left of Pratt's brigade. Also, around midday, Sumner's Second Corps passed through Fredericksburg and assaulted Longstreet's position on Marye's Heights directly behind the town. Both attacks failed, and the one on Marye's Heights did so most tragically.

Between the city and Marye's Heights there was a long and deep sluice running from the canal on the north to Hazel Run below town. There were only two bridges across it, and one was partially destroyed. Beyond that there was an open plain, about half a mile wide and obstructed only in places by fences and buildings. Crossing over Hazel Run and curving around the base of Marye's Heights was the Telegraph Road, which at the hill became a sunken road protected along the Fredericksburg side by a four-foot-high stone wall. Behind that wall, on December 13, stood four ranks of Georgia and North Carolina riflemen, and up the slope above them were well-manned rifle pits. Still farther up, the crest of the hill was heavy with artillery guns. At noon, General William H. French's Union brigades emerged from among the city's buildings, crossed the sluice with some difficulty, and started out across the open field toward the heights. As soon as they were beyond the edge of town, they were hit with devastating fire. A second assault came when Hancock's division surged forward. After only one hour of battle, the plain was littered with thirty-two hundred dead and wounded Northerners. In spite of those awful losses, attempts to take the heights continued. Throughout the afternoon and on into the cold twilight of that December evening, wave upon dark blue wave rushed on toward the stone wall, in each case only to break and fall back, ripped and pounded by Confederate rifle and cannon fire. Thousands of screaming boys collapsed and died as clouds of smoke rose from the ridge and flames flashed from the muzzles and mouths of muskets and guns. It was a brutal day, filled with what one survivor called "the grim and thankless butchery of war." It was "an excellent representation of Hell," an agonizing place of torment in which frightened men sought cover behind the mangled bodies of dead horses and dead comrades, and where, when the slaughter finally ended and darkness fell, Southern soldiers descended the smoking hill to strip naked the Northern dead, piled high before the cold stone wall at the base of Marye's Heights.[57]

Burnside's army had suffered nearly thirteen thousand casualties and gained nothing for the sacrifice. It was an excruciating loss that cut deep into whatever remained of the army's confidence and seriously weakened the will of the soldiers to fight on. "There is no use dodging the fact," admitted Anderson, "the late Fredericksburg disaster disheartened our army greatly and there is not a man who does not dread the idea of going across the Rappahannock to attack the enemy in their fortifications." Evan Jones used the same terms—"the army was disheartened"—and Dr. Castleman, commenting on the dejected mood that took possession of the whole regiment, observed: "I have at no time seen it so depressed." Some days after the battle, James Leonard summed it up when he confessed to friends: "Since the late battle at this point everything has looked dark to me and I have almost given up the last hope."[58]

Some simply refused to take any more. Dr. Castleman quit the army after Fredericksburg. When Anderson learned of his departure he wrote in his journal: "Surgeon Castleman resigned and went home, the Regiment missed him much for as a surgeon he was attentive to his duties and never left anything undone to make the sick comfortable." He was a good man, almost impossible to replace, and Anderson was sorry to see him go. But he was made even sadder by Colonel Amasa Cobb's departure. Anderson believed in Cobb. He admired him and wrote home saying: "I only wish you could see our Colonel, he is as fine a man as ever lived, when in danger he is as cool as a cucumber and [as] brave as a Lion and he never asks a man to go where he would not himself." He was, "in every way," declared another member of the company, "one of the best officers in the army." But in November, Cobb had stood for election to the House of Representatives and had won. Immediately after the Fredericksburg disaster he left the army. He too had had enough, enough of the killing and pain, and more than enough of the poor judgment of the commanding officers. Many others departed as winter set in, including Anderson's friend Fred Borcherdt, who went off to become a second lieutenant with the Twenty-first Wisconsin in Tennessee. That all contributed to a radical change in the character of the regiment, and just after Christmas, Leonard, still in a downcast mood, commented: "We have none of our original field officers left. . . . [and] there are so many of the old hands leaving and new recruits coming in that it scarcely seems like the same regiment."59

It was not the same regiment. Many of the original members were dead, and many more had either been sent home or into army hospitals because of the severity of their wounds or sicknesses. Others had been taken prisoner or had simply wandered off. And those who remained were greatly changed, having been made more callous by their ordeal. There remained far fewer illusions about life and war.

James Anderson had been through it all. He had endured much but had grown to feel more and more as if he and his efforts were unrecognized and unappreciated. No matter what he did, the tension and friction between himself and Captain Walker only seemed to grow more intense. Walker had his favorites and Anderson was clearly not one of them. Other members of the company were promoted while he was passed over, and about that Anderson told his father: "I hate to see men in the company inferior both in Education and Capacity promoted over my head and whom I must obey." As a consequence his contempt for Walker worsened, and he denounced the captain as being "an ignorant, conceited, young fop whose highest ambition is to be considered a 'Gay and Dashing young fellow' and whose greatest boast is that he can drink more whiskey than any other officer in the brigade." Anderson attributed not being promoted to the fact that Walker knew full well he "would not be a spy and tattler for him." Furthermore, he declared: "I do not wish to be considered a pimp and sucker of such a man

and that is the name all his noncommissioned officers bear." James
still had his honor and self-respect. Perhaps his father, who had also
been a soldier, would at least admire him for that.[60]

However, by the end of that hard and bitter autumn campaign,
he was also fed up with the attitudes of most people back home.
Manitowoc newspapers were regularly sent to the company, and
Anderson noticed how frequently they made a great fuss over the
activities of the likes of Captain Charles Walker, Mead Holmes,
and other local members of the Twenty-first Wisconsin. In time he
became considerably irritated by that and "the asses" who, he
complained, were "blowing so much dead wind about the *Gallant
21st*" but had nothing to say about his own unit. Company A had
"never received any favors from the people of Manitowoc," even
though the boys had been brave, fought hard, and suffered much.
"We asked no odds of the Manitowoc people, but," he warned,
"there will be some hard old scores to settle if we ever get back as
we think some will."[61]

Things had changed. Little had turned out as the boys had
expected, and as the struggle lengthened and grew ever more
brutal, their mood had become more somber, more disillusioned,
and more embittered. Since leaving home, the old myths and high
hopes had been dashed, too many of their darkest fears fulfilled.
As the second Christmas of the conflict came and passed, they sat
in camp and wondered what new horrors the winter and the war
might still visit on them.

CHAPTER 6

More of the Fiery Trial

Fellow citizens, we cannot escape history. . . . No personal
significance or insignificance can spare one or another of
us. The fiery trial through which we pass will light us down
in honor or dishonor to the last generation.

—Abraham Lincoln, Second Annual
Message to Congress, December 1, 1862

*I*N PRIMITIVE TIMES winter was a season of special fears. As the
days grew shorter and a cold darkness gained ascendancy over
the light, it appeared as if the sun would vanish forever, leaving all
life to face an eternal night. For James Anderson and his comrades,
however, the winter of 1863 was a season away from death, a time
of quiet rest and regeneration. During that respite they healed and
regained strength, so by the time the light again began to creep
back, holding onto each day for a little longer, they felt some
renewed sense of hope and purpose.

They camped that year near White Oak Church, between the
Rappahannock and Potomac rivers and just a little to the east of
Fredericksburg, where they were surrounded by the drab rolling
countryside of northern Virginia. Their mood, at least at first,
was as somber as the scene of which they were a part. The loss
at Fredericksburg had been emotionally devastating. But with the
arrival of Christmas they began to pull themselves out of the
depression into which that defeat had cast them. In attempts to
be festive, they trimmed their tents with sprigs of holly and

Figure 16. Mead Holmes, Jr., the son of the village's Presbyterian minister and James Anderson's hometown friend, served with the Twenty-first Wisconsin Volunteers in the Army of the Cumberland. (Etching taken from *Soldier of the Cumberland,* courtesy of the Manitowoc Public Library)

bunches of red berries and set up small cedar trees in front of them. After supper on Christmas Day, Anderson and a large number of other hometown boys crowded into Johnny Leykom's tent, where they drank a bucket of hard cider and sang loud and long into the night.[1]

The weather contributed to the improvement of their mood. It was unusually pleasant during the holiday season, and the boys had comfortable quarters. Nothing palatial, just tents, but they were spacious by army standards—ten feet long, six feet wide, and seven feet high at the ridge—and around the bottoms they placed split oak logs to help keep out cold drafts. Inside, the floor space was divided into a sleeping compartment at the rear containing three cots, and in front, where the dirt floor was dug down about two feet below ground level, they had a crude parlor in which they could sit on chairs around a fireplace.[2]

Mead Holmes and his company also enjoyed some pleasant weather around Nashville that year, and on December 25 he informed his family: "It is Christmas, the grass is green, the birds are flitting from bough to bough, the squirrels are chirping, and so it is a 'merry Christmas' even in our camp."[3]

Rosa also felt pleased about the holiday season back in Manitowoc, where the rivers were still open and free of ice. "It is the mildest Winter we have had in the last 12 years" and "the streets are most of the time as free from snow as last August," she noted with much satisfaction in her journal. It was customary to have sledding parties and snowball fights on Christmas, but even without them the members of the Kellners' large extended family who gathered in Michael's farmhouse enjoyed the occasion.

About a week before that, Rosa's older sister Anna, who was back from Texas and again in charge of the hotel, had given her an extra twenty-five cents with which she was to purchase some Christmas presents. It was not very much. With it she could buy almost nothing, and about that she wrote: "I pondered and pondered, thought & thought till my head ached; what could I buy for two shillings to make three presents that I need not be ashamed to give?" At last she came up with the idea of making bookmarks. "I was overjoyed at the idea," she declared. Having decided, she went out and over the bridge to shop on the north side for some cardboard and colored wool yarn. She cut the cardboard into strips and on each sewed with the yarn some bright roses and the initials of the individuals to whom she intended to give each of the bookmarks. On Christmas Day her mother was especially pleased, as much with the thoughtful effort as with the gift itself, and that made it an especially memorable day for Rosa.[4]

It was special for Anderson as well. Not only was it Christmas, but it was also his twenty-first birthday. In spite of all the dangers around him, he had managed to reach the point at which society finally recognized him to be a full-grown man. He had even grown a mustache to better look the part, and the war had aged him in other ways, which began to show on his face and in his attitude about life. His experience in the army, he told his sister Harriet, had been like studying in a "hard school" where he had learned a great deal about himself, the world, and human nature. The lessons since the last Christmas, he said, had been the hardest. "The record of the past year," he wrote in his journal, "is a record of suffering from Hunger, exposure, and fatigue," as well as one of deep and bitter disappointment.[5]

The experience of the war, he told his father, had only made him more determined than ever "to succeed in life." He was convinced that he had "both the talents and energy to do so" if he only managed to survive and get the chance to develop and use his abilities. What he wanted to do, if he ever got home again, he said, was to teach school for a while. Just before enlisting he had been offered a teaching position in a rural school and felt sure he would get other such opportunities when he returned. Then, in time, with savings from the army and teaching, he would attend college. "If I could possibly graduate, then," he informed his father, "when I left college [I would] resume teaching till [I] had again accumulated some money for my maintenance [and] then enter the law office and read Law with some competent Lawyer till I was considered competent to practice." Earlier he had told his father that if he survived the war he wanted to work his way up "to a position in society." Now, after a year and a half in the ranks, he wanted that more than ever.[6]

In fact, that winter Anderson grew impatient about preparing for his future and wrote home requesting that books, especially mathematics books, be sent so he could improve himself. "I am forgetting my education very fast and if I do not rub up my memory a little, I will not know anything at all," he confessed. He was eager to address that, for Anderson, like many other Scots at home and in exile, valued education both for its own sake and for how it enabled them to rise in the world. He also valued it for his sisters, and when, for example, he learned that Harriet might be unable to study English grammar in school because the family lacked sufficient money to buy the book, he immediately sent cash home and declared: "I would rather not be worth a cent and have my sister[s] well educated intelligent women." Furthermore, he urged his parents; "I hope you will buy them anything they actually need to pursue their studies so long as I have a cent of money left."[7]

Harriet appreciated her brother's support and encouragement and she too expressed a strong belief in the importance of her own intellectual development. Likewise, Rosa Kellner described in journal entries her own deep and often frustrated hunger for learning. The long days and even longer nights of drudgery around the hotel consumed most of her time and energy, depriving her of much desired opportunities to learn and grow. "My mind," she lamented on one occasion, "is not cultivated, it is like a neglected garden." "All is business and reading is not to be thought of and so my body is ever active but my mind is not used much and is not improving," she said. "I thought," she concluded, "that if my mind was trained that I might gain a name that would not perish." But she acknowledged, at least to herself, that there was little likelihood of that happening.[8]

The books were sent to Anderson, who took advantage of the wintertime lull to study with some diligence. But not all his free time in camp was spent in serious business. Even after all they had been through, there was still a boyish streak in the soldiers. They loved to play. James Leonard alluded to that in his letters, and

mentioned to Mary Sheldon in one of them: "We have considerable
sports in our camp in the way of jumping, playing ball etc. and
once in a while we have a lively game of snowballing with three
and four hundred in the game at once." Anderson, too, was enthusiastic about such play. He also liked to sing and play his fiddle,
and he, along with Joe Cox, William Turpin, Lewis La Count, and
Wilson Goodwin, hometown friends whose tents were clustered
together in the same part of camp, formed a glee club with some
members of Company F. Anderson sang alto, and in late January,
after getting paid for the first time in seven months, he sent money
home asking that some of it be used to purchase song books for
them—they particularly wanted ones containing the songs "Nellie
Gray," "Nettie More," and "Little Bennie."[9]

The healing effects of play, music, reading, and quiet conversation, along with their own youthful resilience, began to restore their
strength and spirits. By mid-February one member of the company
informed Sewall Smith and the *Tribune* readers: "The boys are fast
recovering from the fatigues of last fall and summer's campaign, and
by the time the roads are again passible . . . the tread of the Army
of the Potomac will be light and buoyant." Anderson also mentioned
that "the Army looked well and in fine condition as to drill, discipline, and appearance." Nevertheless, as spring approached, Anderson felt decidedly uneasy about his own well-being and worried
about his prospects for making it through another season of violent
conflict. That April, in a letter home, he briefly discussed his sense
of foreboding. "I feel strangely about going into this campaign," he
told his family. "Before I have always felt confident of going through
with my part safely, but," he confessed, "now something seems to
say to me that I will not escape as I have done heretofore, unscathed
by the enemy's fire."[10]

Those anxieties must have been the inevitable consequences of
the thousands of terrible sights he had seen during the preceding
months. Not even a peaceful winter's rest could rid his mind of
such memories. Anderson knew only too well what war did to
young men and was naturally concerned for his own safety and
survival. And although such worries were easy to suppress amidst

the quiet and the play of winter camp, as spring brought the inevitable battles closer, they began to reassert themselves.

In helping to prepare for a season of renewed struggle, President Lincoln paid the soldiers a visit at their White Oak Church camp in early April. "Old Abe," observed Anderson, looked "careworn," but he gave the boys some encouraging words and a strong dose of renewed determination. Later that same month, Governor Edward Salomon arrived from Wisconsin and spent a few days with the regiment. Salomon had lived in Manitowoc between his emigrating from Prussia in 1849 and moving to Milwaukee four years later. He knew some of the older men from the northeastern part of the state, and because of that his visit had a personal significance for them and was good for everyone's morale. He "made a speech [and] the Boys cheered him lustily," noted James in his journal.[11]

A week later, at nine in the morning of April 28, 1863, they broke camp and headed back toward the Rappahannock River with orders to take the ground they had failed to capture at the conclusion of their fall campaign. They were returning to Fredericksburg to try again. Even before the opening of this spring campaign, there had already been a second attempt to take Fredericksburg. Burnside, understandably eager to redeem his reputation and with something of an Ahab-like fixation about the conquest of Fredericksburg, had on January 20 ordered two of his three grand divisions to make their way to Banks Ford and there, upstream from Falmouth, cross over to the enemy's side of the river. The plan was to outflank the city and come at it from behind, rather than attempting another frontal assault against the heights.

Anderson and his comrades were participants in that expedition, which set off in midmorning and made camp two miles from Banks Ford later that afternoon. Throughout the whole first half of the month the weather had been fine, but that night it began to rain. It came down hard and the storm continued through the next day. Anderson wrote in his diary: "The army is virtually stuck in the mud, not a piece of artillery can be moved. Rained all day, did not move from where we rested." The next day was just as bad, and Burnside was forced by the circumstance to reluctantly give up the

effort. Early Friday, January 23, the boys started back for their White
Oak Church camp, but along the way they stopped at Falmouth,
where they were issued rations of hard bread, pork, coffee, sugar,
and whiskey. "We had not had anything to eat for 36 hours," noted
James. Their hunger was abated somewhat, but the downpour
remained constant and "the mud was knee deep the whole way,"
wrote Anderson in describing what became known as the "Mud
March." It was a miserable and fruitless experience, and soon after
it was over, Ambrose Burnside was replaced by Major General
Joseph "Fighting Joe" Hooker as head of the Army of the Potomac.[12]

Changes were also made within the regiment. Once Colonel
Amasa Cobb left for Congress, Thomas S. Allen from Mineral Point
was brought in from the Second Wisconsin and promoted up from
lieutenant colonel to take his place. Captain Horace M. Wheeler of
Janesville was also moved up from his leadership of Company E and
raised to the rank of major. At first, in reaction to Allen's appointment, Anderson reported that "the whole Reg[imen]t considered it
an insult to them." That was presumably because of the implication
that no one already in the regiment was worthy of the position.
Once Allen actually joined them, however, it was not long before
he won the respect of the entire regiment. Anderson told his family:
"He seems to be a very fine man and comes very highly recommended by the boys in the 2nd, both for bravery and disposition."[13]

At the same time the Fifth Wisconsin was selected to be part of
the Sixth Corps' newly organized Light Division—or "Light Brigade," as it was most frequently called—which also included the
Sixth Maine, Thirty-first New York, Forty-third New York, Sixty-
first Pennsylvania, and the Third Battery of the New York Light
Artillery. In explaining the nature and purpose of the new outfit,
Anderson said their packs would be hauled by wagons so that they
could "march light having nothing but arms and ammunition and
not more than 1 days rations to carry." They would be fast and
mobile, ideal for skirmishing and lightning-quick assaults.[14]

Once the Light Brigade was formed, the boys were again eager
to take on the enemy. They were therefore excited the morning of
April 28 when ordered to leave their winter camp and commence

the spring campaign. Later that day, on reaching the Rappahannock, they made camp with the whole Sixth Corps just behind Stafford Heights, where they concealed themselves from the enemy. They lit no fires, cooked no food, and after dark quietly came out to carry pontoons down to the river, and did so, reported one officer, "in perfect silence and order." They were once more on the river, right where they had been that previous December—downstream from the town and across from the mouth of Deep Run. There they worked all night, and in the morning stood and watched, said Anderson, while "a line of pontoon boats which we had launched . . . dashed across full of men." Those men were members of two Pennsylvania regiments, and during their crossing they came under heavy fire from Confederate pickets and sharpshooters.

The Wisconsin boys remained on the north side for another two days, camping in the open on the heights, waiting their turn to cross. While they waited, the Union artillery upstream opened fire on Fredericksburg. "We can hear the cannon and see the smoke plain," noted Anderson in his diary that May Day. Frank Haskell, a member of the Sixth Wisconsin who was also there, saw and heard the same thing that day and declared in a letter: "The great voices of those guns, as they echoed and rolled among the hills, and hurled their screeching messages among our enemys, were great music to our ears." They were preparing the way. That night the Fifth Wisconsin once more passed over the Rappahannock River.[15]

Immediately upon reaching the south bank, Anderson and his company were put out on picket duty, and sometime in the night were brought back in and the whole corps began to advance up Bowling Green Road toward the city. General John Newton's Third Division was in the lead, followed by the Light Brigade. General Sedgwick reported that they met with stiff resistance, which "continued all the way to the town, the enemy falling slowly back." "We marched nearly all night and got into the town of Fredericksburg at daylight," noted Anderson. Upon arriving they were greeted by heavy fire from the heights.[16]

It was a frightening place, and the area on the open plain in front of the stone wall at the base of Marye's Heights was known to the soldiers as the "Slaughter Pen" because of the horrors of the preceding December. Memories of that must have haunted the men and made them especially fearful of things to come. This time, too, there were Southern riflemen waiting behind that wall, and above them, as before, were the rifle pits and artillery batteries. On that otherwise pleasant Sunday morning in May it must have still seemed a place of certain doom.

Sedgwick began preparing for battle right away, and organized the assault force he would send into the Slaughter Pen. Company A, along with companies B, F, H, and I of the Fifth Wisconsin, were picked for the front rank of the battle line. They were to lead the charge against the wall and they would be backed up by the Sixth Maine and Thirty-first New York, also taken from the Light Brigade, as well as the six remaining companies of their own regiment. Their right flank would be covered by a storming column made up of the other Light Brigade regiments—the Sixty-first Pennsylvania and Forty-third New York.

As the sun was breaking over Stafford Height to their backs, the men of the assault force stacked their packs in Fredericksburg and headed down the Plank Road to the open plain. Colonel Allen led the companies of the first line out and into position behind a low ridge within about 450 yards of the stone wall. They were protected there and there they remained in suspense for nearly three hours, separated from the enemy only by rows of freshly planted kitchen gardens. And then, just before time ran out, Colonel Allen told them plainly: "Boys! You have seen those heights! You have got to take them! You think you cannot do it; but you can! You will do it! When the order 'Forward' is given, you will start at double quick—you will not fire a gun—you will not stop until you get the order to halt. You will never get that order!" At that point it must have seemed as if they had been unluckily chosen in some cruel lottery for another of the Army of the Potomac's suicide missions.[17]

It was about nine o'clock when the order finally came. They gripped their guns, rose from the ground, and charged toward the heights yelling at the tops of their lungs. They "went forward with fixed bayonets, at a full run over the ground, and in less than three minutes reached the stone wall at the base of the hill, 400 yards distant," wrote an observer. As they expected, there was a devastating storm of fire coming at them from almost every direction—from the cannons on their flanks, the rifles pointed out over the cold stone barricade ahead, and down upon them from the heights above. Many of the Wisconsin boys were hit and collapsed to the ground, but those who made the distance scaled the wall and set about the bloody business of disposing of their enemies. "Our Boys dashed forward furiously . . . Bayonetted many of the Rebels where they stood and taking nearly all the rest prisoners," Anderson later informed his family. They continued up the steep hill, seizing rifle pits and artillery batteries. In the process they also took captive several hundred Confederate soldiers. This time the Slaughter Pen was theirs.[18]

Frank Haskell had witnessed the charge of Sedgwick's Light Brigade. He wrote: "Up went the stormers—The rebel rifle pits flashed and puffed their smoke along the crests, terrible—but Sedgwick's men could not be stopped—they were [out] for blood. Soon we saw the enemy begin to break upon his right, and run from his earth in utter confusion.—Our men could see it, and they roared in cheers." It was an awesome battle, he said: "Cannon thundered,—shells and shot howled and shrieked,—bullets hissed,—men roared and rushed,—and so amid the smoke of sulphur the bloody drama went on."[19]

It was a great victory—their first in a very long time—but it had come at high cost to the company. Three members of Anderson's glee club—Joe Cox, William Turpin, and Lewis La Count—were wounded. "Lewis La Count," Anderson told his family, "was shot down by my side and cried out for me to help him back but I told him I could not then but would come back after we had carried the Heights." When Anderson returned to search for his fallen friend, he was unable to find him among the many dead and wounded strewn over the hillside. James began carrying other injured soldiers down the slope to a makeshift field hospital set up in an abandoned house just beyond the stone wall. Conditions there were bad. "There was no Surgeon on the ground at first so I stayed with the wounded all that afternoon and I assure you I had my hands full," he reported home. "I carried water for them and washed the blood off their Bodies, and dressed their wounds the best way I could."[20]

Other soldiers from Company A were among the wounded. Morris Mullins, John Leykom, Ole Nelson, Frances Stir, James Whalan, William Crocker, Robert Bride, Samuel Dexter, Petro Perbault, and Gottlieb Herman had all been hit by enemy fire. So too had Captain Walker and Lieutenant Aaron Gibson. Most were taken off to army hospitals near Washington. For other lakeshore soldiers, however, the storming of Marye's Heights had been their final battle. Fred Salzman was one. Anderson told Salzman's father that he could be proud of his son, and proud of the fact that he had been "killed instantly, shot through the head by a rifle ball and fell facing the enemy with his rifle still in his hand." Salzman had been the same age as Anderson, just twenty-one. There were others —Thomas Olcott, Franz Harleick, Albert Sommer, James Bride, Albert Boisvert, Joe Biehlie, and Henry Stick—whose young lives ended on the steep hillside that early May morning. Reflecting on those losses, Anderson told his family: "The boys feel proud of their achievements but I have seen more than one coatsleeve drawn over moistened eyes as we gazed on the ghastly features of our slain comrades."[21] Ninety-three of the Light Brigade's officers and men had been killed and another 395 wounded. The Fifth Wisconsin alone lost 44 of its members, and 92 suffered wounds.

During the heat of battle Anderson had been particularly impressed by both Colonel Allen and Lieutenant Joe Goodwin. After it was over he said that Allen was "as brave a man as ever lived," and called Goodwin "as brave a Boy as ever carried a Gun." But not all soldiers there that day were so courageous. There were many, in fact, who were nearing the end of their terms of enlistment and simply refused to risk their lives on what must have appeared a hopeless cause. According to James, they "would not go into the fight with half a will, but ran like sheep." "Indeed," he declared, "some of them refused to march at all and mutinied and threw down their arms." The boys in Company A suffered because of such behavior: "Our co[mpany] lost more than any other owing to a Regiment which should have supported us on the right flank breaking and running in confusion leaving us subject to a cross fire from the rebels." Sometimes Anderson was specific with his accusations of cowardice and, in one example, pointed directly at what he characterized as the disgraceful performance of the Twenty-sixth Wisconsin, which, he claimed, was full of soldiers who had "turned their backs on the Rebels." Most of that regiment were from the Milwaukee area, but its Company F was led by Captain Henry Baetz of Manitowoc, and ninety-nine of its members were from Manitowoc County.[22]

"Not a man in our Regiment was shot in the back and all our dead lay with their heads towards the enemy," boasted Anderson, who felt certain that their brave acts that day would finally win them some much-deserved recognition and praise from the people back home. After all, they had done what no other Union soldiers had been able to do—they had beaten the stone wall and the heights at Fredericksburg. Although Mead Holmes may have diminished the importance of such things—"glory is nothing; an idle hour's brief talk, a flower that blooms to-day and dies to-morrow"—James Anderson did not. He wanted praise, wanted it almost desperately at times, and after their win on Marye's Heights he told his father that he and all the other members of the company were anxiously awaiting newspapers from up north to see what grand things were being said about them. The people back home in Manitowoc, he complained, had thus far in the war given them "the cold shoulder to a great extent," but now, because of the great victory, there was "a chance for them to redeem themselves." Of them all, Anderson thought Jeremiah Crowley was most in need of such redemption. That was, he said, because of Crowley's "dirt[y] slur" concerning the company's "fighting qualities." "Is he satisfied now?" demanded Anderson.[23]

If the boys anticipated lavish praise, reports of the battle in the Eastern newspapers proved disappointing. Although plenty was said about the contributions of the New York and Pennsylvania regiments—and almost always in heroic terms—those of the Wisconsin troops went virtually unmentioned. Reacting to what he considered to be that unforgivable sin of omission, Anderson let fly a blast of anti-Eastern hostility. "The Rats are jealous," he declared, and accused the Easterners of deceitfully trying to steal away what had been pretty much a Midwestern show. Although he regarded troops from Vermont and Maine to be first-rate soldiers, possessing qualities similar to those from the Great Lakes region, he had mostly contempt for those from the big northeastern cities. Most of them were "the Renegades and Outcasts of society . . . [in]capable of feeling the workings of principle within their bosom[s]." It was the New York regiments, he asserted, who "ran like very sheep . . . in disorder and threw themselves on the ground as if dead." Even worse, after the fight was over, those same cowards, said Anderson, made "a business of robbing the dead," their own as well as those of the enemy. They were "a disgrace to humanity," and "the Western men despise[d] the whole crew heartily." And yet, in spite of all that, they had received high praise from all the Eastern newspapers. Of course, the Eastern press and politicians consistently turned a blind eye to the faults of their own soldiers and just as consistently overlooked and ignored the brave deeds and good qualities of the soldiers from farther west.[24]

On the other hand, Anderson expected fairer treatment from the hometown people and newspapers. On several occasions he had complained to his father about the irritating snubs the company had been subjected to and the abundance of praise that had been showered on other local outfits, like Company E of the Fourteenth Wisconsin and Captain Charles Walker's Company K with the Army of the Cumberland. He thought such treatment both unfair and undeserved, and never tried to conceal the envy and resentment it provoked in him.

Much worse, however, was what he regarded as the town's shameful lack of concern for the needs and feelings of the families left behind by the men of Company A. After Marye's Heights, where their casualties had been unusually heavy, Anderson hoped that the people of Manitowoc would finally do the right thing and prove that they had "not altogether forgotten the pledges they made to take care of the Widows and Orphans of those who fell." In other cases, he said, "when men belonging to other companies were killed, assistance was immediately given." "But not so with the relatives of those belonging to Co[mpany] A who required assistance, they have been left to do the best they could for themselves," he angrily pointed out. He also implied that such discrimination was a reflection of the deeply rooted and none-too-subtle class prejudices that existed within the community. Most of the town's elite were from New York and New England. They lived on the north side of the river—up on "Yankee Hill" as it was called—and Anderson, an immigrant who lived on the river flats, was not alone in detecting the haughtiness in their social attitudes, especially toward immigrants and south-side workers. He sarcastically referred to the north-siders as the "Codfish aristocracy" and was convinced that their arrogance was the source of the unfair treatment shown toward both the men of Company A and their families. "There is none of the Codfish aristocracy in Co. A, nothing but a lot of hardfisted farmers and greasy mechanics," he declared.[25]

In the meantime, Mead Holmes and some other members of that local "aristocracy" had spent a difficult winter in central Tennessee. There they experienced no restful reprieve like that enjoyed by Company A. Instead, for Company K and all the soldiers of the Twenty-first Wisconsin Volunteers, that winter was a season of bloodletting and privation.

On the day after Christmas, they left their camp near Nashville and headed southeast on the road toward Murfreesboro. From the very start they were alerted to the possibility of sudden enemy attacks. On the second day of the march, in response to disturbing reports, they were halted and quickly drawn up into battle formation. There they were held all day, ready for a fight, through a cold and steady downpour. The anticipated attack never came, and that night they camped in the mud—"mud to the hubs" said Holmes—and bedded down "without tents, blankets, or overcoats, wet to the skin and rations . . . [all] gone." In the morning the ordeal worsened when they were required to march ten miles through a cedar swamp and to keep slogging on until midnight. The high point of the day came when they found and killed and cooked an ox. When they finally stopped for the night, they were within about ten miles of Murfreesboro.[26]

It was about ten o'clock the next morning—December 30—when they again fell into line and resumed their march down the muddy Nashville-Murfreesboro Turnpike. But they had gone less than half a mile when, without warning, their wagon train came under heavy attack from young Brigadier General Joseph Wheeler's Confederate cavalry. The train was made up of seventy-four wagons hauling their brigade's camp equipment, stores, and provisions, as well as the officers' baggage. They were then part of the Twenty-eighth Brigade, and its commander, Colonel John Starkweather, immediately sent Lieutenant Colonel Harrison C. Hobart and the Twenty-first Wisconsin down the road to deal with the attackers. They rushed to where the commotion was and found there, wrote Holmes, "wagons cross-wise in the road, mules dead, whole teams of six and eight fallen and kicking as only mules can, drivers and men hallooing at the top of their voices." Once on the scene, observed Starkweather, "the Twenty-first Wisconsin was soon hotly engaged." After a vigorous fight of about two hours, Wheeler's cavalry backed off and rode away, but not before Benjamin Tuney of Company D had been killed and twenty wagons destroyed by fire.[27]

That night they made camp near Jefferson, on the north side of Stones River. Most of the Army of the Cumberland was farther down the road, closer to the river and Murfreesboro. At dawn, on the last day of the year, thirteen thousand soldiers of Braxton Bragg's Army of Tennessee hit that main force, striking Major General Alexander McCook's camp with devastating blows. By nine o'clock, the Twenty-first Wisconsin, and the whole of Major General Lovell H. Rousseau's First Division of which it was a part, was sent forward. On the way up, reported Holmes, they "met large numbers [of men] fleeing at full speed, some on artillery, and some on wagon horses, saying they were surprised and terribly cut up." The Wisconsin boys pressed on, sometimes having to push their way through "the vast number of stragglers." "The road was lined with them, each telling some terrible tale," but, Holmes told his parents, all the members of Company K proceeded forward "perfectly self-possessed."[28]

They eventually reached the place where the battle had occurred, but by then the conflict had subsided. They waited for it to resume, and as night fell they took cover in a nearby cedar swamp. It turned bitterly cold, and before dawn the rains returned. That was a Wednesday, and the rain continued, hard, until Saturday. During all that time none of the men had shelter or food, nor were they able to light fires. "Day and night, in the cold, wet, and mud, my men suffer severely," reported General Rousseau. Around them the Confederates were "hovering in the woods," keeping Federal soldiers pinned down with nearly constant rifle and artillery fire. Holmes summed up their condition to his parents: "Much of the time we lay in the mud, the rain often pouring upon us, the most awful . . . artillery thundering above us, balls and shells passing within a few feet, and sometimes inches." To protect themselves, they dug trenches, and at one point, to deal with their hunger, they cut up and ate a young horse that had been killed close by.[29]

On New Year's Day they were sent out to protect some artillery batteries. Around eleven o'clock a Confederate brigade advanced on their position. The soldiers in gray moved to within fifteen yards of the Wisconsin troops, who then opened fire, "killing and wounding two-thirds of the entire brigade and capturing many of the remainder," noted Holmes. The next day, in the middle of the afternoon, there was a similar attack. "It was a hard fight, and the slaughter was dreadful," said Holmes, who also mentioned that when it was through, "the rebels lay piled up, three and four deep, where the canisters and grape had played upon them." It seemed a terrible way to begin the year.[30]

By Saturday night it was finished. After suffering 7,766 dead and wounded, and another 868 men taken captive, the Confederates had finally had enough. General Bragg withdrew to a new position about twenty miles to the south. For the Army of the Cumberland it had been a very "hard earned victory," as President Lincoln put it, and in achieving it, 1,730 officers and enlisted men had died,

7,802 had been wounded, and another 3,717 had been taken captive or were simply missing. In fact, almost a third of the army had been lost. On January 5 the nearly exhausted Union survivors marched through Murfreesboro and made camp near the city, too worn down to resume the offensive.[31]

Although the fighting stopped after that, conditions did not improve. The rain was unrelenting. It was cold, provisions remained in short supply, and at one point Holmes wrote in disgust: "I have not had my coat off in twelve days, and my stockings, so constantly wet, have literally rotted in my shoes. I did not suppose it possible for men to live wet and cold and hungry so long." Even when the rain occasionally ceased, the dampness remained, seeping into everything, chilling the boys to the bone week after week. Then, in late February, conditions became even more arduous when Company K was sent out to escort a fleet of foraging wagons eleven miles down the Shelbyville Pike. Once down the road they fanned out to take on loads before returning to camp. They began at four in the morning and trudged along in the ruts made in the mud by the wagon wheels, continuing without a break until four in the afternoon. It was an uneventful trip, but as they turned to head back, it again began to storm. Throughout the entire return trip the soldiers and mules lowered their heads and pushed on into a dark wall of driving rain. Bogged down with loads, the wagons got stuck, and in the sticky mud churned up by iron-rimmed wheels and hooves, marching became almost impossible. The mud grabbed at the soldier's boots, dragging them down, and soon "the darkness was so great" they "could not see the tracks at all." Wandering like blind men, "down someone would go, up to the knee in a rut full of water and mud," Holmes recounted. Finally, they "arrived in camp at midnight . . . pants soaked, shoes full of mud and water; the mud extended up indefinitely," and there collapsed into an exhausted sleep. The next morning, when they arose stiff and sore, they had no choice but to pull on those same soaked and muddy boots and clothes. It was miserable, but Holmes felt some self-satisfaction in handling the ordeal well, telling his parents, "I begin to pride myself on my powers of physical endurance."[32]

Mead Holmes tried to be optimistic. "My rule," he declared on one occasion, "is to make the best of everything, keep my counsel, mind my own business, and look on the sunny side." But despite all his cheerful, stiff-upper-lip intentions, he saw things that winter that cast a deep gloom over whatever sunny side there might otherwise have been. For one thing, conditions were extremely hard on the horses and mules, and Holmes felt real compassion for them. There was snow and sleet in February and hard, cold rains thereafter. The draft animals frequently became mired in the heavy mud. "Heads low down, they cast such a look of woe upon the passer-by," he observed while commenting on how they strained and pulled when caught, adding that "lying in the mud, six to ten inches deep, soon kills them—poor creatures!" After his trip down and back on the Shelbyville Pike, an experience that also gave him occasion to contemplate the cruel fate of the dumb beasts, he confessed: "I am always glad to see a dead mule. His work is done, and his life of misery and torture is ended." Perhaps, that winter, he also came to feel something of the same for many of the poor wretched men he saw.[33]

As the season wore on, more and more soldiers became sick. For many it was deadly. There were also the victims of enemy raids. At times the tragedy of the war seemed everywhere. At one such point Holmes sadly observed: "How many hundreds of graves are within a circuit of fifteen miles from here; every knoll, almost, has a row of them on it." But although he lamented the losses, he also saw death, at least the right kind of death, as a means of imparting greater significance to life. It was a notion even more ancient than the Christian faith to which he was devoted, but the war had given renewed value to the whole idea of martyrdom. Perhaps that was out of the need to disguise the savagery involved in the killing of hundreds of thousands of young men, and out of a desire to salvage a sense of dignity and meaning for all those boys who died painfully and almost unnoticed as a consequence of poor planning, stupidity, hubris, or just plain bad luck. Whatever the reasons, Holmes, for one, grew increasingly fascinated with the subject of military martyrdom, especially as the time for new battles approached. In late March, for example, when he learned that a boyhood friend had died in Italy, he informed his parents: "I would prefer to bleach on the battle-field slain in my country's cause, than die in Naples, away from my native land, in this hour of her peril." Those same feelings returned just two days later, while he stood by a roadside and intently watched what he described as "a splendid cavalry funeral." He was deeply moved by the solemn procession of mounted and marching soldiers, the riderless horse carrying the fallen warrior's saber and cape, with his spurred black boots fastened backward in the dangling stirrups, the unadorned army ambulance pulled by four horses bearing the body toward the grave, and the military band leading the way. "What glowing and melting music as, with slow tread and muffled drums, they passed. It seemed as if Nature, herself, hushed to hear the cadence," wrote Holmes, clearly moved by the symbols and simple dignity of the ritual.[34]

On April 11 he wrote his family of his mounting excitement over the prospect of renewed fighting. He boasted about the fine condition of the company but closed the letter by remarking: "I guess I am going to have the mumps, my neck feels like it." The next day he was dead.[35]

It was at about 1:30 in the afternoon. He had just finished lunch and was singing with friends around the fire when he suddenly collapsed and died. The army surgeon attributed his death to a "ruptured heart" caused by a congenital defect. He was twenty-one years old.

Rosa Kellner, who admired him deeply, learned of Mead's death when it was announced in the *Tribune* on Monday, April 20. It came as a great shock to everyone, but especially to her. She had "loved him like a brother," she said, and after reading the report in the newspaper, although she busied herself at the never-ending work around the hotel, she was unable to think of much else. The whole mood of the community changed, taking on a downcast appearance, for as Sewall Smith said, the news of his untimely demise fell "with crushing weight upon [all] those who knew his moral worth and manly principle."[36]

The Reverend Holmes, who had, in fact, been on his way to visit Mead in Tennessee, brought his son's body home on the *Comet*.

Flags throughout the village and on the boats in the harbor flew at half-staff, and a crowd gathered on the north pier when the ship arrived on April 21. The funeral took place on Thursday, just four days short of a full year following the spectacular ceremony at the burial of George Waldo. Once again the turnout was huge. Holmes, like Waldo, had been no "ordinary" person. He had been a member of a prominent north-side family, and his death, because of who he was and where it had occurred, magnified his significance. Furthermore, the town's people, for their own reasons and needs, attempted to fashion from his frail-hearted demise something heroic. Young Holmes had long been regarded as a good boy, especially by the Protestant middle-class standards of his society. But in death he became a paragon who reflected the most sacred values of his class and culture. With the sentimentality common to the times, he was eulogized as being "educated, energetic, industrious, with high-toned principles, and irreproachable habits" and was called a "brave young citizen soldier" who had displayed unwavering and "unselfish devotion to the cause of right."[37]

The Presbyterian church was draped with flags and black crepe, and the coffin, placed in front like some high altar, was covered with the same. On top of the coffin rested Holmes's field cap, a sword, and a sweet bouquet of freshly cut flowers. The building was filled to capacity and the windows were left open so that the large crowd of people standing outside could hear the service. Sewall Smith said it was "the largest concourse ever gathered together" in the village.

The ceremony began with the choir singing:

> Oh, wrap the flag around me, boys,
> To die were far more sweet
> With Freedom's starry emblem, boys,
> To be my winding sheet.

They sang all three verses and the chorus two more times, and some of the audience came to tears. From there the drama built, emotions rose, and the ritual climaxed with the funeral oration delivered by the Reverend J. W. Healy, an important Presbyterian cleric from Milwaukee. According to some listeners it was more a hard-hitting partisan harangue than a eulogy, but Rosa thought it was grand: "It was the best patriotic sermon I ever heard setting forth the bright as well as the dark side of the present war." In his message, while of course praising the example set by young Holmes, Healy dealt harshly with the American people. He declared that they were "becoming too effeminate, too rich, too haughty," and were not up to doing their God-given duty. The war itself, he explained, had been sent by God as a painful but necessary cure for those evils that had come to infect the whole body politic. It was, he declared, "a bleeding process to allay the fever of the nation." They were strong words, but his message must have had a powerful impact on the people who heard it; according to the *Tribune,* by the time Healy was finished, "there was hardly a dry eye in that crowded assembly," and even "men, who had faced the dangers of the battle-field, wept like children."[38]

Rosa was also deeply moved by the service and was similarly impressed by the long parade of people and carriages that moved from the church to accompany the hearse over the river and up the hill to the cemetery. "I did not think that there were so many carriages in the place, as with wonder we looked at the number . . . ahead and following us," she remarked. There were also a number of soldiers home on leave. They marched and then gathered with the crowd in the graveyard. Once the body was lowered down, and while a final hymn was being sung, each soldier cast a "handful of earth upon the coffin of their comrade." By then, no one could contain their sobbing. But when it was all over, Rosa, with an uncharacteristic absence of sentimentality, tersely stated: "Mead Holmes with all his talents was created and lived a few years and then sank in the prime of his manhood to feed the worms."[39]

When Anderson learned of Holmes's death he was apparently indifferent in his reaction and indicated that it simply reminded him that he too had to be ready to accept "the will of God without murmuring against His decree." To James and his comrades, death—painful, brutal, and almost always undignified—had become far too common to evoke much attention or emotion. In the face of it the soldiers had become fatalistic. At the same time, death had taken on something of an unreal quality despite, or perhaps because of, it having become a ubiquitous and undeniable fact of life for them. "I can hardly make myself believe that our boys were killed, it seems more like a dream than a reality," wrote Leonard. Perhaps that was the best the mind could do to retain its balance. The fatalism helped them not worry so much. So too did the dreamlike denials. And the ritual and rhetoric that were part of events like Mead Holmes's funeral still tried to turn dying into a dramatic performance so that the viciousness and absurdity of it all might somehow appear noble and fine.[40]

Shortly after the funeral, a blustering snowstorm hit Manitowoc, but it was the last of the season and was soon followed by warm days, budding trees, and the arrival of almost unbelievably good news. On May 10 a ship came in with word that Richmond had fallen. Rosa jubilantly exclaimed: "Then this war will soon be over, blood will cease to flow, and the dreadful scenes of the battlefield will end!" The whole town spontaneously burst into celebration, the noise of which, thought Rosa, "would rend the heavens." Looking out and listening from a window in the Williams House Hotel, she observed, "Shouts of joy are heard and bonfires are send[ing] their blaze up the dusky air."[41]

While others danced and sang, Rosa harbored lingering reservations. The news, she thought, seemed almost too good to be completely true, and therefore, she held back her joy and waited for confirmation. More news did arrive on May 14, and Rosa wrote dejectedly in her journal: "The report was false . . . and I fear that many more of our gallant men will have to lay their lives on the altar of their country." Waldo and Holmes and all the others had not been a sufficient sacrifice.[42]

The war continued in northern Virginia. In early May, after their stunning success at Marye's Heights, Anderson's regiment was to reinforce Hooker at Chancellorsville. But their efforts to push west were frustrated when they were blocked and turned back at Salem Church. Next they moved up to Banks Ford and on May 5 retreated once more to the north side of the Rappahannock and made camp. Soon after that—after Hooker's campaign collapsed into another humiliating Union defeat—they all marched back to an area near their old White Oak Church camp and remained there for the rest of the month.

Once back in camp, the Light Brigade was disbanded. The Fifth Wisconsin and the Sixth Maine were kept together and were put with the Forty-ninth and 119th Pennsylvania regiments to form the new Third Brigade in the Sixth Corps' First Division. The corps remained under the command of John Sedgwick, the much-admired and beloved general whom the boys called "Uncle John." The Third Brigade was put under the leadership of Brigadier General David A. Russell.

Soon it turned hot—terribly, almost intolerably hot—and the men became increasingly irritated with the weather and the repetitious drilling. Other than that, nothing changed until June 7, when, at midnight, they were turned out of their tents and ordered to march back down to the Rappahannock River. At dawn they reached the north bank, right where they had been twice before, and later in the day again crossed over to the south bank near the mouth of Deep Run. As usual, they were fired on by enemy sharpshooters. Once there they did nothing. During the night of June 9, inadvertently leaving behind six members of the company still on picket duty, they crossed back to the north side and again made camp on the bluff. Two days later they began heading north at a killing pace. Back to White Oak Church, up to Stafford Court House, and on to Dumfries, where they arrived at sundown on June 14. That day had been particularly hard. "This is the most severe march I ever was on, the day was hot and sultry, and nine men of our Brigade dropped dead from exhaustion," Anderson noted in his diary. There seemed nothing moderate left in their lives—it was either a tedious lack of action or much more than they could reasonably be expected to endure. They were thankful for the rest at Dumfries, but it was short-lived, and at two in the morning they were up and on the road again, heading up the Alexandria Pike. They trudged on until dusk, until they had reached

Fairfax Station, and there were allowed to rest the whole night and most of the next day.[43]

There was much more of the same for the rest of June—being pushed and pushing themselves unrelentingly along the hot, dusty roads heading north, hearing the monotonous tramping of their own boots for hours and days at a time. On through Drainville, Poolsville, Flattsville, to Monrovia Station and Liberty they marched, with little relief from the heat and almost no time for rest. Through most of it, the sun burnt white-hot in the cloudless sky, draining the men and animals of whatever strength they still possessed.

By the first of July they had made their way as far north as Manchester, Maryland, where they were finally permitted to stop and rest for an entire day. But only one, and not a complete one at that, for just around sunset, soon after they had dined on hardtack and coffee, a rider rushed into camp and minutes later a bugle blew. Lines quickly emerged from the confusion caused by the alarm, and by nine o'clock the foot-sore regiments of the Sixth Corps had resumed their northward journey.[44]

They were on their way to Gettysburg. At least in time that was their destination, for after the first half hour of brisk marching they were halted and informed that they had been heading in the wrong direction. Turning about, they retraced the route they had already covered. Naturally, there was grumbling in the ranks, but the men did what had to be done, and in due time they were moving northward along the road toward Taneytown. They got off the proper route once more before morning, but the mistake was again corrected, and as the sun rose they were making their way up the Baltimore-Gettysburg Pike at a steady pace. Those errors, of course, added extra miles to an already lengthy journey, but the conditions that night were almost ideal for marching. In fact, Anderson found most of it downright pleasant. "The night was cool, the road smooth and clear, and we marched silently and swiftly along," he later recalled. After a while, the silence was broken when a band, just a little ahead of them, began playing what Anderson identified as the "Old John Brown Hymn." It was exciting, almost inspiring, and it summoned up from deep within the boys a chilling martial spirit. The loud, brassy reverberations and the steady drumbeats echoed through the dark and otherwise quiet Maryland country-side, and as the troops became caught up in the cadence, they began to sing—"first a score of voices joined the words to the music, then a hundred, then a thousand, and soon ten thousand voices rolled out the battle song," wrote Anderson.[45]

It was a "happy inspiration" that made the night pass more easily and swiftly than it might otherwise have. At sunrise they stopped briefly for coffee, but by the time wood was gathered and cooking fires kindled, it was time to move on and most of the boys fell back into line before the pots were even warm. After that the sun began to climb in the clear blue sky. As it did, the heat and humidity intensified and choking clouds of dust arose from the road. By midmorning, there was no more singing, no more band music, only the shuffle and thud of thousands of human feet, the clop of hooves, and the rumble of wagons and caissons. By then many of the marchers, observed Anderson, "were fast reaching the limits of human endurance. Men reeled and staggered along as if they were drunken." But still they marched. Around noon they passed from Maryland into Pennsylvania. People there came out to wave from farmhouse porches, and sometimes they rushed to the roadside with food and water and encouraging words for the boys.[46]

At one place a farm family put out a large number of tubs and pails, and while an old man and young boy pulled bucket after bucket from the well, "a portly matron and two handsome girls were keeping the tubs and pails filled with cool sweet water," reported Anderson. They kept it up for a long time and at a rapid pace in spite of the unbearable heat. "Their faces were flushed, and they trembled with exertion," he observed. Like his comrades, Anderson too stopped to drink and took the opportunity to talk with the woman, and from their conversation learned she had two sons among the marchers heading for Gettysburg that day.[47]

About one o'clock they could hear the distant sounds of battle and could see smoke rising above the trees far up ahead. "Where the green of the trees met the skyline we could see the white puffs stand out in the blue sky," Anderson observed. Soon they could also smell the battlefield. They quickened their pace, but the battlefield was still far in the distance. "We went on and on until it seemed as though the road would never end, or as if the hills receded from us as fast as we were able to approach them," he complained. In time, however, they began to descend into a valley where the armies were already gathered for deadly combat. By then it was after three o'clock in the afternoon, and Anderson estimated they had marched about forty-two miles during the previous nineteen hours.[48]

The regiment arrived at Gettysburg at what proved to be a turning point in the war. It was the second day of the battle. At about four o'clock, just as the Sixth Corps was leaving the road and crossing fields toward Little Round Top, General Longstreet unleashed fifteen thousand of his soldiers on General Daniel Sickles's Third Corps, which was out in front of the rest of the Union army, about half a mile from the southern end of Cemetery Ridge. For the next two hours a ferocious struggle took place in the Peach Orchard and Wheatfield between Cemetery and Seminary ridges, down near Devil's Den and Little Round Top. During that same time, decisions were being made about what to do with Sedgwick's newly arrived troops, who were then in the same general vicinity as that battle. About five o'clock, General Joseph Bartlett's brigade was sent up to help plug a hole in the Union line, and the Fifth Wisconsin, along with the Third Brigade, was held in reserve. Anderson and his comrades watched, but were never a part of that violent contest in which each side suffered as many as nine thousand casualties before the Confederate attackers pulled back.

On July 3 Anderson's brigade continued to be held in reserve, and then on Independence Day morning they were moved down to relieve units of George Sykes's Fifth Corps on the slopes of Little Round Top. There too time passed uneventfully. The next morning—July 5—they crossed the valley, moved up the opposite ridge, and occupied the high ground held the day before by the enemy, and from there fired artillery at the retreating Army of Northern Virginia. By then the Battle of Gettysburg was over. It was, wrote

James, "one of the most heavy fights of the war," and it resulted in 23,190 dead, wounded, and missing Northern soldiers, about five thousand fewer than for the South. But no one from Company A, or the Fifth Wisconsin, had been killed or injured.[49]

As Anderson's regiment was beating its way northward through Virginia and into Maryland, John Reed and the Fourteenth Wisconsin Volunteers were closing in on Vicksburg, Mississippi. Reed had been there before, as a prisoner of war with Francis Engle the previous autumn. Now, in the muggy days of May, he had returned to tempt fate once again.

Reed was then regimental sergeant major, and on the morning of May 22 he prepared his troops for an assault on the city. In order to reach it, however, they would have to descend into and pass through a broad but shallow ravine filled with cross-piled trees felled by the Confederate defenders to impede such an attempt. When the orders to advance came, Reed and his company moved down into the ravine but immediately discovered that it was virtually impossible to get through the thick tangle of trunks and limbs while under heavy enemy fire. They remained in that mazelike depression for only about three minutes, but even during that brief spell, 107 members of the regiment were either killed or wounded. Reed himself was hit by a musket ball, which first stuck him on the thumb and then embedded itself in the flesh of his left thigh. He was carried away and put on the Union hospital ship *The City of Memphis.* He was luckier than many, and much luckier than Miron Dill, who was one of the Manitowoc soldiers who died that morning among the fallen trees.[50]

The war was becoming increasingly costly for the village of Manitowoc, even as the economic demands created by the massive conflict produced a great burst of prosperity within the community. By 1863 the tempo of local commerce was quickening, and early that summer Crowley boasted that fifty new buildings, many of them brick, were being erected on both sides of the river. The construction boom had begun the year before and had gathered momentum. Along with the handsome new stores and business establishments there were other improvements in the downtown area, which led Sewall Smith to compare Manitowoc's business section to that of Chicago. He wrote with pride and satisfaction about the more-or-less successful program to rid the streets of the "Hog Nuisance." A pen had been constructed on the south side of town for the confinement of stray pigs, which often ran wild in the streets. Once caught, the pigs' owners were required to pay a fine before they could retrieve their wayward beasts. As a result, declared Smith, "the time has come when ladies can go the length of two blocks without being knocked over by a dirty hog." Aesthetically, at least, this must have contributed to the community's improved business climate, which John Hume, editor of the *Chilton Times,* extolled so liberally during his visit there that June. When Hume passed through town, there were not only no loose pigs but there were no loafers or idlers loitering about either. "Every branch of industry is flourishing and everyone seems to be employed," and "Manitowoc" he observed, "presents a livelier appearance than she has done in years." He specifically mentioned that the shipyards were especially busy. Two vessels were then under construction, the largest of them being built in Rand's yard. It was a 422-ton, 156-foot wooden schooner for the Platt and Vilas Company, a local grain-shipping firm whose business was booming. When completed the ship would cost thirty thousand dollars and would be christened with the utterly prosaic name of the *Chicago Board of Trade.*[51]

All of that—the ships, the new buildings, the full employment—were sure signs of economic growth, and most people saw them as omens of a promising future. Sewall Smith was especially excited about what was happening and proclaimed with all the boosterish enthusiasm of a chamber of commerce brochure: "We are moving steadily ahead; business prospers; lands are cleared; produce raised; buildings are erected; vessels built; the arts and manufactures are progressing; schools flourish and prospects generally were never brighter." Hume had certainly been impressed: "All that Manitowoc wants to start her on the high road to prosperity is a good harbor and a railroad to tap the Chicago and Northwestern Road." Smith, however, believed that the community and surrounding area were already on that high road. "No point in the west is increasing more rapidly in the development of business resources than Manitowoc Co[unty]," he boasted.[52]

Reports on the local lumbering business were especially positive. The war and the economic growth that accompanied it, particularly in Chicago and Milwaukee, had substantially increased the demand for lumber, shingles, barrel staves, and cord wood. As a consequence, prices had also risen sharply and Manitowoc sawmill owners were hustling to make the most of those opportunities. Anderson was personally pleased with that and wrote his father: "I am glad you have plenty of business at the old mill. I hope you will have a steady job all summer and be able to aid me in providing a home for us all."[53]

Of course the new-found prosperity was very popular, but, ironically, it did little to produce harmony or agreement among the citizens. Neither the economic growth nor ritualized events, such as the Holmes funeral, were able to provide the community with a sustained sense of common cause. The deep divisions could not be pasted over for very long, and there was a turbulence just beneath the surface of village life that sometimes erupted with considerable force. That seemed to happen with greater frequency and intensity the longer the war lasted and the more the pressures it exerted disturbed the regular rhythms of community life. For example, there were large numbers of adolescent boys whose fathers were off at war, and who, lacking useful channels for their youthful energy or parental restraints, contributed to an increase in public disorder. As one visitor observed, although most villagers were "inclined to be sociable and friendly," there was "among a certain class of young men a strong disposition to rowdyism." Rowdyism was, of course, common in lumbering settlements with their large numbers of shanty boys and saloons. But by 1863 most of those workers were off at war and most disturbances of the peace were different from the spontaneous barroom brawls that had been part of the lumberman's rough way of life in peacetime.[54]

During the war Manitowoc village youths actually organized competing gangs on the north and south sides of town, and there was nothing very spontaneous about their violent activities. Sewall

Smith contended that those rival "parties of boys" were actually "encouraging a spirit of lawlessness, founded on local jealousies," and warned that "unless speedily checked, [they would] produce results of a serious character." By late February, however, there were disturbing signs that such was already the case, for by then the gangs appeared to be in a state of open warfare. In his February 25 edition of the *Tribune* Smith reported: "On Friday evening last, the north- and south-side boys met in conflict with clubs and stones, instead of their fists as hitherto, and we learned that several on both sides were severely injured." As far as Smith was concerned, the situation was getting completely out of hand. "The jealousy has reached the point that it is no longer safe for a lad to cross the river alone, as he is certain to be assaulted," he declared.[55]

By summertime, property was being vandalized on an ever-increasing scale and personal assaults were no longer confined to the boys beating up on one another. In late June an incident occurred that especially outraged Smith, and it undoubtedly disturbed many other villagers. On July 1 he reported: "Two young ladies stepped into the street on Friday evening last for the purpose of visiting the house of a neighbor close by, when they were rudely assaulted by a party of young vagabonds who commenced throwing stones at them." One of the women was struck hard, knocked down, and badly injured. Smith was quick to point out that her assailants were not children, but youths, who he asserted were clearly "old enough to know better than to bring such disgrace upon . . . [the] village." "These outrages, like several others, have become unendurable," he angrily declared.[56]

The conflicts between the gangs reflected the longstanding divisions within the community, divisions with obvious ethnic and class dimensions and exacerbated by conditions caused by the war. As the armed struggle dragged on, those old enmities festered, sometimes with ugly results.

Emotionally charged disagreements concerning the abolition of slavery and the place of black people in American society continued to divide the community. Mary Sheldon, among others, was troubled by that development and wrote James Leonard about her fears concerning "the negroes that are freed coming up north." He tried to reassure her that their mass migration to places like Wisconsin was highly unlikely. "I think that there is but very little danger of that, [the] Southern climate is better suited to them and if they can live there as free people and get paid for their labor they will stay there in preference to going up North," he explained. Leonard also denied antiwar Copperhead claims that the army was engaged in a war to liberate the slaves. They had it all turned around, he argued, pointing out that the slaves were actually being freed only as a means of more rapidly ending and winning the war. At any rate, he made it clear that he felt no personal sympathy or sense of obligation toward the slaves and concluded by declaring: "For my part I want to see the whole of them out of the country altogether."[57]

Many people in Manitowoc concurred with Leonard's views but brushed aside his somewhat subtle and sophistic ends-and-means distinctions concerning war aims. Some people, and a growing number of them at that, were convinced that the Republicans were wild-eyed fanatics driven by a near-demented sense of mission to alter the racial nature of American society. Jeremiah Crowley, for one, felt sure they would stop at nothing nor tolerate any opposition to achieve their goals. Because of that, he argued, the Republicans had become a serious threat to the rights of the people and the survival of American democracy.

Soon after the beginning of the year, Crowley castigated the Republican regime and "its tools" for its use of bullying tactics to intimidate and silence its critics. He described how two antiwar Democrats in Ozaukee County had been dragged from their homes by the Republican sheriff and his henchmen "in the dead of night and imprisoned." Another incident, quite similar, had occurred in Manitowoc. It involved Andrew Anderson, a Norwegian Democrat. Although Mr. Anderson was normally "a quiet and unoffending" man, he had voiced his disapproval of the government's handling of the war. It was because of that, Crowley asserted, that poor Anderson was soon after "dragged from his residence and incarcerated in the County Jail by three of Abe Lincoln's minions, without any authority of law whatsoever." The attack on his rights and person came without warning on a Sunday morning, and the bewildered Mr. Anderson, said Crowley, was cast into prison without ever being informed of the charges against him. Although released the evening of the same day, Crowley told his readers that Andrew Anderson was given neither an apology nor an explanation for that unlawful and unpardonable violation of his rights. It was, he said, a perfect example of the Republicans' true colors.[58]

Crowley said that signs of the Republicans' wicked conspiracy were everywhere and that even the state government had been drawn into the evil plot. Its compliance with the Militia Act was ample proof of that. Governor Salomon, in assigning quotas to each of the counties, announced that the new system of military conscription would go into effect on November 10, 1862. Immediately, there was widespread and hostile opposition to that policy throughout Manitowoc County. On the day it was to be implemented, a large antidraft demonstration took place in the village. Sewall Smith was particularly upset by the protest and described the event in his newspaper. "A band of men, principally German and Irish came to town in a body from the North part of the County and paraded the streets with the evident intention to intimidate the Draft Commissioner and postpone or prevent the draft," he reported. There was no violence (although the potential for it was clearly present), and after the demonstrators had marched around for some time "uttering threats," they left town. But once again, just before Christmas, Smith stated: "The town is full of men from the country seeking exemptions from the draft." Their efforts had some apparent success, for implementation of the draft in Manitowoc County was postponed for nearly two and a half more months.[59]

It was not until late February that the first man from the county was conscripted into military service. Crowley was outraged. He denounced the coercive character of the policy and saw the whole system as grossly unfair to the affected men and their families. "Most of them were good, able-bodied men . . . sorely needed to attend to . . . agricultural interests at home . . . [and many] had large families dependent upon them and had not the means to procure substitutes," he pointed out. The provision in the law allowing for the purchase of substitutes was controversial simply because it discriminated in favor of the rich. Initially, however, Crowley did not focus on that aspect of the problem because he was convinced that the whole system of military conscription was unconstitutional. He therefore lent his wholehearted support to efforts by District Attorney William Nichols to bring the draft law to the attention of the Wisconsin Supreme Court. He felt certain the High Court would strike it down.[60]

That strategy became irrelevant in March when the Congress— "the Abolition-nigger Congress," Crowley called it—passed the Enrollment Act. It was then that Crowley turned, with a vengeance, to the substitute issue. "The principal point in it," he indignantly charged, "is that every rich man who can spare $300 can stay home while the poor farmer, mechanic, and laborer will have to toe the mark, and make themselves targets for Southern bullets." The class implications clearly touched on very sensitive political nerves in Manitowoc County.[61]

Throughout that winter and early spring those matters were examined and reexamined, defended and denounced, in heated discussions carried on within the village. On one occasion, Almon Mosher, who was, according to Sewall Smith, "ordinarily a quiet, industrious, and sober man," joined in such a public discussion. But no sooner had he begun when Crowley came along and interrupted with an unsolicited antidraft, anti-Republican, anti-Lincoln tirade in which he used liberal amounts of his notoriously purple language. Mosher was offended. He accused Crowley of "talking treason" and told him to stop. Crowley did, leaving abruptly. A short time later, Crowley met one of Mosher's relatives on the street and gave him what must have been a highly biased version of the incident. The relative, in turn, informed Mosher of what Crowley had said, and Mosher became so enraged that he took off in search of Crowley in order to call him "to account for his slanderous reports." When Mosher and Crowley eventually encountered each other it was on the Eighth Street bridge, where they set about shouting and arguing. A crowd soon gathered. The situation grew tense, then exploded when one of Crowley's friends drew a revolver. Mosher's supporters managed to overpower him, but a massive brawl erupted in the street. News of the big fight spread fast, and soon "a number of patriotic Germans crossed the bridge" and joined in the battle. Crowley fled the scene.[62]

Sewall Smith and Crowley were, of course, always on opposite ends of most issues, and the Mosher incident provided Smith with a perfect opportunity to insult Jeremiah Crowley. "This Crowley," he declared, "is so well known as a brawling secessionist, whiskey bloat, the publisher of a dirty sheet devoted to the task of blackening the character of respectable citizens, that we need hardly say much in reference to him." However, just to make sure everyone understood what kind of a person Crowley really was, Smith called him "a bully, a blackguard, and an unmitigated liar" who had "well earned the contempt of the respectable community."[63]

That outburst occurred in February. In April, right after the Holmes funeral, another public disagreement between Smith and Crowley arose. Smith accused District Attorney William Nichols, a staunch Democrat and Crowley's political ally, of making some disgracefully improper comments during the funeral and doing so in a most offensive manner. Smith reported that Nichols had walked up and down the sidewalk outside the Presbyterian church while the solemn ceremony was being conducted inside, loudly denouncing Reverend Healy's sermon, as well as the government and its war policies. His most derogatory language was designed, asserted Smith, to incite even more unfair public opposition to the Republicans. Smith scorned Nichols, questioning his loyalty to the nation, his ability as a lawyer, and labeling him a "Copperhead."[64]

Crowley could not let that pass. He referred to "Tin Horn Smith" as a "political scavenger" who had "no sense of shame." Crowley also provided space in his May 1 edition of the *Pilot* for Nichols to respond to Smith's accusations. Nichols denied all the charges. He admitted being on the sidewalk in front of the church during the funeral, and said that he had indeed taken exception to some of Healy's remarks, thinking their partisan nature inappropriate to the occasion, but he claimed he had never spoken above a whisper and had no intentions of causing trouble. In that same edition, Nichols's explanations were fully corroborated by Perry P. Smith. The fact that this Smith—no relative to Sewall—was a founding father of the community and a prominent north-side Republican greatly strengthened Nichols's credibility. Perry P. Smith testified that Mr. Nichols had "made no noise or disturbance" but had simply leaned over to him and "in a low tone of voice" indicated that "he regretted the subject of politics was introduced by the speaker" and then quietly walked away. Nichols himself concluded his own public statement by accusing Sewall Smith of deliberately distorting the news in a cynical attempt to make political gains at his expense, and, charged Nichols, "to call down upon my head, the malice, hatred, and violence of the community."[65]

Ten days later there was a raid on the *Pilot*. The intruders forced the front door and vandalized the office and print shop, smashing cases, wrecking parts of Crowley's printing press, scattering type about the floor, and destroying the edition of the newspaper that was being composed. Type and other printing equipment was hauled down to the river and cast into the water. The vandals had departed the scene of the crime by the back door and left footprints in the mud revealing that there had been three of them.

Crowley blamed it on "Abolition scoundrels" but placed ultimate responsibility for the attack on Sewall Smith. The night of the raid there had been a meeting of the Union League just down the street from the *Pilot* office. The league was a secret organization, regarded by Crowley as being on the lunatic fringe of the Republican party, and its chief local leader was Sewall Smith. The organization existed, charged Crowley, "for no other purpose than the personal injury of Democrats and the destruction of their property," and he theorized that Smith must have stirred up his followers during the meeting. After fortifying themselves with a bottle or two of cheap whiskey, they had headed down the street to attack his newspaper while there was no one there to defend it.[66]

For the remainder of May, Crowley kept up his attacks on Sewall Smith and his newspaper. "He sinks himself below the depths where manhood dies [but] he boasts of his degradation as though it was a virtue," he proclaimed, calling the *Tribune* "the smut machine" from which poured forth "filth, follies, and infamies."[67] The venom cooled on both sides during early summer, but the attacks were resumed in August when an incident occurred that briefly made Smith the village laughingstock, and Crowley took full advantage of the opportunity it presented him.

On the second Saturday of August, in the afternoon, Smith had walked down to the lake to take a bath in the public bathhouse located about thirty feet offshore, just south of the river. It was a floating structure with a separate chamber for men and another for women, each containing tubs. The whole thing was moored to the shore by several sturdy ropes. Smith was in one side and three of his female friends were in the other. They were all comfortably immersed in the warm, sun-heated water and everything was fine until a sudden gust of high wind blew up. It buffeted the bathhouse and, in doing so, tempted some boys on the beach to shout out that the ropes had broken and that the whole building was being driven out into the lake by the gale. Of course, nothing of the kind had happened, but when the boys sounded the warning even more loudly a second time, Smith panicked. "How the captain's brain was bewildered, how he forgot his bravery . . . and thought only of shipwreck," wrote an amused Rosa Kellner in her journal. According to her report, in a mad rush to escape, Smith bolted out the bathhouse door, leapt into the cold lake water, and ran for shore. On reaching "safety" he stood upon the beach stark naked, or, as Rosa put it, "dressed in the same garment that Adam wore when he first became acquainted with Eve." Soon after his landing, Rosa mockingly added, two of his women friends, "not to be out done in their agility by their gallant leader," also came out and plunged into the lake and up onto the beach wearing nothing more than Smith. And there they stood, all three attempting to cover their nakedness with their hands. To be sure, Crowley reported all the embarrassing details, calling it "the miraculous escape of the brave and peerless *Tribune* man from the watery grave . . . amid the applause and harrahs of numerous men and boys." "It was rich, it was rare," exclaimed Rosa, who, along with Jeremiah Crowley and the rest of town, enjoyed some hearty belly laughs at the expense of Sewall Smith's dignity and pride.[68]

Smith was not amused. He was furious and he blamed the whole thing on Crowley. Smith was so upset and so certain that Crowley had been at the bottom of the whole plot to humiliate him that he declared his intentions of fighting Crowley in a duel. One Thursday evening in late August, while Crowley was out strolling along York Street past the *Tribune* office, he suddenly heard Smith shouting at him from behind. He called him "a G[od] D[amn]ed scoundrel" at the top of his lungs. Then, to Crowley's great surprise, Smith rushed upon him, jumped on his back, and struck him in the face with his fists. They punched and scuffled until forcibly separated. Then, while still swearing at one another, they went their different ways to resume their battles in the public print—their chosen weapons.[69]

The members of Company A were well aware of the Smith-Crowley feud, and most of them, although not necessarily siding with Smith, were highly critical of Crowley. In February, when they learned of his altercation with Almon Mosher, fifty-nine of them—almost all the original Manitowoc members still left—voted in favor of a resolution denouncing Crowley and the *Pilot,* asserting that his newspaper contained "articles of a treasonable and incendiary character." The resolution also commended Mosher for standing up to Crowley's bullying and setting "a good example of how traitors at home should be dealt with." The soldiers did all that, said Anderson, in order "to make Crowley & Co. squirm." But neither their resolution nor their wholehearted support of conscription had noticeable impact on Crowley's attitudes or the increasingly vituperative expression of antiwar, antidraft, and antiblack sentiments in Manitowoc County. As the disagreements heated up there, political fine distinctions faded and more people seemed inclined to identify all Republicans as outright abolitionists and all Democrats as Copperheads. Many villagers appeared to be in agreement with William Nichols, who declared in a speech to the County Democratic Club that "the persons that are responsible for the war are the Nasty, Wicked, Dirty, Stinking, Lousy Abolitionists" who were, he asserted, "negro all over except they have hair where the wool ought to grow." Throughout the spring it was evident that a larger, more militant antiwar movement was taking shape. When Governor Salomon visited Manitowoc in late July, he made a long and impassioned speech at the courthouse in which he denounced "the dirty copperheads" who, he said, "abounded so extensively in Manitowoc County."[70]

At about the same time Salomon was delivering that speech in Manitowoc, massive antidraft and antiwar protests exploded in New York City, turning into three days and nights of violent rioting in which the Irish played a prominent role. Buildings were looted and burned, whole sections of the city were razed, and black people were beaten, burned, and killed. Federal troops were finally sent in to restore order. Anderson and the boys of Company A were among them.

They arrived on August 3, and made camp on Governor's Island. By then, however, the riots had subsided and their intended invasion of New York City turned into what one of them called the "great spree," the "big blow out," and the "grand jollification." It raged for four full days and nights before the boys straggled back into camp "with empty pockets and muddled heads." Some were even arrested and incarcerated. James Leonard, who was a strict teetotaler, reported that most other members of the company were sick "from too free use of liquor and beer."[71]

In time, however, the hangovers cleared up, stomachs settled down, and the company was sent up the Hudson by steamer to Goshen and Albany. There were numerous Irish Democrats in the area, and the soldiers were subjected to a good deal of verbal abuse. But other than that, conditions were far better than anything they had seen at the front. Leonard told Mary Sheldon that it was "the best living . . . [of] any place since leaving Wisconsin." That was especially so during the mellow gold and crimson days of Indian summer along the Hudson River. There the boys were so far removed from the agonies and uncertainties of the war that they sometimes even wondered if such things had ever really been true. Anderson and his comrades hoped they might stay on there for the winter, or perhaps even longer. But deep down they all knew that such peaceful assignments could never last while the conflict still raged. So, while they rested and waited for the unwelcome orders they knew would arrive, they enjoyed what they had and "philosophied," as one of them put it, "on the shortness of human life, and the fleetness of human happiness."[72]

CHAPTER 7

Still This Side of
the Dark River

Through many dangers, toils, and snares
We have already come.
'Twas grace that brought us safe thus far
And grace will lead us home.
—"Amazing Grace"

A FARM WAGON pulled up in front of the Williams House Hotel early Friday morning, September 11, 1863, and the driver jumped down to help a woman and a young man through the door and out onto the board sidewalk along the street. The "poor young boy," as Rosa called him, was the driver's son, the woman, his mother. Although the heat of the day had already begun to rise, the lad was bundled up in heavy blankets. He was a boy of "barely eighteen years" who had served in Tennessee with the Army of the Cumberland, and Rosa, who watched the sad scene from a window, described him as having "beautiful deep blue eyes, . . . a snowy forehead, and a very rosy flush to his cheeks." He had tuberculosis. The army had sent him home to die. His mother had met him the day before on the north pier when the steamship had come in from Chicago, and they had spent the night at Rosa's place. That morning, in setting out for home, the frail young soldier "was too feeble to set up and they had to make him a bed in the wagon," observed Rosa, who matter-of-factly concluded: "He will soon die." Watching the wagon heading away up the dusty street toward the river, Rosa once again wondered just "how many brave noble youths" would have to be "sacrificed on the altar of their country" before the war would finally be finished.[1]

That late summer and early autumn Rosa saw almost a steady stream of returning soldiers. They came back from different areas of the war for different reasons and in a great variety of conditions. Some, like Wilson Goodwin of Company A, came home on leave, got married, and enjoyed some of life's goodness and pleasure before rejoining the company. Many others, with much less to celebrate, were sent home simply because they were too sick, too injured, or too exhausted to keep on with the marching and fighting. The sight of those "poor devils," as she called them, not only evoked a sense of pathos from deep within her but also caused her smoldering anger toward the South to blaze up so that she wished, and even prayed, for a harsh and painful punishment to be inflicted on those people and their whole region. That was especially so one day in early August when a homebound soldier stopped in at the hotel for supper and a night's rest before completing his journey. "He looked very badly," remarked Rosa. In fact his appearance was so pathetic that she attempted, as best she could, not to look at him: "I feared to look at him, for fear I would make him feel badly." The poor fellow, whom she guessed was about twenty-five years old, had lost both an arm and a leg, as well as a part of his jaw, which had been blown away by a piece of shrapnel. That left his face grotesquely disfigured. Rosa helped him with his supper, cutting his food and gently wiping his chin after each bite. When the meal was done they sat together and talked. He told her as best he could how he had been struck while fighting in northern Virginia and knocked unconscious, and how, while in that state, he had been taken prisoner by a rough bunch of Rebels, who with cruel deliberation had cut off his leg and arm. Both limbs had been injured in the fight, he told her, but neither severely enough to warrant amputation. "They dealt so inhumanly with him to destroy all hope of his ever fighting them again," she remarked in disgust. "It made my blood boil with anger, when I heard it, such barbarity, such unheard of wickedness practiced by people who claim to be civilized [and who], in their frantic effort to keep the demon Slavery amongst them they commit deeds that cry to heaven for vengeance."[2]

Although Rosa lamented the suffering, she never seemed to question the importance or rightness of the Union cause, nor did she doubt the North's ultimate triumph. "We are fighting for the right and I have no fear but the dark clouds will clear of[f] and good come of it," she wrote that October. She remained a true believer who frequently wished she was able to do more to assist with the struggle. "I often think about going of[f] to take care of our wounded and sick soldiers," she said, but then admitted: "My health is too delicate." Her health was indeed fragile, and although she was still a young woman of only nineteen, she suffered from painfully swollen joints, especially in her right hip and arms, as well as from severe bouts of both physical and emotional exhaustion.[3]

Rosa's conviction about the rightness of the Union cause was shared wholeheartedly by James Anderson. But that autumn he, along with James Leonard and undoubtedly the other members of the company, felt some growing concern about the possible harm being done to that cause by the increasingly militant antiwar Democrats. "The disaster that I and most soldiers fear the most," Leonard told Mary Sheldon that October, "is that these copperhead party [advocates] may succeed in carrying the election in two or three of the large states through lies and misrepresentations and thus assist in prolonging the war by working against the Authorities in Washington." Although Wisconsin was clearly not one of those "large states," the soldiers of the Fifth Regiment were uneasy about the potential consequences of that year's state and local elections. The Democrats totally dominated politics along the lakeshore, but Anderson hoped the Republicans might rebound with some strong showings in many of the county races. He was especially pleased that Perry P. Smith was running for the Republicans for the state assembly. "He is the right sort of man to send there," and he would be, James told his family, a major improvement over the Democrats then representing the area, who, he said, were "disgracing the County by their ignorant twaddle at Madison." He also hoped that

Smith's considerable personal prestige would benefit other Republican candidates. But above all else, it seemed, Anderson wished to see the lakeshore's arch-Democrat, Jeremiah Crowley, beaten and humiliated in his race for county superintendent of schools. That was the office that Anderson's uncle, Henry Sibree, had sought the year before, when Crowley had been so vicious in his attacks on him. Anderson hoped for revenge, and that September he wrote home urging his father on, exhorting him: "Do everything in your power to defeat the Traitor Crowley."[4]

Previously, in 1861, Crowley had been elected clerk of court after a fiery campaign. The next year he was easily reelected, but decided in 1863 to attempt to move up to the school superintendent's position. Perhaps he was motivated by his conviction that the county's educational system was in danger of being taken control of by a conspiracy of radical Republicans and abolitionists who intended to use the schools for political indoctrination. He certainly warned the voters often enough that such a sinister plot was afoot. That was at the core of his intensely negative campaign against his opponent, William Eldridge, and the whole local Republican establishment. But beyond that Crowley probably had more positive reasons, for, like so many other immigrants both before and after him, he undoubtedly had a deep faith in the transforming and democratizing powers of public education and therefore wished to advance that cause. On one occasion he expressed some alarm about the large numbers of children he observed in Manitowoc who were not attending school at all. They were, he said, "receiving so large a part of their education in our streets, and are thus forming habits of immorality and vice, and as such can only be regarded as candidates for our jails and prisons." He was clearly convinced that sound schools and good teachers were essential for the shaping of children into "useful members of a well regulated society," and was therefore eager to contribute to and, indeed, become the leader of such efforts in Manitowoc County.[5]

Whatever his personal goals and motives may have been, Jeremiah Crowley was at the center of the viciously partisan political storm that swept through the county that fall. He was, no doubt, one of the primary forces that whipped it up and appeared to revel in the blast and bluster of the campaign. On the other hand, he was himself an object of attacks. Predictably, Sewall Smith made Crowley his favorite target, and Crowley returned the attack. Their hard-hitting give-and-take produced a series of grossly inflated rhetorical exchanges in the public print. At times Crowley portrayed himself as the victim of an unfair and dishonest campaign designed to ruin his reputation and complained that he had become "the subject of constant abuse and vituperation." On other occasions he was defensive, declaring among other things that the "charges of habitual drunkenness" leveled against him by his opponents were "totally and wickedly false." Often he was aggressive in his own accusations against Eldridge, who, he pointed out, had been charged with embezzlement and had been expelled from the Order of Good Templars on account of his violation of their temperance oath. Candidates "in glass houses must not throw stones," he mockingly advised the Republicans in reference to the drinking issue, and in November Crowley convincingly triumphed over Eldridge and his enemies. He was elected superintendent of schools by 1,951 to 1,238 votes. Eldridge was clearly the favorite candidate within the village, outpolling Crowley there by 353 to 198 votes. Among the soldiers of Company A, Crowley's candidacy did not fare at all well, and from the whole lot of them, Anderson informed his family; "Our Friend, Unhappy Jeremiah, did not get a [single] vote!" On the other hand, Crowley's support was extremely strong in the rural areas, where he carried all but three of the townships, and some of those by wide margins. But besides that, all other Democratic candidates in the county won their contests. Not even the venerable Perry P. Smith survived what turned out to be an unqualified routing of the county's Republicans that year.[6]

The outcome of that election made Manitowoc County a political oddity. Everywhere else in the state Democratic candidates were discredited and defeated by a reconstituted and revitalized Republican organization, which included a good many war Democrats eager to put political distance between themselves and the Copperheads. They had combined to form a new Union Republican coalition.

Even their candidate for governor that fall, James T. Lewis of Columbus, had been a Democrat until 1861. As a Union Republican, Lewis beat Milwaukee lawyer and insurance executive Henry L. Palmer by an impressive 72,717 to 49,053 votes. The whole Fifth Wisconsin Regiment favored Lewis over Palmer by a gigantic margin of 418 to 1. But in Manitowoc County, Lewis lost by 647 votes. Even war hero Lucius Fairchild, elected secretary of state by a landslide as a Union Republican, lost in Manitowoc County. Crowley was, of course, delighted with the victories on the homefront and understandably disgruntled about the results around the rest of the state. There he attributed Republican success to "fraud and corruption darker and more damnable than ever disgraced a political party in this or any other country."[7]

There were apparently a good many people in Wisconsin willing to give the Republicans credit for the upsurge of economic prosperity. More importantly, many had become convinced that the war had finally turned in the North's favor and that steadfast support of the Republicans and the boys in the field would hasten its victorious conclusion. Although a different political logic prevailed in Manitowoc County, there, too, people believed they saw signs of the struggle's end. Such beliefs were often reinforced by news sent home by local soldiers, as was the case that October when Captain Joseph Rankin wrote from Arkansas: "The rebels are coming in every day in large numbers and giving themselves up." "Most of them seem tired of the rebellion," he noted.[8] But there were no signs of impending Confederate collapse in northern Virginia when the Fifth Wisconsin returned there from New York in mid-October.

After passing through Philadelphia, Baltimore, and Alexandria, where they remained confined to their coaches and stalled along a railroad siding for an entire night and day, they again took to the road and marched off to Fairfax Court House. For the next three weeks they seemed to ramble aimlessly around, marching and camping in various places in the general area of Warrenton, Virginia. It was at Warrenton that Anderson received news of the death of his boyhood friend Edward Lyon, who had been a member of the Twenty-seventh Wisconsin Volunteers and had succumbed to sickness in Little Rock, Arkansas, that September. Anderson was sadly philosophical in his reaction: "Poor Ed, [but] such is the causalties [*sic*] of war. Salzman is gone, Mead Holmes gone, and many others whom I shall miss if I ever return but God only knows who is to be next."⁹

The next morning, November 7, "just as the sky began to redden in the east" and after they gulped down cups of strong black coffee, "the columns filed into the road and swung out with a long steady marching step southward towards the enemy." They were heading for Rappahannock Station, located on the north bank of the Rappahannock River, some distance upstream from Fredericksburg, where the Confederates had positioned themselves within a formidable complex of earthworks, redoubts, and rifle pits, all of which were guarded by black banks of cannon. The Union troops arrived there about four in the afternoon, and while opposing artillery batteries boomed back and forth, Brigadier General David Russell, commander of the Third Brigade of the Sixth Corps' First Division, decided that he had "two regiments in his brigade that could take those works." They were the Fifth Wisconsin and the Sixth Maine, the two core outfits of the old Light Brigade. "No better regiment than the 6th Maine ever marched," claimed Anderson, who also said that "between them and the 5th Wisconsin there was a peculiar affection." They had been through much together. And that November afternoon, just as the sun touched the far-off western horizon, they once again moved forward to engage the enemy. They would have to ascend and descend a series of ridges in between in which, like a succession of shallow moats, water had accumulated from recent rains. They had been ordered to make their initial strike using only bayonets. In response to that order there was, said Anderson, a "hoarse murmur along the line and the rattle of rods" as the boys defiantly bit off and rammed cartridges down their barrels as they advanced toward the barricades of logs and dirt that lay ahead.

Up and down they went in their advance, and when they cleared the last ridge and were finally free of the mud and water, they flung aside their haversacks and broke into an open run, letting out with a "terrible shout" as they rushed on through an area studded with stumps and littered with cut tree limbs. In the shadowy half-light of dusk they seemed to float forward, and when the phantom figures huddled behind the earthworks saw and heard them approach, they responded with flashing lines of fire and smoke. "The shell and shot went howling around us at a dreadful rate; as we came nearer, canisters and their deadly rifle bullets commenced dropping our men thick and fast," Anderson later reported. Those not hit pressed on, seemingly undistracted by that lethal storm or the cries of falling comrades. "But our boys went on at a run, cheering loudly and carrying the fort and rifle pits for the whole breadth of our line of battle, and then commenced the tug of war," declared Anderson. The opposing forces clashed and merged into a chaos of hand-to-hand combat in which men beat upon one another with rifle butts, stabbed ferociously with bayonets and knives, and fired lead into each other's bodies from scarcely more than an arm's length away. While that was happening, Sergeant Joe Goodwin of the Manitowoc company pushed his shoulder against the wheel of a Confederate cannon, moving it around and discharging it into a crowd of gray-coated soldiers. It tore them to pieces. Goodwin then rammed in and fired off a thunderous succession of loads until he was himself shot in the head. He died by the side of the cannon, but until the very end, Anderson informed his family, Sergeant Goodwin behaved "with the bravery which has always been characteristic of him."[10]

In time, reinforcements were rushed up. Some of the Southerners made a desperate attempt to escape across the pontoon bridge spanning the river just behind them. Others threw away their packs and weapons and tried to swim across to safety. Some were killed in the water. Most were taken prisoner. Eight regiments in all gave themselves up that evening. It was a decisive win for the Northerners, but a particularly costly encounter for Company A. Joe Goodwin, along with Captain Horace Walker and Private Joseph Beth, lost their lives at Rappahannock Station. Walker had been only twenty-four years old, and Joe Goodwin just twenty. Also, James Leonard had been wounded in both an arm and a leg, and

Albert Burbridge, Albert Payne, and John Schmoke all had been struck by enemy fire. All were original volunteers who had joined up so eagerly during the spring of 1861.[11]

The victory at Rappahannock Station was followed by an embarrassing fiasco at Mine Run in the area known as the Wilderness, just south of the Rappahannock River. After that, it being too late in the season to undertake a full-scale campaign, the Army of the Potomac went into winter camp at Brandy Station, in the rolling countryside between the Rappahannock and Rapidan rivers. It was then early December and, as in the past, the troops worked to make themselves as comfortable as conditions would permit. At first they were housed in tents, but, in time, they "erected huts and cabins of logs and mud" and settled in to "make war against the monotony of camp life." All the usual activities and diversions were again employed in that effort. But also, during those long idle months, members of the opposing armies frequently engaged in "interesting conversation with utmost good nature" with one another while manning their picket lines. Sometimes the Northern boys even joined forces with the Rebels to hunt stray sheep, sharing together the fun of the chase as well as the pleasant sharp taste of the freshly roasted mutton.[12]

It turned out to be an exceedingly boring and uneventful winter. Even the weather remained dull for most of the season, and other than the usual complaints about stale biscuits, tainted salt pork, and too much drilling, the soldiers had few challenges with which to contend.

While most of the company tediously passed the time at Brandy Station, Leonard recuperated in Havenwood Hospital in Washington. He complained by letter to a hometown friend about his aches and pains, which he said were aggravated by the chilling dampness and drafts of the place. His wounds did not heal as rapidly as expected, but he remained optimistic about keeping both injured limbs and eventually getting well. He also informed his friend that he had become well acquainted with some wounded Confederate soldiers with whom he shared a ward. They were pleasant "associable fellows," he said, who "receive just the same treatment as our own men," and one of them, whose company he especially enjoyed, was "a very smart intelligent young man," who, Leonard remarked, "is quite a contrast to the most of the Southern soldiers." The old stereotypes persisted. Yet the men passed the winter with hardly a hint of the animosity one would expect of enemies. Perhaps that was because, as soldiers, they understood one another better than the civilians ever could. Then, too, for most of them the war was finally over.[13]

Most members of Company A spent the winter of 1863–64 out of harm's way, but back in northeastern Wisconsin, Rosa Kellner faced some truly mortal dangers. Early New Year's Eve afternoon Rosa's oldest brother Joseph came to town with a sleigh and team of horses to take her, Anna, and their young nephew Johnny Choupek, who lived with them at the hotel, back to the parental homestead near French Creek. Most family members intended to gather there to celebrate the arrival of the new year. It was a familiar journey of scarcely more than twelve miles along a well-marked road and, although somewhat cold, it was otherwise a pleasant day when they started out. Just a short way out of town, however, conditions changed abruptly. The sky turned slate black as scowling clouds rolled in from the north and the wind picked up. It began to snow, then to storm. "It grew colder and colder and the fast falling snow was drifted right in our faces by the wind that blew right against us," Rosa later wrote. The horses strained and tugged at the harness, plodding on through the deepening drifts. In no time it became impossible to tell where the ground and sky met, or even where the road ran and fence posts stood. The wind howled and moaned and the cold became almost unbearable. Joseph, who had carelessly neglected to bring along a hat, attempted to tie a scarf about his stinging ears but could not manage to do so. "His fingers were stiff with cold although he had a good warm pair of mittens on," remarked Rosa, who took off her own mittens and tied the scarf about Joseph's head for him.

At the same time, little Johnny, she said, "began to cry, saying his lame limb was so cold he could not feel it." Once more, Rosa took charge, wrapping an old quilt around the boy's legs. But no sooner was that done than he began to sob and complain about his hand. With tears freezing on his red cheeks he told her that he had lost a mitten and that his hand was fast growing numb. "Sure enough," exclaimed Rosa, "the mitten had slipt off and the poor hand was icy cold." She rubbed it vigorously to get the circulation going and then gave him one of her own mittens. Almost immediately, her exposed hand began showing signs of frostbite. She tucked it beneath her shawl but that was of little help. Then, "in despair," she recounted, "I unhooked my dress and pushed it in [and, in time,] it began to feel better."

All the while the blizzard grew worse. "The cold was not only piercing but great angry gusts came one after the other and drifted snow into our poor benumb faces and seemed to pierce through all our clothing," she wrote. Joseph clutched and jerked at the reins, snapping them down upon the horses' broad backs, shouting at them over the wind, urging them on into the swirling whiteness, hoping they were still heading in the right direction. All the while it grew darker and darker, and then, with what Rosa estimated to be about five more miles to go, Joseph began to complain about his feet. By then the team was wearing down. But they dare not stop for fear they would never get the horses moving again. "I feared that some great calamity would happen to us for it surely grew colder every moment," she said. More immediately, and just for an instant, Rosa felt the panic of self-concern: "I feared my nose was gone and I thought how dreadful you will look without a nose." However, her attention was once again diverted by Joseph, who turned and told her: "I fear my feet are gone!" Rosa exhorted everyone to fight back, to struggle against the cold, killing darkness, and to maintain their stubborn determination to make it through. "I tried to be active and make others so," she recalled, saying: "I moved my toes all the time and felt thankful that my shoes were so large and roomy. I think that saved my feet. I would not let Joseph rest but kept calling to him to move his toes and stamp his feet." As she did so she continued to squint anxiously into the night, and then, as they were almost unable to withstand any more, she spotted a light. Soon after that, declared Rosa, "we reached Joseph's house all safe and sound." "I will never forget how thankful and pleased we all were," she added in something of an understatement.

In time, after eating a hot supper in Joseph's warm kitchen, they again headed out into the night, across Polifka Road to their father's farmhouse. "The snow was so deep that we fell in over our knees," noted Rosa. But when they were once more safely inside they celebrated the occasion with unusual exuberance. "We had a great time, wishing Father and Mother a happy new year and tried to make everyone happy," she wrote. They were happy, of course, just to be alive and out of the storm. It continued to rage outside, and after retiring to bed, Rosa lay awake and shivered until dawn. "It was dreadful cold [and] I could not get warm all night although covered with a heavy feather bed," she remarked.[14]

Rosa and the other Kellners survived their encounters with the Wisconsin winter, and while they did so Anderson and the other members of Company A loafed about camp near Brandy Station. James eventually began to complain and feel sorry for himself again. It was predictable. It was simply part of army life and was in part the verbal release of frustrations brought on by the unmet emotional needs that were the soldier's inevitable lot. As usual, James became upset by what he regarded as the shamefully ungrateful lack of recognition the village showed toward the company. Once again he expressed his personal resentment about the praise he thought was being lavished upon other, less deserving local troops. He also continued to protest the unfair and unwarranted treatment he had been subjected to by Captain Horace Walker, even long after Walker had died at Rappahannock Station. On the very night before the captain met his death he had confessed to his abusive treatment of Anderson, James informed his family. Nevertheless, a deep sense of unredressed injustice persisted, disturbing Anderson's thoughts and making him ever more sullen and moody. And even as late as April he declared: "I have always endeavored to do my duties as a soldier to the best of my ability and I have never been reprimanded or under arrest (except once in N.Y.) although I have had an officer who hated me as heartily as I despised him and who lost no opportunity of putting a slight upon me in the presence of others."[15]

Anderson felt that virtually all his good qualities and contributions had been overlooked while Walker had been in command of the company. Immediately after the captain's death, he was promoted to corporal, and although that was some measure of recognition, he considered it to be far too little, too late, and, therefore, almost an insult. Comrades of his had been promoted much faster. Fred Borcherdt, for example, who had joined the company with Anderson in April of 1861, had been made a lieutenant in the Twenty-first Wisconsin two summers earlier. What's more, he pointed out, "many whom I knew to be my inferiors in education and ability, as well as soldierly conduct were placed over me." His status, or lack of it, caused him to brood and feel anxious about what people back home thought of him. "I have no doubt," he told his father, that "many of my old friends wonder why I did not make my way up faster in the Army, [but] they have no idea of the jealousies, spites, and petty annoyances which is put on one who does not happen to suit an Officer or who is too independent to submit to all his whims and caprices." He worried, desperately hoping that people in Manitowoc would not erroneously assume that his lack of advancement was evidence of any lack of courage and ability, for, he again asserted, the fault was in Walker and not in himself, and the fact he "was not flunky enough to suit the powers that were" alone accounted for his still-modest standing.[16]

In order to clear up any remaining doubts and rescue his reputation, Anderson eagerly sought an officer's commission. That, he felt certain, would bring vindication. Besides, he wanted the extra money for his family and, he plainly stated, he wanted "to spite certain ones who have twitted a little on my being in the ranks so long." He would show his detractors how wrong they were, and getting a commission, he thought, could be the start of something big for him. "I believe I am fitted for it and would rise high . . . if I once had a start," he told his father.[17]

Becoming an officer became something of an obsession for Anderson. The wish was, of course, natural for a youth like himself, so eager to prove his worth as a man and so hungry for approval and recognition. In late March he felt certain that it was about to be fulfilled. In a much-appreciated show of support, both the commissioned and noncommissioned officers of his regiment enthusiastically recommended him for a lieutenant's position with one of the new regiments then being formed up in Wisconsin. That vote of confidence did much to bolster Anderson's morale, and with considerable pride he wrote home: "I got this recommendation from my officers unasked and unsought for and cannot help looking upon it as a recognition of my merits as a soldier." Likewise, he appreciated the political influence being exerted on his behalf by his Uncle Henry, as well as by Ben Jones and Perry Smith, about which he commented: "It gives a soldier a great deal of encouragement to know that his friends at home speak well of him."[18]

All those efforts proved ineffective, however, and Anderson's quest for a commission met with repeated frustration. He even sought assistance from Amasa Cobb, his old colonel, then serving in Congress, and in the meantime informed his folks: "I can get a recommendation for a Colored Regiment commission easy but I will put that off until last." Although a strong opponent of slavery, he was not at all eager to serve with black troops, even as an officer. There was not much prestige in that. "Of course," he said, "I would prefer a white Reg[imen]t, but I will never serve in the ranks again." There no longer seemed enough in it for him.[19]

His hopes for advancement went unrealized, contributing more than ever to his glumness. But that notwithstanding, there was plenty else to annoy him that season. He was weary of the whole war, jaded with the army, and the stress and strain was clearly beginning to tell on him. That Christmas he turned twenty-two. But even at that young age his hair had begun to grow gray. "Well it is enough to turn anything gray to be roasted, frozen, soaked, starved, and worked as I have been the last two years," he declared in a letter home. Besides all that, there were the constant vacillations between periods of hyperactivity and prolonged idleness, between extremes of excitement and numbing boredom. Then, too, there were all the real and imagined dangers and the recurring rushes of fear and anger that had to be controlled. It was not possible to submit to such conditions for as long as Anderson had without losing one's emotional resilience and becoming downcast and ill-tempered. As a consequence, the winter of 1863–64 found him beset by even more irritations than usual, and he complained, often bitterly, about friends and relatives who did not answer letters, about long overdue paydays, bad food, inconsiderate comrades, and hometown draft dodgers like Will Hoye, who had fled to Canada to evade service in the army. About such people he derisively declared: "They are loyal enough so long as they do not have to suffer the hardships of war: But when they are called upon to pick up a Gun they turn tail and head for another Country instead of honestly discharging the debt they owe."

Anderson also complained about women. Maybe he still harbored hurt feelings about Addie Carpenter, but whatever it was, it provoked a scorn in him for nearly all of womankind. That March he informed his parents: "I never had any great liking for but one girl and I have got bravely over that [and] am indifferent towards *all* of them as an old Bachelor of sixty, that is so far as *marriage* is concerned." In fact, he referred to marriage as "moral suicide" and at one point declared: "I have seen enough of women in the last three or four years to know that good wives are scarce . . . [and] in fact I have a rather poor estimate of woman in general and were it not for the fact I have a good mother and sisters I would denounce the whole sex."[20]

His mood grew even darker as spring came on and another campaign season approached. There was still no satisfaction on the issue of his commission, and because of that he became increasingly dissatisfied and more eager than ever to be done with soldiering altogether. He admired and respected Captain Wilson Goodwin, who had led the company since Walker's death, and when Goodwin resigned and returned home that April, James developed some serious second thoughts about staying on past his own original term of enlistment, even if he were offered an opportunity to become an officer, and even if it was with an all-white regiment. Finally, that same month, his feelings of exasperation nearly reached a breaking point when the army, with neither warning nor explanation, arbitrarily extended the term of service for all members of the Fifth

Wisconsin another two full months—from May 10 to July 13. That simply was not fair, especially after all they had been through and endured for the cause. Enough was enough, and Anderson declared: "It would not surprise me in the least if the Regiment would mutiny about it."[21]

During that same long and tedious winter, Jeremiah Crowley also grew increasingly cantankerous, carping about a good many things but complaining most about Lincoln, the Republicans, and their mishandling of the war. He characterized the president as "the nation's greatest misfortune" and accused him of "retelling old jokes" while the country was "steeped to its very lips in blood." He also warned readers that the Republicans had "avowed themselves in favor of a general mixture of their own blood with that of negroes and entitled their party a miscegenous one." Others of his insulting attacks struck closer to home, and in early winter he took obvious delight in holding the Reverend L. N. Wheeler up to special scorn and public ridicule. Lucius Wheeler, a militant Republican member of the Union League, was the village's outspoken and somewhat self-righteous Methodist minister who had taken it upon himself to denounce local people opposed to the military draft. Since coming to town two years earlier, claimed Crowley, Wheeler had tirelessly preached "blood and thunder from the pulpit, on the streets, in the byplaces of the town and country—advocating the war as a blessing and dealing death and damnation to everyone who did not believe in John Brown being the second Christ and Abe Lincoln his successor on earth." Furthermore, charged Crowley, "many of the dirtiest articles defaming the character of some of our respectable citizens which have appeared in [Sewall Smith's newspaper] the *Smut Machine* are from his pen." Of course, it was Crowley himself and some of his cronies who were the objects of such attacks, and therefore Crowley made no effort to conceal his considerable delight when he learned that Wheeler had been drafted. It was such poetic justice, he thought, such sweet nemesis, but Crowley scornfully predicted that the preacher would probably use his political connections to get himself excused from the very duty he insisted other men not be allowed to evade. In the end, Wheeler would "turn tail on his Father Abraham, and try to remain home."[22]

As the season wore on, partisan feuding intensified. Sometimes it became downright ugly, and Sewall Smith was every bit as vicious at it as Crowley. At one point Smith characterized Crowley's paper as overflowing with "slang, slime, lies, treason, blackguardism, and a copious sprinkling of magnificent Piety." The insulting exchanges went on all winter and into the spring, and then in June the conflict went from harsh words to malicious deeds when, one night, some men, suspected to be members of the Union League, caught and hanged Crowley's dog. Smith reported the incident in the *Tribune* with obvious relish, indicating that "the late dog's master feels himself in danger, and is fearful, lest perhaps, a mistake has been made, and the wrong dog hung." A few weeks later Crowley himself was grabbed and threatened with a severe beating by Wyman Murphy, who had served as a lieutenant in the Union army. It happened, said Smith, when "the *Pilot* blackguard, steaming as usual with whiskey, impudently put in his filthy tongue" into a somewhat private conversation about the war. There had been an animated discussion on one of the downtown streets, and Crowley, who was passing by, butted in, to which Murphy took angry exception. Apparently neither man had much respect for the other, and only the sheriff's timely intervention saved the controversial editor from a hard thrashing.[23]

That spring even nature turned hostile. At first, as April returned, the villagers were optimistic, as was usually the case that time of year. Even Anderson, after being morose most of the winter, wrote home from Virginia in an upbeat mood: "I am glad you are having such good weather and hope that the logs are all down by this time, and the old mill clanking away as merrily as ever giving work to those who need it and making money for its owners." Anderson had worked in Jones's sawmill and somewhat nostalgically added: "I love to think of that old mill and wish all in it well." Unfortunately, all was not well. Before the end of the month both the mill workers and the whole village were facing some threatening conditions. First of all, the weather turned against them. In mid-April it became unusually dry, and after that there was no rain at all—not a drop—until the very end of June. As a consequence, river levels dropped so low that the logs cut upstream during the winter could not be floated over Cato Falls or Manitowoc Rapids and down to the mills that lined the river bank within the town.[24]

Matters were made worse when, to everyone's surprise, it suddenly turned unseasonably cold in the middle of June. That double blow made people deeply concerned. On June 15, Smith reported in the *Tribune:* "The Great Drouth still continues, and we greatly fear there will not be grain enough raised in this county, this season, to supply the wants of our inhabitants." Some of their worst fears, he said, had already been realized five nights earlier when a hard frost had hit and "laid out, pretty much, all the potatoes, corn, beans, and, we fear, the little fruit grown around us." That combination of frost and drought would have been plenty bad enough, but on Monday, May 30, just around noon, "the wind began to blow from off the land with great violence; and of such intense heat, that it was like the breath of a furnace." "Shortly afterward," continued Smith, "smoke was seen curling sky-ward, south west of the village; and the forked flames of fire came madly forward." Fire bells were sounded in the village, and their clanging was kept up throughout the afternoon and on into the night.[25]

Meanwhile, just beyond the settlement a great moving wall of flames, observed Crowley, was "sweeping away grass, trees, fences, and other property." Inhabitants of the countryside headed for town, seeking safety along the edge of the lake. Unfortunately for many of them, reported Crowley, "the smoke was so dense that few persons could reach the place." The situation grew even more perilous when other fires blazed up and out of control north of town, up near Two Rivers, from where they soon spread southward toward Manitowoc. On the way they consumed a tannery, along with a Bohemian farmer's house, barn, and oat crop. On June 3, Crowley declared with alarm that "a most devastating fire was raging in the woods a few miles north of the village, burning and destroying everything in its path." Clouds of smoke and ash blew over and through the settlement. People coughed and choked and wrapped wet rags about their faces. Animals snorted and struggled for air. Eyes watered and stung and the fearful suspense mounted.[26]

Then, abruptly and almost miraculously, that same day, the third of June, the winds, which like huge bellows had blown on the flames for the better part of a whole week, suddenly died out. The fires diminished and eventually sputtered out among the charred brush and tree stumps. By month's end even the drought had passed. On June 29, right about supper time, the sky turned black and a soft rain began to gently pelt the dry ground. It was the first rain in well over two months, and as the cool night closed in, the mild refreshing shower turned into a driving downpour that continued until dawn.[27]

During those natural trials along the lakeshore, Anderson and the other survivors of Company A commenced their final campaign. The winter camp at Brandy Station was evacuated the afternoon of May 4 and the boys marched off to Germania Mills, where they crossed over the Rapidan River. From there they carried on for about another two miles before stopping for the night in the midst of a broad, still-unplowed field. Next morning the regiment and the rest of the Sixth Corps moved cautiously along the Old Verdiersville Road, on which, before long, they were caught in a brisk skirmish with Confederate troops sent out to slow down their advance. The resistance, although spirited, was overcome when, at about ten o'clock, companies A, C, and I of the Fifth Wisconsin opened the way. "We charged at them on a dead run and drove them out from behind trees and logs in a hurry, but not until they had killed and wounded quite a number of our men," wrote Anderson. In that attack two members of his company went down; Michael Pelcha was killed and Levi Croissant wounded.[28]

Following the skirmish, the army plowed ahead, pushing the enemy farther and farther back until about four in the afternoon. Then the Confederates launched a bold counterattack, smashing through the Forty-ninth New York just to the left of the Fifth Wisconsin, opening a hole that enabled the Southerners to circle around behind the Union forces. Anderson and his comrades beat a hasty retreat. In a short time they regrouped and struck back. In doing so they managed to scatter most of their opponents and take nearly three hundred prisoners.[29]

By then the Army of the Potomac was deep into the Wilderness, an area Evan Jones described as being "covered by thick brush and dwarfish trees, and cut up by ravines and narrow streams." It was like a natural labyrinth in which men became easily confused and lost, a place, according to Anderson, where "the brush was so tangled that you could not see over 20 or 25 yards ahead of you." There the opposing forces fired on one another almost unseen as visibility was made even worse by the billows of smoke that hung densely among the leaves and branches in the fading twilight. Finally, after a full day of chaotic violence, wrote Jones, "night closed in and the bloody conflict between invisible foes ceased."[30]

"We lay all that night in the line of battle and the next morning the Rebels attacked us and were repulsed with heavy loss, but we also suffered much from their batteries which threw canisters at us when we tried to follow them. This took place in a dense thicket and our ranks were broken at every step," Anderson informed his father. At one point in the pursuit, the boys of Company A advanced to the swampy edge of a small creek, where enemy fire forced them to stop and fall back. They scurried to take cover behind a nearby hill, where they quickly constructed a breastwork of logs and dirt. There they lay in wait for a long while, and then, at dusk, the Confederates rose and rushed at them from out of the shadows.[31]

By that point in the campaign the Army of the Potomac had suffered more than seventeen thousand casualties, even though its spring offensive had been in progress for less than a full week. Their losses soon became worse, when, during the night of May 6, Confederates set fires in the dry underbrush of the Wilderness. Flames cracked and flashed and both soldiers and draft animals panicked. Some men, in fearful confusion, became lost and, along with wounded comrades unable to flee, they suffocated in the smoke, their bodies burned in the onrushing blaze. By the time the sun rose again, a long train of heavy army wagons bumped and jolted eastward toward Fredericksburg, hauling away yet another dreadful "cargo of tortured bleeding patriots."[32]

Ulysses S. Grant, their latest in a long and discouraging succession of commanding generals, was a man without any romantic illusions about the nature of war who well understood that great amounts of suffering, slaughter, and bullheaded determination were required before the struggle could be ended. He also realized that the Rebels could not be beaten in the Wilderness, and therefore, during that awful night of May 6–7, decided to move his army to a new position. He marched the soldiers hard until dawn, at which time they were drawn up in a line across the Fredericksburg and Gordonsville Plank Road at a place about three miles west of Robertson's Tavern. There they stood tense and ready, but there was no fight because, explained Anderson, enemy forces "did not dare to attack our front that day." They remained in place until well after nine o'clock that night, when they moved off in what they and their adversaries assumed was a retreat to Fredericksburg. But it was no retreat. After another hard night of marching, they discovered, much to their surprise, that they were in fact pressing rapidly toward Spotsylvania Court House.[33]

There, for twelve terrible days, the armies savaged one another. On the second day's encounter, as the Fifth was burrowing into trenches, an ambulance rushed past. Soon a message went through the corps, passed from man to man—"Johnny is wounded," they repeated one to another in hushed voices. They were referring to John Sedgwick, commander of the Sixth Corps, their big, barrel-chested general who had become a much-beloved father figure to the boys. Something of an eccentric, he wore a crumpled broad-brimmed black hat and a red shirt beneath his dark blue Union tunic, and he exuberantly shared much of the common soldier's lot. He had a hearty laugh, a thunderous voice, and exerted a profound influence upon the troops he led. It seemed he would do almost anything for them, and they for him. Like the other soldiers, Anderson greatly admired Sedgwick, cherished his approval and praise, and in letters home attempted to explain to his family the nature of the unusual bond that existed between the general and his troops. Early that May he had tried to illustrate that by recounting an incident: "I shall never forget him as he looked on that night of the 6th [of May], when part of his line was broken and he rode up to our regiment, and when he saw our part of the line so cool and determined, he took off his hat and bowed. The men jumped to their feet and cheered as they never did before right in the face of the enemy who advanced about the same time but met a volley that sent them back much quicker."[34]

Just three days later, at Spotsylvania, John Sedgwick stood and watched some of his men ducking to evade enemy fire. After briefly observing them, he strode up, and in his own characteristically blustering style, shouted out, "Why, what are you dodging for? They could not hit an elephant at that distance!" Just then a rifle cracked. The general was hit in the head. He thudded to the ground and did not move. "We could not believe for a long time that our kindly old leader had fallen but soon it was confirmed that he was indeed gone," Anderson sadly recounted.[35]

The slaughter continued with appalling ferocity, going on day after day, thousands of soldiers suffering and dying. Some of those struck simply crumpled and collapsed without a sound; others fell and felt their lives slowly ebb away as their blood trickled out and death gradually crept over them; still others were ripped apart in explosive agony. Many more lost parts of themselves, going down in shock with bleeding wounds. On May 10, Anderson was himself hit on the right cheek by a hot piece of shell fragment. Luckily, it first struck and shattered his rifle stock, greatly diminishing its velocity. Otherwise it might well have blown away the whole side of his face. As it was, he suffered nothing more than a painful bruise just below his eye.[36]

That same day, a little before dusk, the Fifth was again teamed up with the Sixth Vermont Volunteers, and they were sent out to storm a part of the enemy's line. They took considerable ground but were unable to hold it, eventually being driven back when other units failed to come to their support. They were "much disheartened by their failure," confessed Anderson, but, he went on, "we knew it was none of our fault or lack of courage." Believing that might have been some consolation as they rushed back into their trenches and lay there in the dirt "sadly counting over the missing ones."[37]

They were back in the thick of the Spotsylvania fighting on May 12, and in that engagement, after firing off most of his ammunition, Anderson threw aside his rifle and rushed forward to seize control of an enemy artillery piece. John Hinman of Company E helped him, and turning it about, they discharged it into the midst of an advancing regiment from South Carolina. The results were grotesque. At least forty of the Southern boys were killed or wounded by that first blast. After that, Anderson reported, "we worked the gun on them until we fired all the ammunition there was in two limbers and this at a distance of about 10 rods from their rifle pits." Logs were splintered and dirt blown about, exposing the Confederates to devastating direct fire. Many crouched in the debris and died with their arms over their faces. The brutal combat went on through a heavy rain until midafternoon. During the fighting John Hinman was killed. Eventually, Anderson and his company were relieved and sent to the rear for a decent night's sleep. It had been an exhausting day, in the course of which Union forces had taken more than three thousand Confederate captives. Since arriving at Spotsylvania, they had inflicted perhaps as many as twelve thousand casualties on the Confederate army.[38]

In spite of such numbers the struggle was far from finished. Yet after a few more days in that place, where neither army was able to break the bloody deadlock, the Northern troops once again moved out. On May 19, they marched down the Po River Valley southeastward to Holladay Plantation and on to Guiney's Station. After that they traveled due south, crossing the North Anna River on May 23, then on through Oxford to Beaverdam Station, where they tore up railroad tracks and burned train cars. They then crossed back over the North Anna, moving up to Golansville, then moved east to Mangohick, down across the Pumunky River at Nelson's Ford, through Hanover Court House destroying three railroad bridges, to Cold Harbor, where they arrived in the early afternoon of the first day of June. Along the way, Bill Crocker got separated from the company and was left behind, and Anderson, finding himself unable to keep up, lagged far behind the others during the stretch between Golansville and Hanover Court House. He was nearly exhausted by the time he managed to catch up. "Threw myself down on the ground as soon as I joined the Regt. and when the orderly woke me later this morning I had slept 13 hours," he wrote in his diary on May 28. From then on, until they reached Cold Harbor, the going got much tougher as they encountered determined Confederate resistance.[39]

Once they reached Cold Harbor on June 1 they were again back in the area of the Chickahominy River and Gaines' Mill, closer to Richmond than at any other time since the disastrous Peninsula campaign of two years before. Although weary from their long, hot march, they almost immediately mounted a massive assault in which the regiment managed to gain control of the Confederate's first row of trenches and earthworks. Next evening, as the attack was resumed, Anderson described how the whole Sixth Corps "charged in three lines of battle and drove the rebels from their advanced positions." In doing so, however, the regiment suffered another nineteen casualties. By then, there were only five officers left and Captain Charles Kempf of Company C, being the most senior, was put in command of the regiment.[40]

The Confederates remained stubbornly dug in, their lines of trenches stretching from Topopotomy Creek about five miles above Cold Harbor all the way down to the Chickahominy, a little more than two miles south of town. The Army of the Potomac was also strung out just west of Cold Harbor in a parallel line of trenches facing the enemy, with the Sixth Corps positioned at the northern end of that line. There the scene must have greatly prefigured those along the Western Front in France, and at dawn on June 3, much like those Tommies and doughboys yet to be, they arose from the earth to move up and over the top in a screaming charge with fixed bayonets out across "no-man's-land" toward the opposite trenches. The consequences were deadly, and by early afternoon, after losing another seven thousand men, the attack was called off. It seemed every bit as bad as the slaughter at Marye's Heights behind Fredericksburg a year and a half earlier. The ground was again littered with broken bodies, the air once more filled with the cries of suffering men. Fortunately for Anderson and his company, they were spared from participating in that assault, but nonetheless they felt the emotional shock of it. Anderson reflected their growing sense of frustration and futility: "This is a terrible campaign, neither side will yield and although we drive the rebels from position to position they fall back and fight us as wicked as ever. . . . It is a bitter fight and God only knows how it will end."[41]

They stayed on at Cold Harbor until June 12. For much of that time Anderson was in the front row of rifle pits exchanging fire with Confederates a few hundred yards away. On the twelfth, they pulled out just after dark, crossing the Chickahominy under the cover of night. Since leaving camp at Brandy Station on May 4, about sixty thousand of their army had fallen.

In the middle of June, James Leonard was well enough to rejoin the regiment in its new position near Petersburg, and there became a participant in what he described as its "arduous, long, and over-burdening campaign." Their conditions were becoming increasingly miserable due to the intense heat of another southern summer. Day after day the sun burnt fiercely in an empty sky, draining the soldiers of whatever strength they might still possess. "The weather is exceedingly and Tremendously hot and fearfully dry, the ground is fairly baked to a crust," complained Leonard. The drought in Virginia was every bit as severe and many times more scorching than the one back home, and by June 26 Leonard told Mary Sheldon that he was unable to recall when it had last rained. In that heat, the boys seemed to burn and crack like the ground beneath them, as the scene of which they were a part grew increasingly distorted in rising ripples of heat haze. But still they battled on.[42]

By then there was little left of the company's flag. "It is very conspicuous and wherever it flies, there the lead and iron goes thickest," Anderson told his family that June. But even well before that their "Dear Old Flag," as he called it, was in tatters and "dropping to pieces every time it is unrolled." Good men had been killed and wounded carrying it and keeping it from enemy hands, and by the spring of 1864 it had become like some sacred relic, so much so, said James, that "the pieces, as they fell, were eagerly sought after by the Boys." Even though "shell and bullets and the winds . . . claimed their share of the fragments," he was able to get a piece for himself, which he sent home to his parents. "I want you to treasure it carefully and prize it highly," he instructed them.[43]

By the time they dug in at Petersburg, little was left of the original company. In the beginning, in that long ago April of 1861, there had been 104 of them—96 from the village of Manitowoc alone—but by late June of 1864 James Leonard noted: "We have twenty-eight of the old men all told, sick, well, wounded & detached to go home to Manitowoc, provided no more get killed." But even the survivors, like Anderson and Leonard, seemed to be only half-alive. Leonard complained that he felt "threefourths sick all the while," and Anderson scribbled in his diary on June 24: "hardly able to crawl I am so sick."[44]

Anderson was worn out. At Petersburg his strength and spirit were so low he completely lost interest in even the prospect of getting a commission, even one in a white regiment. He simply wished to endure long enough to fill out his term and go home to Wisconsin. "I have been quite sick and am run down to a mere skeleton," he informed his family in late June. The "hardship, fatigue, and bad water" had finally become too much for him, and he confessed, "When the corps moved 10 or twelve miles I have to take two days to travel the distance they go in one." Furthermore, he knew the very worst of the summer heat was yet to come. It would kill him if he tried to stay. Stubbornly he fought back against what was becoming a condition of near-terminal weariness, counting the days, and hoping he might hang on long enough to make it back to the cool air of the Lake Michigan shoreline. If he could do that, if he could return to the North, he felt certain he would eventually regain his lost strength.[45]

Finally, on Wednesday, July 13, he joyfully wrote in his diary: "Our term of service is expired and we have bid farewell to our comrades." He had survived. The next day he wrote home, announcing, "I thought I would drop you a line to let you know that

I am still this side of the 'Dark River' and with every prospect of soon being with you."[46]

On the way out of Virginia they again glided down the James River, past "Lordly Mansions" and "the Huts of Negroes," past Harrison's Landing, where they had awaited death that awful early summer of 1862, and then on past the site of Jamestown, which, he observed, was "completely deserted and only a few Ruined Log Huts marked the spot around which so many Memories of Historic Adventure Linger." Soon after that, after once again churning up the Chesapeake and Potomac by steamship, they were back in Washington, back to where they had once set out from to make war on the South. Both they and the city had changed much in the meantime, and the dome of the Capitol had been completed during their absence. After some rest and decent food, James went touring, revisiting the Patent Office and the Smithsonian Institution and stopping this time at the graves of fallen friends in the Georgetown Cemetery. On July 20 they boarded a northbound train, which, after some delay at Baltimore where Rebels had blown up tracks, raced on through the night, reaching Tyron, Pennsylvania, just as it began to grow light. After that the war swiftly receded into the distance as they climbed up the country along the iron rails that led away from the smoking guns and dying men. By suppertime, July 21, they were back in Chicago, and the next morning they passed safely over into Wisconsin.[47]

When they crossed the border at Beloit they cheered, and then rumbled on in their "emigrant cars" through the ripening midsummer grain fields, reaching Madison around two in the afternoon, where they "met with a pretty fair reception." Early that evening there was a parade. "We then formed and marched around town headed by a Brass Band and a Delegation of Milwaukee Turners. The Governor and his staff led the Procession [and] while we were on the march all the Bells of the town was ringing and the Battery in the Park fired its Guns." They ascended the hill to the state capitol building, where, for the last time, they were drawn up into their dark blue ranks and rows. There they stood as Governor Lewis welcomed them home. Everyone cheered and the boys then returned to Camp Randall for refreshments and to collect their pay.[48]

The next day was Saturday. It was a sweet, warm summer's day during which the sunburned soldiers began thinking about once more becoming farmers, teachers, and mill hands. James "went down to one of the Lakes and bathed in the afternoon" and the next morning took a long solitary walk in the wooded countryside, letting its peacefulness settle upon him and soak back into his being. Although it was a Sunday, he chose not to attend church. "My appearance with my old campaign clothes is hardly respectable," he wrote in his diary. Even after all he had been through, appearances still mattered. Besides that, he was still not fully ready to rejoin the gatherings of civilians.[49]

Nine days later, Rosa Kellner mentioned their homecoming in her journal: "The Fifth Wisconsin company, or rather what is left of it, returned yesterday or the day before." Crowley also mentioned it almost in passing in the August 5 issue of the *Pilot,* observing that only fifteen of the company's original members had made it back. But as they were part of "the first Company that left our place," he said, "the returned members met with more than an ordinary welcome." But it was not much more than ordinary. There was a concert and reception for them that next Thursday at Glover Hall, then it was done. Their war was over, their time as soldiers finally finished. They were home and could again feel the cool lake breezes and once more hear the waves peacefully lapping along the shore.[50]

Epilogue

April is the cruellest month, breeding
Lilacs out of the dead land, mixing
Memory and desire, stirring
Dull roots with spring rain
                    —T. S. Eliot, "The Waste Land"

*T*HE WAR, although over for the survivors of Company A, raged on in northern Virginia, Georgia, and other places in the South. There the guns thundered on through the fall and into another winter. At the same time, within Manitowoc County, partisan political conflicts continued. They provided an outlet for venting the hostility and fear that built up within its communities, which, that autumn, came pouring forth in the 1864 election. The village, along with the townships of Cato and Liberty, stood by Lincoln and the Republicans, but the voters throughout the rest of the county gave strong support to George B. McClellan and the Democrats. Some months before returning home Anderson had bluntly expressed his personal opinion about the Democrat's presidential candidate, referring to him as "Gen. McClellan, my old Commander whom I hate and despise as I do Jeff Davis or any other traitor." Those sentiments did not change after he left the army, but they were clearly not ones shared by most voters in Manitowoc County, where McClellan received 2,248 votes compared to the 1,179 cast for President Lincoln. Furthermore, Democratic candidates once again won every office up for election in the county that

year. That was, as before, in sharp contrast to the political prefer-
ences expressed around the rest of Wisconsin, where Lincoln won
by a comfortable margin and Republican candidates carried five out
of six congressional districts.[1]

That autumn Anderson joined his father and Uncle Henry to
work on behalf of Republican office seekers. But as engaging as that
must have been, he also had to concern himself with the urgent
issue of making a living. The family was in a condition of near
poverty when he returned home. Jean, his oldest sister, had appren-
ticed with a milliner and was working as a clerk, but she alone had
steady, albeit poorly paying, employment. Their father remained
caught in the uncertain cycles of the sawmill business, seldom
working more than part time and often not working at all. There
had been some hope that he might be appointed village lighthouse
keeper, but when that met with disappointment, Anderson took
most of the savings he had left and purchased two teams of horses,
some harness and equipment, and went off into the forest to haul
logs throughout the winter for some local lumber companies with
which he had arranged contracts.[2]

One early winter day, soon after the first snowfall, Anderson was
back in town and was called over to John D. Markham's law office.
Markham was a member of the Union League, as were Anderson's
father and uncle, and so too was John Guyles, the deputy provost
marshall for Manitowoc County, who was there at Markham's waiting
with an agent of the federal secret service. As soon as introductions
were made and Anderson was sitting down, he was sworn to secrecy
and asked if he would work with them in tracking down and appre-
hending deserters, draft dodgers, and bounty jumpers. They suspected
a considerable number of such men to be hiding out in the county's
forests, awaiting the arrival of spring and the reopening of navigation
when they could get passage on local schooners to Canada. Helping
Guyles would earn James some much-needed additional money and,
besides that, would provide another opportunity to actively support
the Union cause. For those reasons he accepted the offer.[3]

During the winter they made a number of raids, most being
carried out at night in the dark forest and deep snow, which

sometimes involved dangerous encounters with desperate men who were likely to face firing squads if caught. Anderson's first such experience was a late-night strike on the workers' bunkhouse at Week's Mill in the southern part of the county. There they caught one deserter, although a second man they sought escaped into the darkness. Soon after that, the number of such clandestine expeditions increased, especially after Guyles retired due to the painful infirmities of old age and rheumatism and was replaced by Frederick Borcherdt, another Union League member whose son had served with Anderson in Company A. Borcherdt was something of a zealot, who, said Anderson, "worked men and horse to the limit" and was himself "tireless in following up any clue" that might help in hunting down suspected deserters and draft dodgers.[4]

Under his leadership, their biggest and most daring assignment was a raid on a deserters' camp well concealed within a swampy area in the northern part of the county. It was up near Cooperstown, where some years before a tornado had torn up and twisted several thousand acres of trees into huge piles and rows of broken roots, trunks, and branches, and up through which new growth had begun to protrude. The men within, they knew from informers, were well armed and dangerous, and because of that, Borcherdt, Anderson, and the others moved cautiously into the "Big Windfall," as the area was called, with army revolvers and Enfield rifles, closing in on the camp from different directions in two parties. It was early afternoon when they started, and they had not gone very far before Anderson's party was sighted by one of the suspected deserters, who fired his rifle and shouted warnings to the other members of his camp. There was a brief outburst of gunfire from both sides. Then James, wearing Indian moccasins and being a fast runner, dashed ahead and captured the man, who had alerted the others, and was soon followed by the other members of his raiding party, who, with guns blazing, made their way through the tangled uprooted trees and stormed into the camp. There they found a cabin in the middle of the clearing. "With a revolver in my hand, I burst open the door, but no one was there," Anderson later recalled. Looking around, he said, "everything showed they had just left suddenly and in the utmost confusion." Two of the fugitives were picked up the next day near De Pere, but the others got away.[5]

After that, there were other raids, some more successful than the one on the "Big Windfall" and others even less so, and Anderson continued to be a participant in most of them right down to the end of the war in April.

That February, while Anderson was still in the bush hauling logs or helping Borcherdt hunt down deserters, the United States Telegraph Company completed the stringing of a line from Milwaukee into Manitowoc. It was along that wire that the news of Lee's Palm Sunday surrender at Appomattox Court House was flashed into town on Tuesday morning, April 11. With the arrival of that message the whole community spontaneously burst into uproarious celebration with people banging on pots, firing guns, and blasting off steam whistles. That afternoon a jubilant meeting was held in the north-side park, the same park in which the boys had once drilled in preparation for war. Among the many speakers, the village's Episcopal rector, the Reverend Lyman Freeman, evoked the most intense response when he delivered a rousing address and gave thanks for the long-awaited victory and the much appreciated return to peace. Although most people present cheered and applauded throughout the afternoon, not everyone expressed good will. Hard feelings persisted, and antiwar Democrats who tried to join the gathering were made to feel uncomfortable and unwanted, and some prominent Republicans made that most apparent. "It seems," complained Crowley, "that the little clique which always controls the destiny of this village, could not let their party malice [to] one side even for a day like that." But his own partisan feelings remained as intense as ever, and he was not only upset by the attempts to exclude people like himself from the celebration but also indignant about how the Republican speakers, the Reverend Freeman in particular, had mentioned the freeing of "the nigger" far too frequently.[6]

Even the next week, when news of Abraham Lincoln's assassination reached town, Crowley still found it virtually impossible to put aside his partisanship. Although he called the killing of the president "a fiendish crime," he could not, or would not, bring himself to offer up even the faintest praise of Lincoln as a leader or a man. He could only go so far as to call the dead president "the legal representation of the nation" and to declare: "However weak, however deep in error his policy may have been founded, whatever private wrongs he may have inflicted in the past, an attack upon his person was an attack upon the sovereign people of our free Union."[7]

The rest of the village, however, seemed almost overwhelmed by grief. Even though the president's body lay in state more than a thousand miles away, and in spite of the fact that most of the county's voters had cast ballots against him in the most recent election, the community staged an elaborate funeral-like ceremony to commemorate the fallen leader. On Wednesday, April 19, according to the account in the *Pilot,* people began "flocking in" from throughout the surrounding countryside just after dawn, coming to the village "on foot, on horseback, and by wagon." There were thousands of them. Many had been there in other Aprils, to attend those dramatic early war meetings and to watch the first companies of volunteers drill in the park, and then to witness the somber burials of George Waldo and Mead Holmes; but their reasons for coming this time seemed even more compelling. It was as if something profound had just been decided, something affecting the fate of the whole human race, and that someone much greater and far more significant than a chief magistrate tragically had been taken from them. The people, moved by their own deep and mysterious inner needs, responded once more with ritual to the violent events and their own sense of wonderment and loss. Crowley commented that it was "the most imposing of any demonstration which had ever taken place in the community."[8]

At one o'clock in the afternoon, with church bells clanging out a slow, sad cadence, a solemn procession, which eventually stretched out for well over a mile, set out from the courthouse. It included the Manitowoc Brass Band, the county's returned soldiers led by Captain Wilson Goodwin, a hearse drawn by six white horses, the public officials from the village, county, and nearby communities, all the settlement's fraternal societies and fire companies, as well as all its schoolchildren and teachers and hundreds of ordinary citizens.

They all made their way along Eighth Street, past the Williams House Hotel, over the river, and up the hill to the north-side park. There the Reverend S. S. Smith, who had succeeded the drafted L. N. Wheeler at the Manitowoc Methodist Church, delivered the funeral oration. "It was a mournful ceremony, and the many who participated in it seemed heartily bereaved at the national loss," observed Crowley.[9]

After that, people once more went about their normal business, resuming their struggles with nature, the economy, and one another. That fall James Anderson went off to Lawrence University in Appleton. Rosa continued on with her long and often arduous days and nights at the hotel. Her life had become more empty and her thoughts more morose following the death of her father that January. She had loved him dearly and his passing, although not unexpected, caused her to descend into another deep and prolonged melancholy mood, during which she no longer wrote in her journal. James Leonard returned to teaching school just west of town, in the village of Branch. His long-distance relationship with Mary Sheldon, whose wartime letters, he told her, had "driven away the lonesomeness of camp life and mad[e] bright and joyful hours which otherwise would have been dark and weary," did not ripen into a long-term association. She became the wife of P. J. Pierce, the county clerk of court, and in 1867, Leonard married Martha Gould of Kenosha. In April of the following year, he left Manitowoc on board the *Sea Bird* for Chicago with intentions of looking into the possibility of purchasing a grocery store there.[10]

The *Sea Bird* was a steamship owned and operated by the Goodrich Company of Manitowoc. It was a 190-foot wooden sidewheeler that traveled between the village and Chicago twice a week throughout the navigation season. By the time Leonard boarded it on Monday morning, April 6, the first two voyages of the new spring schedule had already been completed. Both were uneventful, as was the first leg of his own trip as far as Milwaukee, where he got off to spend Tuesday and Wednesday in the city before reboarding the *Sea Bird* to complete his voyage to Chicago when it returned on Thursday evening, April 8.

When the *Sea Bird* had set out from Manitowoc that Thursday morning, Captain John Morris was on the bridge and there was a crew of eighteen. Seven of its crew, as well as the captain, were residents of Manitowoc. The exact number of passengers remains unclear, but at least eighteen were also from the village, and four others had come in from the communities of Newton and Mishicot, which were located within the county.

Conditions were fine when the voyage commenced, but no sooner had they rounded South Point and were underway than the weather changed, a storm suddenly blowing in from the northeast. The wind picked up and soon became a roaring gale, driving the waters up into rolling banks that rose and broke against the flanks of the ship. Snow began to fall, and before long the *Sea Bird* was caught in a full-scale blizzard. By the time they reached Sheboygan the squalls were so fierce and the swells so violent that they were unable to dock and new passengers had to climb up nets strung from the harbor tug to get aboard. Heading downlake after that was treacherous, and by the time they pulled into Milwaukee they were nearly three hours behind schedule and most of the passengers were wretchedly seasick. It was ten o'clock at night when they departed the Milwaukee harbor, and by then, to everyone's great relief, the storm had abated and the lake was calm. It had, in fact, turned into a pleasant early spring night, and by midnight, when they docked briefly at Racine, most passengers were sound asleep secure in their cabins.

About five hours later, just before dawn, while plowing southward through rising swells, disaster struck.

That afternoon—about three o'clock, Friday, April 9—a telegram reached Manitowoc informing the village that there had been a fire on board the *Sea Bird* that morning, but the message implied that it had been minor, and reported that everyone was safe and well. "ALL SAVED," it declared. However, as afternoon turned into evening and the daylight faded without further details coming in, a fearful suspense began to build within the community. After supper, reported the *Pilot*, "the telegraph office, and the sidewalk in front of it, were crowded until a late hour by an eager . . . yet patient throng who watched and waited for further tidings until it was evident that nothing more would be learned that night, when they turned away with heavy hearts." The following morning there was more news. All of it was bad—much worse, in fact, than anyone had feared. The fire had been a major one and had actually turned the vessel into a floating inferno. All on board, except for two, the telegram made unequivocally clear, had gone down dead with the ship, and neither survivor was from Manitowoc. Later that day another message came in over the wire. A third survivor had been found. He was James Leonard.

Leonard had been up early that morning, well before the other passengers, had talked with one of the mates, and eaten some breakfast, but because the weather had again turned miserable he had returned to his cabin, where he lay on his bunk with the blankets pulled up over him. Less than a quarter hour later he was startled by the sound of an alarm, and within minutes, the whole ship seemed to go mad. Just the sound of the alarm sent some people into a panic, and passengers, said Leonard, began "knocking down the partitions and doors of their staterooms" in frantic attempts to break out. Once on deck they discovered the ship was ablaze, and when Leonard emerged from his cabin he was immediately swept up in a terrified crowd surging forward toward the ship's bow so as to be as far from the flames as possible. The *Sea Bird*'s three lifeboats were plenty large enough to hold everyone. However, all were at the stern of the ship where the fire was most intense, and the smoke and flames prevented the crew from getting to them. "The whole after part of the boat was burning up, and the [life]boats themselves were on fire," reported another of the ship's passengers.

There was a bitter cold northwestern wind. The lake was in turmoil, gray-green swells mounting up and breaking into frigid white spray. Leonard remain on deck less than ten minutes, and in that brief time, he said, "the boat was covered with flames." Unable to stand the heat and smoke any longer, he pulled tight the ropes of his cork life preserver and hurled himself out and over the side and down into the water.

Unlike most passengers, Leonard was fully dressed and wearing a long heavy overcoat, and although that threatened to pull him under it also protected against the cold. Fortunately, within minutes he was able to grab hold of a large rectangular piece of wreckage. Pulling himself up onto it, he punched holes in the wreckage with his pocket knife through which he tied the ropes of his life preserver. The wind immediately caught and pushed him southward, up and down the crests and troughs, swiftly moving him away from the burning ship. By the time the lumber schooner *Cornelia* came down the lake and drew near the *Sea Bird*, he was already well over a mile away. Although he waved and shouted he went unnoticed.

The *Sea Bird* was at least six miles out when Leonard jumped overboard, and once he was on the wreckage the wind drove him downlake rather than in toward shore. Consequently, he remained in the water a long time. In an attempt to deal with the intense cold he cut long strips out of the lining of his overcoat with his knife and bound them around his exposed head and hands. That helped only a little. He floated on all day. The waves constantly dashed over him, coating him with ice. He faded in and out of consciousness. Once the sun began to sink, his feelings of desperation gave way to resignation as he then believed he would die on that board, frozen stiff in the brutally cold darkness. But no sooner had his mood thus shifted when his piece of wreckage banged against something. It startled him back to alertness so that he quickly realized he had collided with the posts of the breakwater just offshore, northeast of Evanston, Illinois. Frantically he severed his ropes, cut himself free of his stiff frozen overcoat, and painfully pulled himself up and over the ice-covered posts. On the other side, to his great relief, he was able to touch bottom, and although one of his legs was partially frozen, he managed to wade ashore and climb the high sand bluff along the top of which he limped and staggered his way southward to the edge of Evanston. There he found shelter in a farmhouse and was saved.

Leonard returned to Manitowoc on the steamship *Orion,* Sunday morning, April 19. He never did go into the grocery trade in Chicago, but stayed on in Manitowoc, working as a clerk in George

Figure 17. Joseph Kapitan and Rosa Kellner were married in Manitowoc in October 1866. (Courtesy of Lynda Dvorachek)

Glover's store until 1874, when he and his family moved to Green
Bay. There he returned to teaching school and eventually became
superintendent of schools for the city. After that he enjoyed some

comfortable success in the insurance business, living on in Green Bay until his death at age 62 in 1901.[11]

By the springtime of the *Sea Bird*'s sinking, Rosa had also endured more tragedy. Before that, however, and after recovering from her spell with depression brought on by the death of her father, her life had grown pleasurable, and even sweet again, when she commenced a courtship with Joseph Kapitan. Kapitan, who like herself was a Bohemian immigrant, came to work at the Williams House Hotel shortly after the war and eventually became a co-proprietor of the establishment with Rosa's sister Anna. Rosa and he soon developed a warm affection for each other, and in mid-October of 1866 they were married in the First German Lutheran Church.

For some time before that Rosa had all but given up on the possibility of marrying, and on one occasion had written: "[I] wonder how any one can fall in love with my plain face, at least Anna said my nose was too large." After the war, when single women significantly outnumbered eligible bachelors, there were many young women in Manitowoc who resigned themselves to spinsterhood. But though she was decidedly plain, Rosa was unusually intelligent, sensitive, and caring. For her, love was vital. "How I would despise myself if I married for money and not for love. No I shall never marry unless it is to one who loves me and whom I love," she declared.[12]

She apparently held fast to her conviction. She recorded her love of Joseph, and for a time Rosa seemed more deeply contented than she had been in years. She soon became joyfully pregnant. In June she gave birth to twin daughters whom she named Rosa and Josephine. But both were weak and died within a few days. The profound pain of that plunged Rosa back into a despondent state of mind, which deepened and grew darker with time, filling her days with sorrow, troubling her sleep with morbid and fearful dreams. She retreated into herself, taking refuge in her journal, writing long rambling passages in which she poured out her private grief so that the act of writing became a form of therapy. Writing was one of the few things she was still able to enjoy, and at one point she wrote on a loose leaf of paper: "I love to write. When I have pen in hand, the black fluid near me, of course, paper and books scattered around me, I am at home in my element." But, as before, she wanted to do more than just keep a personal journal. "I would love to write a book," she said, declaring, "would I had the opportunity some have I would earn a name for myself that would probably outlive this frail body." As she had done so often in the past, however, Rosa sowed self-doubts among her own hopes, and although the idea of becoming an author excited her, she nonetheless seemed fatalistically resigned to her humble situation. Again, referring in that same passage to her desire to write, she declared: "[I] fear it would not benefit my fellow beings much, my education is not good, I have no time to read and study, my health is not very good, [and] I fear a rose tree and a little mould will mark my resting place before the hope of my life is accomplished."[13]

She continued to engage in such private dialogues with herself and slowly her spirits began to revive. Early in 1868 she became pregnant again. That September she gave birth to a healthy son and named him Joseph. She was undoubtedly very pleased and deeply happy. However, in giving life to him she had used up what remained of her own, and on September 26, poor frail Rosa closed her eyes and gave up the struggle. She was only twenty-four. She left behind a fine son and a long, thoughtful journal.

Jeremiah Crowley sold his beloved newspaper that next summer. He was suffering from a lingering illness and had been "slowly passing away" for some time. He had hung on for as long as he was able. But in June of 1869, after the warmth of the spring failed to revive his strength, he issued his final editorial in which he informed his readers that failing health was forcing him, as he said, "to close up, we fear, forever, our career as a journalist." The *Pilot* was sold to E. B. Treat, a Democrat of more mellow temperament than his own, and Crowley lived on almost unnoticed through another winter and died quietly at home on April 11, 1870. Throughout the village flags on public buildings were lowered to half-staff, and two days later a large funeral was held for him on the south side at the Catholic church. There, the fire-eating editor from County Cork was finally laid to rest. Everyone was there, even most of his old enemies.[14]

So ran the endless cycles of April along the lakeshore—birth, death, and rebirth; melancholy memories mixing with renewed hopes.

James Anderson graduated from college that spring and returned to Manitowoc. The community had grown and changed considerably since the beginning of the war, and in 1870 its population exceeded five thousand. During the 1860s the county population had also increased by nearly tenfold. The local economy had expanded and become more diversified and developed, and in 1872 a railroad running west, connecting Manitowoc with Appleton, was completed. The following year, in September, at Centerville in the southern part of the county, officials of the Lake Shore and Western Railroad Company drove the last spike into the line running between Manitowoc and Milwaukee. After that the old isolation was gone and the village was more connected with the life beyond its clearing. Major improvements to the harbor also contributed to that. The sandbar that accumulated where the river entered the lake was removed, and the channel was dredged so that ships could move upstream into the midst of the community. The lumber industry, around which the settlement had originally been built, declined rapidly, especially following the devastating forest fires of October 1871, which swept down out of Kewaunee County and consumed thousands of acres of timber in the northern townships. But the demise of lumbering was compensated by the rise of agriculture, shipbuilding, and industries such as brass and iron foundries, brick yards, and tanneries, and, as a consequence, the town's population increased by another third during the 1870s and 1880s.[15]

Anderson became part of that growth and change. While at Lawrence he had supported himself by teaching school, and at one point his finances became so strapped that he was compelled to suspend his studies for a year in order to work full time as principal of the elementary school in De Pere. But he returned to college, and during those summers at college he also read law with Judge Meyers in Appleton. After graduating in 1870, he returned to Manitowoc, where he continued his legal training with John D. Markham. His wartime aspirations to get a college education, to "take up the study of law," and eventually to work his "way up to a position in society" were diligently pursued. After a year clerking for Markham, Anderson was admitted to the bar. He went on to have a long and successful career, first in private practice, then as Manitowoc's city attorney, and finally as a county judge. In 1888 he was elected to the Wisconsin state assembly and served a term in Madison. Throughout those years he also retained a keen interest in writing, which, for a while, he gave expression to by becoming the owner and editor of the *Lake Shore Times,* a newspaper he published from 1883 to 1886. That simply became too much work while dealing with the increasing business of his law office, but even after getting out of journalism he wrote some articles about his boyhood and Civil War experiences and authored a book entitled *Pioneer Courts and Lawyers of Manitowoc County.* Along the way he also lost his wartime aversion to the idea of marriage. While at Lawrence he met Eva Mills, a literature student who was the daughter of Judge J. T. Mills of Grant County, and after a courtship of about four years, much of it carried on by correspondence, they were married on July 17, 1873. They raised a son and a daughter— Joseph and Jean Harriet—accumulated an impressive private library, and had a large experimental orchard and fruit farm just north of town.

In the early winter of 1872 Anderson's father died at age sixty-six, and the following summer, just a few weeks after his marriage to Eva, his mother also passed away. Both his sisters, Jean and Harriet, died in their thirties, but James lived a long and good life. After escaping death in the war and returning home to Manitowoc, he saw the ice in the river form and break up and the lilacs along the shore bloom again and again for nearly another sixty years. In that time he and the town made it through the hard times that came and went, and came again, and he was there to watch two more generations of boys march down Eighth Street and off to war, first to the Caribbean and then to France. He was also there in March of 1926 when Company A's "Dear Old Flag" was again returned to Manitowoc. By then he was a much-revered white-haired man.

In those times, and especially in the spring of the year, Friday nights downtown were busy, almost festive, occasions. Men were out

Figure 18. Judge James S. Anderson was a much respected citizen and lawyer in Manitowoc during the late nineteenth and early twentieth centuries. (Courtesy of the Manitowoc Public Library)

of the factories and shipyards with their week's pay. It was a night for cold beer and fried perch freshly caught in the clear waters just offshore. Women shopped in the crowded stores and children met friends on the streets. It was such an evening on Friday, May 5, 1927, and Judge Anderson, who was still a tall, straight, distinguished-looking man, was downtown. Shortly after supper, he stepped off the sidewalk on Eighth Street to cross over toward the Williams House Hotel. No sooner had he done so when a boy on a bicycle struck him. In the collision the judge was knocked down, hitting his head hard on the pavement. He never regained consciousness. Through the weekend he lingered on at his own house, where, just before dawn on Monday morning, he quietly died. He was eighty-seven.

"There was no man better known or more respected" in the town, wrote the editor of the *Manitowoc Herald News*. "He was a warrior to the end," remarked a friend, who also called him a man of "majestic character" whose "integrity was as unquestionable as his courage." James Anderson was one of the last of his kind to go, for with his death only three veterans of the Civil War remained alive in the county. As the old soldiers departed, the connections between the living and what Whitman had called the "real war" fell away. Memory—especially of the common soldier's part in the struggle—faded, and Anderson's own sudden passing, declared that same friend, left "a lonely place against the sky, as when a lordly cedar goes down with a great shout upon the hills."[16]

Notes

PROLOGUE

1. James Anderson to his Parents and Sisters, Brandy Station, Virginia, Jan. 19, 1864, from the James S. Anderson Papers, Archives of the State Historical Society of Wisconsin (hereafter cited as Anderson Papers). All letters cited are from this collection unless otherwise indicated. Well after completing my own research in the papers of James S. Anderson, Dennis R. Moore of Manitowoc edited and self-published Anderson's Civil War papers: Dennis R. Moore, ed., *The Civil War Diaries and Letters of James S. Anderson, Company A, 5th Wisconsin Volunteers, Manitowoc, Wisconsin* (Manitowoc: Dennis R. Moore, 1989). Mr. Moore did very careful work, which I have used in checking my original notes.

2. Hamlin Garland, "The Return of the Private," in *The American Tradition in Literature,* ed. Sculley Bradley, Richard Croom Beatty, and E. Hudson Long (New York: Norton, 1967), 1:932.

3. Walt Whitman, "The Real War Will Never Get into the Books," in *Complete Prose Works, Walt Whitman* (New York: Mitchell Kennerly, 1914), 74. Some of the "real war" has gotten into some books, and perhaps the most noteworthy examples are Reid Mitchell's *Civil War Soldiers: Their Expectations and Experiences* (New York: Viking, 1988) and Bell I. Wiley's *The Life of Johnny Reb: The Common Soldier of the Confederacy* (Indianapolis: Bobbs-Merrill, 1943) and *The Life of Billy Yank: The Common Soldier of the Union* (Indianapolis: Bobbs-Merrill, 1952). However, these are general works, describing general conditions, and do not look at the experiences in the context of actual day-to-day events.

4. Winston S. Churchill, *My Early Life: A Roving Commission* (New York: Charles Scribner's Sons, 1930), 65; Thomas Jefferson to Colonel William Steven Smith, Paris, Nov. 13, 1787, *The Life and Selected Writings of Thomas Jefferson,* ed. Adrienne Koch and William Peden (New York: Modern Library, 1944), 436.

5. William Shakespeare, *The Life of King Henry the Fifth,* act 3, scene 1.

6. Mark Twain, "The Private History of the Campaign that Failed," in *The Portable Mark Twain,* selected and introduced by Bernard DeVoto (New York: Viking Press, 1946), 142; Ambrose Bierce, "A Son of the Gods," in *The Complete*

Short Stories of Ambrose Bierce, ed. Ernest Jerome Hopkins (Garden City, N.Y.: Doubleday, 1970), 286; Twain, "Private History of the Campaign," 139.

7. Stephen Crane, *The Red Badge of Courage* (Boston: Houghton Mifflin, 1960), 230; Bierce, "One of the Missing," in *Complete Short Stories of Ambrose Bierce,* 266; Farley Mowat, *And No Birds Sang* (Boston: Little, Brown, 1979), 211; Ernest Hemingway, *A Farewell To Arms* (New York: Collier Books, Macmillan, 1929), 249.

8. Bierce, "Son of the Gods," 286; Erich Maria Remarque, *All Quiet on the Western Front* (Greenwich, Conn.: Fawcett Crest, 1959), 237, 55.

9. Mowat, *No Birds Sang,* 93; Philip Caputo, *A Rumor of War* (New York: Ballantine Books, 1977), 218; J. Glen Gray, *The Warriors: Reflections of Men in Battle* (New York: Harper and Row, 1959), 52, 51; Crane, *Red Badge of Courage,* 135; Gray, *Warriors,* 51.

10. Crane, *Red Badge of Courage,* 143; Remarque, *All Quiet on the Western Front,* 237.

11. Gerald F. Linderman, *Embattled Courage: The Experience of Combat in the American Civil War* (New York: Free Press, 1987), 223; see also John Keegan, *The Face of Battle* (Harmondsworth, Eng.: Penguin Books, 1976).

12. Whitman, "Real War," 75.

CHAPTER 1: A PLACE TO BEGIN AGAIN

1. Rosa Kellner's Journal, Apr. 18, 1861, May 18, Aug. 22, 1860. This valuable and lengthy journal is now in the possession of Rosa Kellner's great-granddaughter, Lynda Dvorachek, who still lives in Manitowoc County (hereafter cited as Kellner Journal).

2. Notes on the Kellner Journal prepared by Lynda Dvorachek and Carole M. Bethke Dolato, July 1988.

3. Kellner Journal, July 20, 1860.

4. Ibid., June [?], 1863, Aug. 22, 1861.

5. Ibid., Apr. 18, 1861; *Manitowoc Herald,* Apr. 25, 1861; *Manitowoc Daily Tribune,* Apr. 19, 1861; James S. Anderson, "Manitowoc County in the Civil War," paper read before the meeting of the Manitowoc County Historical Society, Feb. 1911, p. 2, Anderson Papers.

6. Kellner Journal, Apr. 18, 1861.

7. Anderson, "Manitowoc County in the Civil War," 2.

8. Louis Falge, ed., *History of Manitowoc County Wisconsin* (Chicago: Goodspeed Historical Association, 1911), 2:182; "Certificate, Statement of Service," from the British army, and "Statement of Conduct," by Lieutenant Colonel A. Jones, York, Upper Canada, Aug. 12, 1829, both in Anderson Papers.

9. See J. M. Bumsted, *The People's Clearance: Highland Emigration to British North America, 1770–1815* (Edinburgh: Edinburgh University Press and the University of Manitoba Press, 1982); T. C. Smout, *A Century of the Scottish People, 1830–1950* (London: Collins, 1986).

10. Friedrich Engels, *The Conditions of the Working Class in England,* trans. and ed. W. O. Henderson and W. H. Chaloner (Stanford: Stanford University Press, 1968), 45; quotations from Archibald Alison and J. C. Symons, 142, 46.

11. Gerhard Kremers, "An Immigrant's Letter: Manitowoc Rapids, in the State of Wisconsin, July 26, 1848," Manitowoc County Historical Society Occupational Monograph 59, 1986 (reprinted from *Wisconsin Magazine of History* 21 [Sept. 1937]: 68–84); John M. Berrien to Lieutenant Colonel J. J. Abert, Chief of the Topographical Bureau, Detroit, Oct. 1837, in *U.S. Congress, House of Representatives. War Department. Harbor at Manitowoc: Letter from the Secretary of War: Report of the Colonel of the Topographical Engineers, Relative to the Importance of a Harbor at Manitowoc, in the Territory of Wisconsin,* Apr. 19, 1844 (serial set 444), 3–4.

12. James Sibree Anderson, "Indians of Manitowoc County," *Proceedings of the State Historical Society of Wisconsin,* Fifty-ninth Annual Meeting, Oct. 26, 1911 (Madison: State Historical Society of Wisconsin, 1912), 165.

13. Ibid., 166.

14. Ibid., 167.

15. Ibid., 168–69.

16. Reference to the Anderson's house, Kellner Journal, June 25, 1861.

17. John Schuette, "An Ideal City," chap. 19 in Falge, ed., *History of Manitowoc County* 1:391.

18. Kremers, "Immigrant's Letter," 3; Nils Williams Olsson and Jonas Oscar Backlund, ed. and trans., *A Pioneer in Northwest America, 1841–1858: The Memoirs of Gustaf Unonius* (Minneapolis: University of Minnesota Press, 1950), 2:154, 155.

19. G. C. Wellner, "In Pioneer Days," chap. 5 in Falge, ed., *History of Manitowoc County* 1:54.

20. Harlan Hatcher, "Sails," in *The Great Lakes Reader,* ed. Walter Havighurst (New York: Collier Books, 1966), 350–51; Kellner Journal, Apr. 28, 1861.

21. Shipping and export report for the Village of Manitowoc for 1859, reported in the *Manitowoc Pilot,* Jan. 27, 1860.

22. Census information published in the *Manitowoc Pilot,* Aug. 31, 1860; see also Wellner, "In Pioneer Days" 1:52, 51.

23. Demographic information on the village of Manitowoc taken from the *Federal Census Manuscripts for 1860,* State Historical Society of Wisconsin Library.

24. Wellner, "Pioneer Days" 1:53, 49.

25. *Mortality Schedule, 1860, for Manitowoc County from the Federal Census,* transcribed from census records by the Manitowoc County Genealogical Society, May 1984, Manitowoc Public Library.

26. Ibid.

27. Packard death reported in the *Manitowoc Pilot,* Feb. 10, 1860; suicide of the Bohemian girl and the death of the Bohemian farmer reported in the *Manitowoc Pilot,* Mar. 23, 1860; other specific deaths in the *Mortality Schedule, 1860, for Manitowoc County.*

28. Wellner, "Pioneer Days" 1:51.

29. Olsson and Backlund, eds., *Memoirs of Gustaf Unonius* 2:155.

30. See Caroline Hubbard, *History of the City of Manitowoc . . . From 1850 to 1860* (Manitowoc: Manitowoc Public Library Board, 1904).

31. Margaret Fuller, *Summer on the Lakes, in 1843* (Urbana: University of Illinois Press, 1991), 12; Andrew R. L. Cayton and Peter S. Onuf, *The Midwest and the Nation: Rethinking the History of an American Region* (Bloomington: Indiana University Press, 1990).

32. George C. Brown, ed. and trans., "A Swedish Traveler in Early Wisconsin: The Observations of Fredrika Bremer," *Wisconsin Magazine of History* 61 (1978): 308; also see John D. Buenker, "Wisconsin as Maverick, Model, and Microcosm," in *Heartland: Comparative Histories of the Midwestern States,* ed. James H. Madison (Bloomington: Indiana University Press, 1988), 59–85.

33. See Falge, ed., *History of Manitowoc County,* vol. 1, chap. 15; Kellner Journal, July 13, Sept. 18, 1860.

34. *Manitowoc Pilot,* Jan. 4, Feb. 22, 1861, Mar. 30, 2, Nov. 9, 1860.

35. *Manitowoc Pilot,* Oct. 26, June 22, 1860, Jan. 4, 25, 1861.

36. *Manitowoc Daily Tribune,* Apr. 19, 1861; *Manitowoc Pilot,* Apr. 19, 1861.

37. *Manitowoc Daily Tribune,* Apr. 22, 1861; James S. Anderson, Journal, April 1861 to December 31, 1861, p. 2, Anderson Papers (hereafter cited as Anderson Journal 1).

CHAPTER 2: RITES OF PASSAGE

1. *Manitowoc Herald,* May 2, 1861; Anderson, "Manitowoc County in the Civil War," 2; *Manitowoc Daily Tribune,* Apr. 22, 1861.

2. *Manitowoc Pilot,* Dec. 21, 1860; *Manitowoc Herald,* Apr. 25, July 4, 1861; also see Walter Stix Glazer, "Wisconsin Goes to War, April 1861" (Master's thesis, University of Wisconsin–Madison, 1963).

3. *Manitowoc Daily Tribune,* Apr. 27, 1861.

4. See Cayton and Onuf, *Midwest and the Nation;* also, Michael Barton Goodmen, *The Character of the Civil War Soldiers* (University Park: Pennsylvania State University Press, 1981); *Manitowoc Weekly Tribune,* July 3, 1861; *Manitowoc Daily Tribune,* Apr. 15, 1861.

5. *Manitowoc Pilot,* Apr. 26, May 3, 1861.

6. *Manitowoc Herald,* May 9, 1861; the information about the composition of Company A, Fifth Wisconsin Volunteers derived from the Muster Rolls in the Archives of the State Historical Society of Wisconsin, Madison.

7. For a general discussion of motivations of the men and boys who volunteered for military service early in the Civil War, see Mitchell, *Civil War Soldiers,* and the early chapters of James W. Geary, *We Need Men: The Union Draft in the Civil War* (De Kalb: Northern Illinois University Press, 1991); *Manitowoc Daily Tribune,* Apr. 22, 23, 1861.

8. See George L. Mosse, *Nationalism and Sexuality: Respectability and Abnormal Sexuality in Modern Europe* (New York: Howard Fertig, 1985), 114; Mitchell, *Civil War Soldiers*, 17; Linderman, *Embattled Courage*.

9. Peter Scherfins's name is spelled a number of different ways in different sources, but the spelling here, taken from the Muster Rolls, will be used consistently throughout the text.

10. *Manitowoc Pilot*, Apr. 26, May 17, 1861.

11. James S. Anderson, "Speech," Mar. 23, 1925, printed in *Record of the Proceedings on the Occasion of the Presentation of the Flag of Co. A, Fifth Wisconsin Volunteer Infantry to the Manitowoc County Historical Society* (Manitowoc: Manitowoc County Historical Society, 1925).

12. *Manitowoc Herald*, June 20, 1861; also see discussion of the symbolic importance of such flags in Mitchell, *Civil War Soldiers*, 19.

13. *Manitowoc Pilot*, May 17, 1861.

14. For discussion of the "knightly" images and imagination and their impact on nineteenth-century public opinion, see George L. Mosse, *Nationalism and Sexuality*. *Manitowoc Pilot*, May 17, 1861.

15. *Manitowoc Herald*, May 9, 23, 1861; *Manitowoc Pilot*, May 17, 1861.

16. Kellner Journal, June 25, 1861; Anderson Journal 1, June 23, 1861, 4–5.

17. Kellner Journal, June 25, 1861.

18. Anderson, "Speech."

19. Ibid.

20. Anderson to Family, from the *Comet*, June 24, 1861; Anderson to Family, Camp Randall, June 24, 1861.

21. See Carolyn J. Mattern, *Soldiers When They Go: The Story of Camp Randall, 1861–1865* (Madison: State Historical Society of Wisconsin, 1981); also, John K. Driscoll, "Wisconsin in the American Civil War," *Wisconsin Academy Review* 30 (1984): 30–35.

22. Anderson to Family, Camp Randall, June 24, 1861.

23. *Madison Journal* comments published in the *Manitowoc Pilot*, July 5, 1861; letter from John Leykom in *Manitowoc Pilot*, July 12, 1861; Anderson to Family, Camp Randall, June 24, 1861; Anderson to Family, Camp Randall, June 3, 1861.

24. Anderson Journal 1, n.d., 10; Letter from "S," Camp Randall, in *Manitowoc Tribune*, July 24, 1861.

25. Anderson to P. P. Smith, Camp Randall, June 27, 1861; Anderson Journal 1, n.d., 10; Anderson to Family, Camp Randall, July 3, 1861.

26. Anderson to Family, Camp Randall, July 5, 1861; Anderson Journal 1, n.d., 10; Leykom letter in *Manitowoc Pilot*, July 12, 1861.

27. Anderson Journal 1, July 4, 1861, 11; Anderson to Family, Camp Randall, July 5, 1861.

28. Anderson to Family, Camp Randall, July 5, 1861.

29. See Mattern, *Soldiers When They Go*; July 21, 1861, Alfred L. Castleman, *The Army of the Potomac: Behind the Scenes, A Diary of Unwritten History* (Milwaukee: Strickland, 1863), 7 (hereafter cited as *Castleman Diary*).

30. Anderson to Family, Camp Randall, July 11, 1861.

31. "J. E." letter, Camp Randall, July 12, 1861, in *Manitowoc Tribune*, July 24, 1861; "S" Letter, Camp Randall, July 18, 1861, in *Manitowoc Tribune*, July 24, 1861.

32. Anderson Journal 1, n.d., 12–13.

33. Anderson Journal 1, July 24, 1861, 13.

34. Ibid., 14, July 25, 1861, 15; Anderson to Family, Harrisburg, July 29, 1861; "J. E." letter, Harrisburg, July 28, 1861, in *Manitowoc Tribune*, Aug. 7, 1861; *Castleman Diary*, July 27, 1861, 7.

35. *Castleman Diary*, July 29, 1861, 7, 8.

36. Ibid., July 31, 1861, 9.

37. Anderson to Family, Camp Cobb near Baltimore, Aug. 2, 1861.

38. *Castleman Diary*, Aug. 19, 1861, 17.

CHAPTER 3: MARCHING ALONG AND WAITING AROUND

1. Anderson to Family, Georgetown Heights, Aug. 10, 1861.

2. Margaret Leech, *Reveille in Washington, 1860–1865* (New York: Harper and Brothers, 1941), 12; also see Constant McLaughlin Green, *Washington: Village and Capital, 1800–1878* (Princeton: Princeton University Press, 1962), and Stanley Kimmel, *Mr. Lincoln's Washington* (New York: Coward-McCann, 1957).

3. James H. Leonard to Mary Sheldon, Camp Cobb near Washington, D.C., Aug. 15, 1861, R. G. Plumb, ed., "Letters of a Fifth Wisconsin Volunteer," *Wisconsin Magazine of History* 3 (1919): 51–83 (hereafter just the letter and page number will be cited).

4. George B. McClellan to Mary Ellen McClellan, Washington, D.C., July 27, Aug. 9, 16, 1861, *The Civil War Papers of George B. McClellan: Selected Correspondence, 1860–1865*, ed. Stephen W. Sears (New York: Ticknor and Fields, 1989), 70, 81–82, 85; see also Bruce Catton, *Terrible Swift Sword* (New York: Washington Square Press, 1963), 74–87; Linderman, *Embattled Courage*, 202.

5. The quotation from McClellan is taken from James M. McPherson, *Battle Cry of Freedom: The Civil War Era* (New York: Ballantine Books, 1988), 359–60; Linderman, *Embattled Courage*, 203.

6. *Castleman Diary*, Nov. 20, 1861, 56.

7. Anderson to Family, Camp Advance, Sept. 10, 1861; Leonard to Sheldon, Camp Advance, Sept. 12, 1861, 56; Evan R. Jones, *Personal Recollections of the American Civil War* (Newcastle-on-Tyne: M. and M. W. Lambert, 1872), 6.

8. Leonard to Sheldon, Camp Advance, Sept. 12, 1861, 56.

9. Unidentified author, letter from a soldier in the Fifth Wisconsin Volunteers, Sept. 6, 1861, in *Manitowoc Pilot*, Sept. 27, 1861; Anderson to Family, Camp Advance, Sept. 10, 1861.

10. Anderson to Family, Camp Advance, Sept. 10, 1861.

11. Anderson to Family, Camp Advance, Sept. 10, 1861; Anderson Journal 1, Sept. 10, 1861, 22; Letter from Company A, *Manitowoc Herald*, Oct. 11, 1861.

12. Anderson Journal 1, Sept. 15, 1861, 23; Letter from Company A, *Manitowoc Herald,* Oct. 11, 1861; Anderson to his Sisters, Camp Advance, Sept. 25, 1861.

13. Anderson to his Sisters, Camp Advance, Sept. 25, 1861.

14. Anderson Journal 1, Sept. 28, 1861, 25–26.

15. Anderson to Family, Camp Advance, Sept. 30, 1861.

16. Anderson to Family, Camp Griffin, Oct. 14, 1861.

17. Anderson to his sister Jean, Camp Advance, Sept. 17, 1861.

18. Anderson to Family, Camp Griffin, Oct. 14, 1861; Anderson Journal 1, Oct. 14, 1861, 30; Letter from "Volunteer," Camp Griffin, Oct. 17, 1861, in *Manitowoc Herald,* Nov. 14, 1861.

19. Letter from "Volunteer," Camp Griffin, Oct. 17, 1861; Anderson to Family, Camp Griffin, Oct. 14, 1861.

20. Anderson to his sister Jean, Camp Griffin, Oct. 28, 1861; Anderson to Family, Camp Griffin, Oct. 20, 1861.

21. Letter from Company A, Fifth Wisconsin Volunteers, Camp Advance, in *Manitowoc Herald,* Oct. 11, 1861.

22. *Castleman Diary,* Dec. 2, 1861, 62.

23. Anderson to Family, Camp Griffin, Nov. 30, 1861; Leonard to Sheldon, Camp Griffin, Nov. 5, 1861, 58; Anderson to Family, Camp Griffin, Dec. 8, 1861; unidentified member of the Fifth Wisconsin Volunteers, Camp Griffin, Jan. 30, 1862, Edwin B. Quiner, ed., *Correspondences of the Wisconsin Volunteers* (Madison: State Historical Society of Wisconsin, 1865), 3:155.

24. See Kerry A. Trask, "The First Full Measure: Manitowoc Enters the Civil War," *Voyageur* 3 (1986): 5–14.

25. A Letter to Fitch from the Fourteenth Regiment, Camp Wood, Dec. 6, 1861, *Manitowoc Herald,* Dec. 19, 1861; James Newton to his Parents, Camp Wood, Feb. 24, 1862, in Stephen E. Ambrose, ed., *A Wisconsin Boy in Dixie: The Selected Letters of James K. Newton* (Madison: State Historical Society of Wisconsin, 1961), 9.

26. There was a series of very well-written, descriptive letters sent to Fitch of the *Manitowoc Herald* from a member of Company C, Fourth Wisconsin Volunteers printed under the pseudonym "Camp." Almost all the members of that particular company were from Sheboygan; Paleman Smalley and Orin S. Kittell were the only members from Manitowoc. Because of the high quality of the writing in these "Camp" letters, and because Smalley was a well-educated and highly articulate individual who went on to a successful career in journalism after the war, I have concluded that Smalley was the author of the "Camp" letters.

27. "Camp" from Snow Hill, Worcester County, Maryland, Nov. 7, 1861, in *Manitowoc Herald,* Nov. 21, 1861.

28. "Camp" from Drummondtown, Virginia, Nov. 25, 1861, in *Manitowoc Herald,* Dec. 12, 1861; "Camp" from Baltimore, Dec. 14, 1861, in *Manitowoc Herald,* Dec. 26, 1861.

29. "Camp" from Baltimore, Jan. 1, 1862, in *Manitowoc Herald,* Jan. 16, 1862.

30. Kellner Journal, Sept. 14, 1861.

31. Kellner Journal, Oct. 29, Nov. 22, Dec. 8, 13, 1861, Feb. 15, 1862, Oct. 2, 1864.

32. Anderson to his Sisters, Camp Griffin, Oct. 28, 1861; Anderson to Parents, Camp Griffin, Dec. 5, 1861.

33. Kellner Journal, June 25, 1861.

34. Anderson to Family, Camp Randall, July 5, 1861; Anderson to Family, Harrison Landing, Aug. 13, 1861; Anderson to his sister Jean, Camp Advance, Sept. 12, 1861; Anderson to his sister Jean, Camp Advance, Sept. 17, 1861; Anderson to his Mother, Camp Griffin, Dec. 28, 1861.

35. Anderson to Family, Camp Randall, June 27, July 11, 22, 1861; Anderson to his sister Jean, Camp Kalorama, Sept. 1, 1861; Anderson to his sister Jean, Camp Advance, Sept. 17, 1861.

36. Anderson to his sister Jean, Georgetown Heights, Aug. 10, 1861; Anderson to his sister Jean, Camp Kalorama, Sept. 1, 1861; Anderson to Family, Camp Griffin, Dec. 8, 1861; Anderson to his Sisters, Camp Griffin, Dec. 17, 1861; Anderson to Family, Camp Griffin, Jan. 12, 1862.

37. Anderson to Family, Camp Griffin, Dec. 25, 1861; Leonard to Sheldon, Camp Griffin, Nov. 5, 1861, 157.

38. Anderson Journal 1, Jan. 1, 1862, 34; Anderson to Family, Camp Griffin, Jan. 7, 1862.

39. *Castleman Diary*, Feb. 15, 1862, 83; Nov. 8, 1861, 50; Anderson to Sisters, Camp Griffin, Dec. 28, 1861.

40. Anderson to Family, Camp Griffin, Dec. 5, 1861; Leonard to Sheldon, Camp Griffin, Dec. 5, 1861, 61; Anderson to Family, Camp Griffin, Dec. 5, 1861.

41. Anderson to Sisters, Camp Griffin, Nov. 30, 1861; *Castleman Diary*, Nov. 29, 1861, 56; Anderson to Sisters, Camp Griffin, Dec. 17, 1861.

42. Anderson to Family, Camp Griffin, Jan. 26, 1862; letter from Captain Temple Clark, Camp Griffin, Feb. 4, 1862, printed in *Manitowoc Pilot*, Feb. 28, 1862; Anderson to Family, Camp Griffin, Feb. 19, 1862; J. Crowley's comment was in *Manitowoc Pilot*, Feb. 28, 1862; Anderson to Family, Camp Griffin, Jan. 26, 1862.

43. Anderson to Family, Camp Griffin, Mar. 28, 1862.

CHAPTER 4: SPRING OFFENSIVES

1. James Leonard to Mary Sheldon, Camp Griffin, Mar. 9, 1862, 64.

2. *Manitowoc Weekly Tribune*, Mar. 12, Apr. 23, 1862; Kellner Journal, Feb.–Mar. 1862.

3. Leonard to Mary Sheldon, Camp Griffin, Mar. 9, 1862, 65; Anderson to Family, Camp Griffin, Feb. 19, 1862; Anderson to Family, camp in Field No. 2, Mar. 17, 1862.

4. Anderson to Family, Camp Griffin, Jan. 26, 1862; reference to the "Harpers Ferry Musket," Anderson Journal 1, Aug. 3, 1861, 18; Anderson to Family, Camp Griffin, Jan. 26, 1862.

5. *Castleman Diary*, Mar. 10, 1862, 94; Anderson to Family, Camp Griffin, Feb. 27, 1862.

6. *Castleman Diary*, Mar. 10, 1862, 94.

7. Ibid., 95.

8. Ibid., Mar. 16, 1862, 99.

9. Ibid., Mar. 23, 1862, 102.

10. Anderson Journal 1, Mar. 22, 1862, 41–42; Anderson to Family, camp at Little Bethel Fort Monroe, Mar. 31, 1862.

11. Anderson to Family, camp at Little Bethel Fort Monroe, Mar. 31, 1862; *Castleman Diary*, Mar. 23, 1862, 104, 105; Anderson to Family, camp at Little Bethel Fort Monroe, Apr. 3, 1862; *Castleman Diary*, Mar. 31, 1862, 108; Anderson to Family, camp at Little Bethel Fort Monroe, Mar. 31, 1862.

12. Anderson Journal 1, Apr. 5, 1862, 46.

13. *Castleman Diary*, Apr. 17, 1862, 113.

14. Ibid., Apr. 8, 1862, 113.

15. Anderson to Family, near Yorktown, Apr. 14, 1862.

16. Ibid.

17. Ibid., Apr. 20, 1862; *Castleman Diary*, Apr. 17, 1862, 124.

18. *Castleman Diary*, Apr. 28, 1862, 128–29.

19. See Trask, "First Full Measure."

20. Ibid.; *Manitowoc Tribune*, Apr. 16, 1862; Kellner Journal, Apr. 27, 1862. See also a very good short study of the uses of rhetoric and ritual in dealing with class conflicts within communities: Teresa A. Thomas, "For Union, Not for Glory: Memory and the Civil War Volunteers of Lancaster, Massachusetts," *Civil War History* 40 (Mar. 1994): 25–47.

21. Anderson to Family, camped somewhere in Virginia, May 21, 1862; Anderson to Family, camp near Chickahominy, May 28, 1862.

22. Catton, *Terrible Swift Sword*, 264.

23. Anderson to Family, Camp Griffin, Feb. 27, 1862; Scherfins's letter printed in the *Manitowoc Pilot*, Apr. 11, 1862.

24. Anderson to Family, camp at Little Bethel Fort Monroe, Mar. 31, 1862.

25. Letter from "M. C. G.," camp near Richmond, June 18, 1862, in *Manitowoc Tribune*, July 16, 1862.

26. Thomas Wagener to William Henry, May 8, 1862, in *Manitowoc Pilot*, May 30, 1862; *Castleman Diary*, May 5, 1862, 137, 138.

27. Anderson to Family, near Williamsburg, May 6, 1862; *Castleman Diary*, May 5, 1862, 138; Edwin B. Quiner, *The Military History of Wisconsin: A Record of the Civil and Military Patriotism of the State* (Chicago: Clarke, 1881), 511.

28. Anderson to Family, near Williamsburg, May 6, 1862; George B. Engles to Parents, n.d., in *Manitowoc Herald*, May 22, 1862; Thomas Wagener to William Henry, May 8, 1862, in *Manitowoc Pilot*, May 30, 1862.

29. Anderson Journal 1, May [?], 1862, 56–57.

30. *Castleman Diary*, May 9, 1862, 141; Anderson to Family, near Richmond, June 19, 1862; Letter from "C. A.," in *Manitowoc Tribune*, May 28, 1862.

31. *Castleman Diary*, May 11, 1862, 144; Anderson to Family, somewhere in Virginia, May 21, 1862.

32. *Castleman Diary*, May 26, June 8, 1862, 155, 159.

33. Anderson Journal I, early June 1862 at Golden's Farm, 69; Anderson to Family, near Chickahominy, May 28, 1862.

34. Anderson to Family, on the Chickahominy, June 4, 1862.

35. "Camp" to William Fitch, Ship Island, Mississippi, Mar. 20, 1862, in *Manitowoc Herald*, May 1, 1862; Letter from "A. C. B." from the Fourth Wisconsin, Ship Island and on the Steamship *Colorado*, Apr. 23, 1862, in *Chilton Times*, May 17, 1862; "Camp" to Fitch, from U.S. frigate *Colorado*, on the Mississippi River, Apr. 23, 1862, in *Manitowoc Herald*, May 15, 1862; "Camp" to Fitch, Vicksburg, June 29, 1862, in ibid., July 17, 1862.

36. Anderson Journal I, June 1, 1862, 66–67.

37. Anderson to Family, on the Chickahominy, June 1, 1862.

38. Anderson to Family, camp near Richmond, June 12, 1862; Leonard to Sheldon, near Chickahominy River, June 15, 1862, 66.

39. Anderson to Family, camp near the James River, July 8, 1862; Catton, *Terrible Swift Sword*, 309.

40. Anderson Journal I, June 26, 1862, 72.

41. Ibid., June 27, 1862, 73.

42. Ibid., June 28, 1862, 73; Evan Jones, *Four Years in the Army of the Potomac: A Soldier's Recollections* (London: Tyne Publishing, 1872), 66.

43. Catton, *Terrible Swift Sword*, 319; Anderson Journal I, June 29, 1862, 76; letter from Horace Walker, from Harrison's Landing, July 13, 1862, in *Manitowoc Tribune*, Aug. 6, 1862; list of sick and wounded soldiers left behind at Savage Station printed in *Manitowoc Herald*, Aug. 7, 1862.

44. Anderson Journal I, June 28, 30, 1862, 77, 78.

45. Jones, *Four Years in the Army of Potomac*, 70.

46. Anderson Journal I, June 30, 1862, 79–81.

47. *Castleman Diary*, July 1, 1862, 173; Anderson Journal I, June 30, 1862, 81; Anderson to Family, Harrison's Landing, July 8, 1862.

48. Anderson Journal I, July 1, 1862, 83.

49. *Castleman Diary*, July 1, 1862, 83; Siegfried Sassoon's poem, "A Working Party."

50. Jones, *Four Years in the Army of Potomac*, 73, 71; *Castleman Diary*, July 2, 3, 1862, 175, 177.

51. *Manitowoc Tribune*, July 2, 1862; Jones, *Four Years in the Army of Potomac*, 74.

CHAPTER 5: AUTUMN STORMS

1. *Castleman Diary*, Aug. 23, 1862, 202; July 13, 1862, 186.

2. Anderson Journal I, Aug. 30, 1862, 92.

3. *Castleman Diary,* Sept. 1, 1862, 213; Sept. 12, 1862, 222; Sept. 13, 1862, 224; Sept. 17, 1862, 228; Anderson Journal 1, Sept. 14, 1862, 97–98.

4. *Castleman Diary,* Sept. 13, 1862, 222.

5. Anderson Journal 1, Sept. 14, 1862, 98–99.

6. Ibid., Sept. 17, 1862, 100; Jones, *Four Years in the Army of the Potomac,* 80–81, 85.

7. Anderson Journal 1, Sept. 17, 1862, 100; Report of Brigadier General Winfield S. Hancock, on the Battles of Crampton's Pass and Antietam, near Sharpsburg, Maryland, Sept. 21, 1862, in *The War of the Rebellion: Compilation of the Official Records of the Union and Confederate Armies,* 128 vols. (Washington D.C.: Government Printing Office, 1888), ser. 1, vol. 19:406 (hereafter cited as *OR*); Anderson Journal 1, Sept. 17, 1862, 100. The manuscript written by Anderson, with no place or date given, is a report on the Battle of Antietam and is clearly by James Anderson and included in his papers at the Archives of the State Historical Society of Wisconsin.

8. Antietam MSS, Anderson Papers.

9. *Castleman Diary,* Sept. 18, 1862, 230; Antietam MSS, Anderson Papers.

10. Antietam MSS, Anderson Papers.

11. Statistical information taken from McPherson, *Battle Cry of Freedom,* 544. The quotation of the Wisconsin soldier is taken from a letter written by Frank Haskell, Sept. 19, 1862, from the Haskell Papers, Archives of the State Historical Society of Wisconsin, here taken from Catton, *Terrible Swift Sword,* 434.

12. McPherson, *Battle Cry of Freedom,* 545; *Castleman Diary,* Sept. 18, 1862, 232.

13. Kellner Journal, July 24, Aug. 25, 1862.

14. Ibid., Sept. 3, 4, 1862.

15. There is much written about myths and stereotype images associated with Native Americans, but a good single standard work of this subject is Robert F. Berkhofer Jr., *The White Man's Indian: Images of the American Indian from Columbus to the Present* (New York: Vintage Books, 1978). Specifically on the panic in Wisconsin, see Milo M. Quaife, "The Panic of 1862 in Wisconsin," *Wisconsin Magazine of History* 4 (Dec. 1920): 166–95.

16. *Manitowoc Herald,* Nov. 17, 1857.

17. Ibid.

18. Kellner Journal, Oct. 18, 1860, Apr. 14, 1861, Aug. 12, 1863.

19. Anderson to Family, Camp Cobb near Baltimore, Aug. 2, 1861; Anderson to Family, camped somewhere in Virginia, May 21, 1862.

20. *Manitowoc Pilot,* Oct. 3, 31, 1862, Jan. 30, 1863.

21. Ibid., Nov. 7, 1862, Apr. 15, 1864.

22. "Camp" to Fitch, Vicksburg, June 29, 1862, in *Manitowoc Herald,* July 17, 1862; "Old Soldier" to Crowley, Columbus, Kentucky, Apr. 18, 1863, in *Manitowoc Pilot,* Apr. 24, 1863.

23. "Manitowoc Boy" to Crowley, Belle Plains, Virginia, Apr. 1, 1863, in *Manitowoc Pilot,* Apr. 24, 1863.

24. Richard N. Current, *The History of Wisconsin: The Civil War Era, 1848–1873* (Madison: State Historical Society of Wisconsin, 1976), 80, 389.

25. *Manitowoc Tribune*, Sept. 3, 1862; *Manitowoc Pilot*, Sept. 5, 1862.

26. *Manitowoc Pilot*, Oct. 24, 1862.

27. Ibid.

28. Ibid.

29. Falge, ed., *History of Manitowoc County* 2:180; Anderson to Family, near Manassas Junction, Nov. 8, 1862; *Manitowoc Tribune*, Oct. 15, 1862.

30. *Manitowoc Pilot*, Oct. 17, 1862.

31. Anderson to Family, near Manassas Junction, Nov. 8, 1862.

32. Election results in *Manitowoc Pilot*, Nov. 7, 1862.

33. Lovina Classon, "Dear Brother," ibid., Aug. 15, 1862.

34. *Manitowoc Herald*, Aug. 21, 1862; Kellner Journal, Sept. 24, Nov. 23, 1862.

35. Kellner Journal, Sept. 26, 1862; Anderson to Family, camped near Alexandria, Sept. 5, 1862.

36. Don Shove to T. C. Shove, near Corinth, Mississippi, Oct. 13, 1862, in *Manitowoc Herald*, Oct. 23, 1862; details of Temple Clark's condition reported in the *Manitowoc Pilot*, Nov. 21, 1862.

37. Andrew Sloggy to Harry G. Edwards, Corinth, Mississippi, Oct. 22, 1862, in *Manitowoc Herald*, Nov. 6, 1862.

38. Ibid.

39. Francis Engle to his Father, n.p., n.d., in ibid., Nov. 13, 1862.

40. Letter from Captain Charles H. Walker, on the march, Oct. 19, 1862, in ibid., Dec. 4, 1862.

41. Ibid.; Report of Colonel John C. Starkweather, on the battlefield at Chaplin Hill, Oct. 11, 1862, *OR* 16:1156.

42. Anderson to Family, camp near Alexandria, Sept. 11, 1862.

43. Kellner Journal, Aug. 25, 1862. The wartime letters of Mead Holmes Jr., along with an introduction written by his father, the Reverend Mead Holmes Sr., were published in *Soldier of the Cumberland: Memoir of Mead Holmes Jr.* (Boston: American Tract Society, 1864), 60 (hereafter cited as *Soldier of the Cumberland*); Kellner Journal, Aug. 25, 1862.

44. Holmes to Parents, Kentucky, Oct. 23, 5, 1862, and to Friends, on the battlefield, Oct. 9, 1862, *Soldier of the Cumberland*, 100, 91, 93.

45. Holmes to Friends, Oct. 9, 1862, and to Parents, Oct. 13, 1862, ibid., 94, 96.

46. Holmes to Friends, Mitchellville Station, Tennessee, Nov. 14, 1862, and to Parents and Friends, seven miles from Lebanon, Kentucky, Oct. 23, 1862, ibid., 102, 98–99, 100, 103.

47. Holmes to Parents, near Nashville, Dec. 3, 1862, and to Sewall Smith, near Nashville, Dec. 25, 1862, ibid., 116, 126–127.

48. Leonard to Sheldon, near Aquia Creek, Virginia, Dec. 1, 1962, 68.

49. Ibid., 68; Anderson to Family, camp near Aquia, Virginia, Nov. 30, 1862.

50. Anderson Journal 1, Dec. 11, 1862, 112.

51. *Castleman Diary*, Dec. 12, 1862, 260; Anderson to Family, near Fredericksburg, Dec. 17, 1862.

52. Anderson to Family, near Fredericksburg, Dec. 17, 1862; Jones, *Four Years in the Army of the Potomac*, 100.

53. Anderson to Family, near Fredericksburg, Dec. 17, 1862.

54. Ibid.

55. Ibid.

56. Report of Brigadier General Calvin E. Pratt, camp on Stafford Heights, Dec. 18, 1862, *OR* 21:532.

57. Thomas Francis Galwey's Diary (of 8th Ohio Infantry), parts published under the title "An Irishman's View of Battle," in Edward J. Stackpole, *The Battle of Fredericksburg* (Harrisburg, Pa.: Eastern Acorn Press, 1981), 49, 50.

58. Anderson to Family, camp on the Rappahannock, Jan. 19, 1863; Jones, *Personal Recollections*, 11; *Castleman Diary*, Dec. 20, 1862, 274; Leonard to Sheldon, near White's Church, Virginia, Dec. 28, 1862, 69.

59. Anderson Journal 1, Dec. 24, 1862, 119; Anderson to Family, Harrison's Landing, Aug. 1, 1862; "Union" letter, from the banks of the James River, July 4, 1862, in *Manitowoc Tribune*, July 16, 1862; Leonard to Sheldon, White's Church, Dec. 28, 1862, 70.

60. Anderson to Family, Harrison's Landing, Aug. 1, 1862; Anderson to Family, on the Rappahannock, Jan. 6, 1863.

61. Anderson to Family, Aquia Creek, Nov. 30, 1862.

CHAPTER 6: MORE OF THE FIERY TRIAL

1. Anderson to Family, near Belle Landing, Dec. 26 1862.

2. Anderson to Family, on the Rappahannock, Jan. 6, 1863.

3. Mead Holmes to S. Smith, near Nashville, Dec. 25, 1862, *Soldier of the Cumberland*, 145.

4. Kellner Journal, Jan. 27, 1863, Dec. 21, 1862.

5. Anderson to Harriet Anderson, Rappahannock River, Dec. 26, 1862; Anderson Journal 1, Dec. 27, 1862, 120.

6. Anderson to Family, Rappahannock River, Jan. 6, 1863; Anderson to Family, Camp Griffin, Dec. 5, 1861.

7. Anderson to Family, near Belle Plains, Virginia, Feb. 14, 1863; Anderson to Family, near Belle Plains, Virginia, Mar. 9, 1863.

8. Kellner Journal, Apr. [?], 1863.

9. Leonard to Sheldon, near Belle Plains, Virginia, Apr. 1, 1863, 72; Anderson to Family, White Oak Church, Jan. 28, 1863; Anderson to Family, Belle Plains, Virginia, Apr. 12, 1863.

10. "Rifle" to S. Smith, Belle Plains, Virginia, Feb. 17, 1863, *Manitowoc Tribune*, Mar. 4, 1863; James S. Anderson, Apr. 8, 1863, Journal (unpaginated), Jan. 1–Dec. 31,

1863, Anderson Papers (hereafter cited as Anderson Journal 2); Anderson to Family, Belle Plains, Virginia, Apr. 27, 1863.

11. Anderson Journal 2, Apr. 8, 21, 1863.

12. Ibid., Jan. 21, 23, 1863.

13. Ibid., Jan. 27, 1863; Anderson to Family, White Oak Church, Jan. 29, 1863.

14. Anderson to Family, White Oak Church, Jan. 29, 1863.

15. Report of Major George W. Dawson, Sixty-first Pennsylvania Infantry, Light Division, camped on the Rappahannock, May 10, 1863, *OR*, vol. 25, 1:625; Anderson Journal 2, Apr. 29, May 1, 1863; Frank Haskell's letter, opposite Fredericksburg, May 3, 1863, in Frank L. Byrne and Andrew T. Weaver, eds., *Haskell of Gettysburg: His Life and Civil War Papers* (Kent, Ohio: Kent State University Press, 1989), 71.

16. Report of Major General John Sedgwick, Commander of the Sixth Army Corps, on the Rappahannock, May 15, 1863, *OR*, vol. 25, 1:558; Anderson Journal 2, May 3, 1863.

17. Quiner, *Military History of Wisconsin*, 514; see also Dennis R. Moore, *Manitowoc Herald Tribune Times*, May 3, 1988.

18. "The Storming of Fredericksburg Heights," May 3, 1863, in Quiner, ed., *Correspondences* 8:282; Anderson to Family, near Fredericksburg, May 4, 1863.

19. Haskell letter, May 3, 1863, in Byrne and Weaver, eds., *Haskell of Gettysburg*, 72.

20. Anderson to Family, near Fredericksburg, May 9, 1863.

21. Ibid.; Anderson to Family, May 4, 1863.

22. Anderson to Family, near Fredericksburg, May 9, 1863.

23. Anderson to Family, near Potomac Creek, May 25, 1863; Mead Holmes to Parents, Murfreesboro, Tennessee, Mar. 1, 1863, *Soldier of the Cumberland*, 157; Anderson to Friends at home, Potomac Creek, May 15, 1863; Anderson to Family, near Fredericksburg, May 9, 1863.

24. Anderson to Family, Potomac Creek, May 25, 1863.

25. Anderson to Friends at home, Potomac Creek, May 15, 1863; Anderson to Family, Potomac Creek, May 25, 1863.

26. Holmes to Parents, Murfreesboro, Jan. 7, 1863, *Soldier of the Cumberland*, 128.

27. Holmes to *Tribune*, Murfreesboro, Jan. 13, 1863, *Soldier of the Cumberland*, 134; Report of Colonel John C. Starkweather, First Wisconsin, Commander of Third Brigade, Camp Jefferson, near Stones' River, Tennessee, Dec. 31, 1862, *OR*, vol. 20, 1:391.

28. Holmes to Parents, Murfreesboro, Jan. 7, 1863, *Soldier of the Cumberland*, 129.

29. Report of Major General Lovell H. Rousseau, Nashville, Jan. 11, 1863, *OR*, vol. 20, 1:379; Holmes to Parents, Murfreesboro, Jan. 27, 1863, *Soldier of the Cumberland*, 130.

30. Holmes to *Tribune*, Murfreesboro, Jan. 19, 1863, *Soldier of the Cumberland*, 136, 137.

31. McPherson, *Battle Cry of Freedom*, 582.

32. Holmes to Parents, Murfreesboro, Jan. 7, 1863, *Soldier of the Cumberland*, 130.

33. Holmes to Parents, Murfreesboro, Mar. 22, Feb. 5, Mar. 1, 1863, ibid., 181, 144, 155.

34. Holmes to Parents, Murfreesboro, Mar. 22, 20, 1863, ibid., 180, 173.

35. Holmes to Parents, Murfreesboro, Apr. 11, 1863, ibid., 185.

36. Report of Mead Holmes death in the *Manitowoc Tribune*, Apr. 22, 1863, the announcement originally made on Apr. 20, 1863.

37. Ibid., Apr. 22, 1863.

38. Ibid., Apr. 29, 1863 (full account of the funeral from the *Manitowoc Tribune* in *Soldier of the Cumberland*, 206–10); summary of Healey's sermon, Kellner Journal, Apr. [?], 1863; *Manitowoc Tribune*, Apr. 29, 1863.

39. Kellner Journal, Apr. [?], 1863.

40. Anderson to Family, Belle Plains, Virginia, Apr. 27, 1863; Leonard to a Friend, White Oak Church, May 14, 1863, 73.

41. Kellner Journal, May 11, 1863.

42. Ibid., May 14, 1863.

43. Anderson Journal 2, June 14, 1863.

44. James S. Anderson, "The Marching of the Sixth Corps to Gettysburg," *Military Order of the Loyal Legion of the United States: War Papers—Wisconsin* 4 (1904): 77–84.

45. Ibid., 79–80.

46. Ibid., 81.

47. Ibid.

48. Ibid., 82.

49. Anderson Journal 2, July 4, 1863.

50. John Reed to Mother, from the hospital steamer *City of Memphis*, May 26, 1863, in *Manitowoc Pilot*, June 12, 1863.

51. *Manitowoc Pilot*, July 10, 1863; *Manitowoc Tribune*, July 9, 16, 1862; "Stranger's Opinion of Our Village," *Manitowoc Pilot*, July 3, 1863.

52. *Manitowoc Tribune*, Mar. 4, 1863; "Stranger's Opinion," *Manitowoc Pilot*, July 3, 1863.

53. The positive condition of the lumbering business discussed in the *Manitowoc Tribune*, Aug. 5, 1863; Anderson to Family, Potomac Creek, May 15, 1863.

54. "Manitowoc as It Appears to a Stranger," *Manitowoc Tribune*, Oct. 1, 1862.

55. Ibid., Feb. 25, 1863.

56. Ibid., July 1, 1863.

57. Leonard to Sheldon, Belle Plains, Virginia, Apr. 1, 1863, 71.

58. *Manitowoc Pilot*, Jan. 16, 1863.

59. *Manitowoc Tribune*, Nov. 17, 1862.

60. *Manitowoc Pilot*, Feb. 20, 1863.

61. Ibid., Feb. 13, 1863; also see Geary, *We Need Men*, a very fine comprehensive study of the whole Civil War draft system in the North.

62. *Manitowoc Tribune*, Feb. 4, 1863.

63. Ibid.

64. Ibid., Apr. 29, 1863.

65. *Manitowoc Pilot,* May 1, 1863.

66. Ibid., May 12, 1863.

67. Ibid., May 22, 1863.

68. Kellner Journal, Aug. 14, 1863; *Manitowoc Pilot,* Aug. 14, 1863.

69. *Manitowoc Pilot,* Aug. 21, 1863.

70. "Speech by William M. Nichols at the Meeting of the Democratic Club at the Courthouse," Feb. 21, 1863, *Manitowoc Tribune,* Mar. 4, 1863; Anderson to Family, Belle Plains, Virginia, Mar. 23, 1863.

71. Letter from "Stew," near New York City (from the Wisconsin Fifth Infantry Regiment), Quiner, ed., *Correspondences* 8:331; Leonard to a Much Respected Friend, New York, Aug. 8, 1863, 77.

72. See Jones, *Four Years in the Army of the Potomac,* 119–26, on their experience in upstate New York; Leonard to Sheldon, Goshen, New York, Oct. 8, 1863, 78; letter from "Stew," Quiner, ed., *Correspondences* 8:331.

CHAPTER 7: STILL THIS SIDE OF THE DARK RIVER

1. Kellner Journal, Sept. 11, 1863.

2. Ibid., Aug. 12, 1863.

3. Ibid., Oct. 4, Aug. 4, 1863.

4. Leonard to Sheldon, Goshen, New York, Oct. 8, 1863, 79; Anderson to Family, Albany Barracks, Sept. 26, 1863.

5. *Manitowoc Pilot,* Sept. 21, 1860.

6. Ibid., Oct. 30, 1863; Anderson to Family, Warrenton, Virginia, Nov. 26, 1863.

7. See Current, *History of Wisconsin: The Civil War Era;* Anderson to Family, Warrenton, Nov. 6, 1863; *Manitowoc Pilot,* Nov. 20, 1863.

8. Captain Joseph Rankin, letter from Helena, Arkansas, Oct. 11, 1863, in *Manitowoc Pilot,* Oct. 30, 1863.

9. Anderson to Family, Warrenton, Nov. 6, 1863.

10. J. S. Anderson, "The Battle of Rappahannock Station," a tattered and incomplete printed account of the battle. Publication title is not indicated, nor is the date of publication. This document was included among Anderson's Papers in the Archives of the State Historical Society of Wisconsin. There is also a letter written by James Anderson from Rappahannock Bridge, Nov. 8, 1863, in Quiner, ed., *Correspondences* 8:337. The quotation here is from the last paragraph of the letter printed by Quiner.

11. Anderson letter, Rappahannock Bridge, Nov. 8, 1863, Quiner, ed., *Correspondences* 8:337.

12. Jones, *Personal Recollections,* 13.

13. Leonard to a Respected Friend, Havenwood Hospital, Washington, D.C., Dec. 13, 1863, 80.

14. Kellner Journal, Jan. 16, 1864.

15. Anderson to Family, Brandy Station, Virginia, Apr. 17, 1864.

16. Ibid.; Anderson to Family, Brandy Station, Virginia, Dec. 9, 1863.

17. Anderson to Family, Brandy Station, Virginia, Apr. 14, 1864.

18. He informs his family that he has been recommended for a commission by the officers of his regiment in a letter from Brandy Station, Virginia, Mar. 23, 1864; the comment about that recommendation being unsolicited is made in a letter to his family from Brandy Station, Virginia, Apr. 17, 1864.

19. Anderson to Family, Brandy Station, Virginia, Mar. 23, Apr. 13, Mar. 20, 1864.

20. Anderson to Family, Brandy Station, Virginia, Dec. 9, 27, 1863, Mar. 26, Apr. 4, 1864.

21. Anderson to Family, Brandy Station, Virginia, Apr. 22, 1864.

22. *Manitowoc Pilot,* May 27, June 24, Apr. 15, 1864, Nov. 27, 1863.

23. *Manitowoc Tribune,* June 22, Aug. 3, 1864.

24. Anderson to Family, Brandy Station, Virginia, Apr. 17, 1864.

25. *Manitowoc Tribune,* June 15, 1, 1864.

26. *Manitowoc Pilot,* June 3, 1864.

27. *Manitowoc Tribune,* June 29, 1864.

28. Anderson to Father, n.p., May 13, 1864.

29. Ibid.

30. Jones, *Four Years in the Army of the Potomac,* 129, 130; Anderson to Family, near the Po River, Virginia, May 15, 1864.

31. Anderson to Father, May 13, 1864.

32. Jones, *Four Years in the Army of the Potomac,* 145.

33. Anderson to Father, May 13, 1864.

34. Anderson to Family, Po River, May 15, 1864.

35. General Sedgwick's comment quoted from Linderman, *Embattled Courage,* 141; Anderson to Family, Po River, May 15, 1864.

36. Anderson to Family, Po River, May 15, 1864.

37. Ibid.

38. Ibid.

39. James S. Anderson, Journal, May 9 to June 25, 1864, Anderson Papers (hereafter cited as Anderson Journal 3).

40. Anderson to Family, Cold Harbor, June 4, 1864.

41. Ibid.

42. Leonard to Sheldon, Petersburg, June 26, 1864, 82.

43. Anderson to Family, Cold Harbor, June 4, 1864; Anderson to Family, Brandy Station, Virginia, Apr. 4, 1864. The flag he is referring to may not be the original one presented to the company by the women of Manitowoc in June of 1861. There is some confusion still on this matter. See *The Flag of Company A* (Manitowoc: Manitowoc County Historical Society, 1925).

44. Leonard to Sheldon, Petersburg, June 26, 1864, 82; Anderson Journal 3, June 24, 1864.

45. Anderson to Family, n.p., June 25, 1864; Anderson to Uncle Walter [Sibree], near Petersburg, June 25, 1864.

46. Anderson Journal 3, July 13, 1864; Anderson to Family, Soldiers' Rest, Washington, D.C., July 14, 1864.

47. James Anderson, "A Trip Down the James River," Anderson Papers. This undated handwritten document appears to have been written during his trip out of Virginia on July 11, 1864. There is also a brief description of this same trip in Anderson Journal 3, July 11, 1864. The Washington visit is described in ibid., July 14–16, 1864.

48. Anderson to Family, Madison, July 23, 1864.

49. Anderson Journal 3, July 23, 24, 1864.

50. Kellner Journal, Aug. 2, 1864; *Manitowoc Pilot,* Aug. 5, 1864.

EPILOGUE

1. Anderson to Family, Warrenton, Virginia, Nov. 6, 1863; report on the election results of 1864 in *Manitowoc Pilot,* Nov. 11, 1864.

2. See reference to Jean Anderson's situation in letters, Anderson to Jean, Brandy Station, Virginia, Apr. 13, 1864, and Anderson to Family, Brandy Station, Virginia, Apr. 22, 1864. And see reference to the possibility of his father's appointment as lighthouse keeper in Anderson to Family, Washington, D.C., July 14, 1864. On his own activities of buying the horses and going into the forest to work for the winter, see Anderson, "Manitowoc County in the Civil War," 17.

3. Anderson, "Manitowoc County in the Civil War," 17.

4. Ibid., 18.

5. Ibid., 19, 20.

6. *Manitowoc Tribune,* Apr. 12, 1865; *Manitowoc Pilot,* Apr. 14, 1865.

7. *Manitowoc Pilot,* Apr. 21, 1865.

8. Ibid.

9. Ibid.

10. Leonard to Sheldon, Petersburg, July 26, 1864, 83.

11. See the complete story of Leonard and the sinking of the *Sea Bird* in Kerry A. Trask, "Fire on the Lake: James H. Leonard and the Sinking of the Sea Bird," *Manitowoc Maritime Museum: Anchor News* 25 (1991): 92–95, 112–14.

12. Kellner Journal, Feb. 10, 1861.

13. This passage, written on a loose leaf of paper, is included in the Kellner Journal, without a specific date but inserted among the pages written during 1867.

14. *Manitowoc Pilot,* July 9, 1869, Apr. 14, 1870.

15. See Falge, ed., *History of Manitowoc County* 1:375–78; and Walter Vogl, "Forest Fires in Manitowoc County—1871," Manitowoc County Historical Society Occupational Monograph 58, 1986.

16. *Manitowoc Herald News,* May 6, 1927; "An Appreciation," by "A Friend," ibid., May 10, 1927.

Bibliography

PRIMARY SOURCES

Manuscripts

Anderson, James S. Papers. State Historical Society of Wisconsin Archives, Madison.

Civil War Muster Rolls, Wisconsin Volunteers. State Historical Society of Wisconsin Archives, Madison.

Federal Census of Wisconsin Manuscripts for 1860. State Historical Society of Wisconsin Library, Madison.

Kellner, Rosa. Journal. Private collection of Lynda Dvorachek, Manitowoc County, Wisconsin.

Personal Papers, Memoirs, and Records

Ambrose, Stephen E., ed. *A Wisconsin Boy in Dixie: The Selected Letters of James K. Newton.* Madison: State Historical Society of Wisconsin, 1961.

Anderson, James S. "The Marching of the Sixth Corps to Gettysburg." *Military Order of the Loyal Legion of the United States: War Papers—Wisconsin.* Vol. 4. Milwaukee: Burdick and Allen, 1904. 77–84.

Anderson, James Sibree. "Indians of Manitowoc County." In *Proceedings of the State Historical Society of Wisconsin, At Its Fifty-Ninth Annual Meeting, October 26, 1911.* Madison: State Historical Society of Wisconsin, 1912. 160–69.

Baensch, Emil, trans. "The Letters and Diary of Joh. Fr. Diederichs." *Wisconsin Magazine of History* 7 (1923–24): 218–37, 350–68

Bjerke, Robert A., ed. *Manitowoc County Declarations of Intent, 1848–1929.* Manitowoc: Manitowoc County Genealogical Society, 1992.

Brown, George C., ed. and trans. "A Swedish Traveler in Early Wisconsin: The Observations of Fredrika Bremer." *Wisconsin Magazine of History* 61, 62 (1978): 41–56, 300–318.

Byrne, Frank L., and Andrew T. Weaver, eds. *Haskell of Gettysburg: His Life and Civil War Papers.* Kent, Ohio: Kent State University Press, 1989.

Castleman, Alfred L. *The Army of the Potomac: Behind the Scenes, A Diary of Unwritten History from the Organization of the Army by General George B. McClellan, to the Close of the Campaign in Virginia, About the First Day of January.* Milwaukee: Strickland, 1863.

Fuller, Margaret. *Summer on the Lakes, in 1843.* Urbana: University of Illinois Press, 1991.

Holmes, Mead, Sr., comp. *Soldier of the Cumberland: Memoir of Mead Holmes Jr.* Boston: American Tract Society, 1864.

Jones, Evan R. *Four Years in the Army of the Potomac: A Soldier's Recollections.* London: Tyne Publishing, 1872.

————. *Personal Recollections of the American Civil War.* Newcastle-on-Tyne: M. and M. W. Lambert, 1872.

Kremers, Gerhard. "An Immigrant's Letter: Manitowoc Rapids, in the State of Wisconsin, July 26, 1848." Occupational Monograph 59. Manitowoc: Manitowoc County Historical Society, 1986.

Lowenfels, Walter, ed. *Walt Whitman's Civil War.* New York: Alfred A. Knopf, 1961.

Mortality Schedule, 1860, for Manitowoc County, Wisconsin from the Federal Census. Manitowoc: Manitowoc County Genealogical Society, 1984.

Olsson, Nils William, ed., and Jonas Oscar Backlund, trans. *A Pioneer in Northwest America, 1841–1858: The Memoirs of Gustaf Unonius.* 2 vols. Minneapolis: University of Minnesota Press, 1950.

Plumb, R. G., ed. "Letters of A Fifth Wisconsin Volunteer." *Wisconsin Magazine of History* 3 (1919): 51–83.

Quiner, Edwin B., ed. *Correspondences of the Wisconsin Volunteers.* Madison: State Historical Society of Wisconsin, 1865.

Rusk, Jeremiah M., and Chandler P. Chapman, eds. *Roster of Wisconsin Volunteers, War of the Rebellion, 1861–1865.* 2 vols. Madison: Democrat Printing, 1886.

Sears, Stephen W., ed. *The Civil War Papers of George B. McClellan: Selected Correspondence, 1860–1865.* New York: Ticknor and Fields, 1989.

War of the Rebellion, The: Compilation of the Official Records of the Union and Confederate Armies. 128 vols. Washington, D.C.: Government Printing Office, 1880–1901.

Whitman, Walt. "The Real War Will Never Get into the Books." In *Complete Prose Works, Walt Whitman.* New York: Mitchell Kennerly, 1914.

Newspapers

Manitowoc Herald
Manitowoc Pilot
Manitowoc Tribune

SECONDARY SOURCES

Books, Articles, and Theses

Buenker, John D. "Wisconsin as Maverick, Model, and Microcosm." In *Heartland: Comparative Histories of the Midwestern States*. Ed. James H. Madison, 59–85. Bloomington: Indiana University Press, 1988.

Caputo, Philip. *A Rumor of War*. New York: Ballantine Books, 1977.

Catton, Bruce. *Glory Road: The Bloody Route from Fredericksburg to Gettysburg*. Garden City, N.Y.: Doubleday, 1953.

———. *Terrible Swift Sword*. New York: Washington Square Press, 1963.

Cayton, R. L., and Peter S. Onuf. *The Midwest and the Nation: Rethinking the History of an American Region*. Bloomington: Indiana University Press, 1990.

Churchill, Winston S. *My Early Life: A Roving Commission*. New York: Charles Scribner's Sons, 1930.

Crane, Stephen. *The Red Badge of Courage*. Boston: Houghton Mifflin, 1960.

Current, Richard N. *The History of Wisconsin: Volume II: The Civil War Era, 1848–1873*. Madison: State Historical Society of Wisconsin, 1976.

Driscoll, John K. "Wisconsin in the American Civil War." *Wisconsin Academy Review* 30 (September 1984): 30–35.

Falge, Louis, ed. *History of Manitowoc County Wisconsin*. 2 vols. Chicago: Goodspeed Historical Association, 1911.

Fries, Robert F. *Empire in Pine: The Story of Lumbering in Wisconsin, 1830–1900*. Sister Bay, Wisc.: Wm. Caxton, 1989.

Fussell, Paul. *The Great War and Modern Memory*. London: Oxford University Press, 1975.

Garland, Hamlin. "The Return of a Private." In vol. 1 of *The American Tradition in Literature*, 2 vols. Ed. Sculley Bradley, Richard Croom Beatty, and E. Hudson Long. New York: W. W. Norton, 1967.

Gass, Otto. *The History of the City of Manitowoc, Wisconsin: Its Pioneer and Early Industries Prior to 1850*. Manitowoc: Manitowoc Public Library Board, 1903.

Gay, Peter. *The Cultivation of Hatred*. New York: W. W. Norton, 1993.

Geary, James W. *We Need Men: The Union Draft in the Civil War*. De Kalb: Northern Illinois University Press, 1991.

Girard, Rene. *Violence and the Sacred*. Trans. Patrick Gregory. Baltimore: Johns Hopkins University Press, 1972.

Glazer, William Stix. "Wisconsin Goes to War, April 1861." Master's thesis, University of Wisconsin–Madison, 1963.

Goodmen, Michael Barton. *The Character of the Civil War Soldiers*. University Park: Pennsylvania State University Press, 1981.

Gray, J. Glen. *The Warriors: Reflections of Men in Battle*. New York: Harper and Row, 1959.

Green, Constant McLaughlin. *Washington: Village and Capital, 1800–1878.* Princeton: Princeton University Press, 1962.

Hatcher, Harlan. "Sails." In *The Great Lakes Reader.* Ed. Walter Havighurst. New York: Collier Books, 1966.

Hemingway, Ernest. *A Farewell to Arms.* New York: Collier Books, Macmillan, 1929.

Hopkins, Ernest Jerome, ed. *The Complete Short Stories of Ambrose Bierce.* Garden City, N.Y.: Doubleday, 1970.

Hubbard, Caroline. *The History of the City of Manitowoc, Wisconsin from 1850 to 1860.* Manitowoc: Manitowoc Public Library Board, 1904.

Keegan, John. *The Face of Battle.* Harmondsworth, Eng.: Penguin Books, 1976.

———. *The Mask of Command.* New York: Viking, 1987.

Kertze, David I. *Ritual, Politics and Power.* New Haven: Yale University Press, 1988.

Kimmel, Stanley. *Mr. Lincoln's Washington.* New York: Coward-McCann, 1957.

Leech, Margaret. *Reveille in Washington, 1860–1865.* New York: Harper and Brothers, 1941.

Linderman, Gerald F. *Embattled Courage: The Experience of Combat in the American Civil War.* New York: Free Press, 1987.

McPherson, James M. *Battle Cry of Freedom: The Civil War Era.* New York: Ballantine Books, 1988.

Mansfield, Sue. *The Gestalts of War: An Inquiry into Its Origins and Meanings as a Social Institution.* New York: Dial Press, 1982.

Mattern, Carolyn J. *Soldiers When They Go: The Story of Camp Randall, 1861–1865.* Madison: State Historical Society of Wisconsin, 1981.

Mitchell, Reid. *Civil War Soldiers: Their Expectations and Experiences.* New York: Viking, 1988.

Mosse, George L. *Nationalism and Sexuality: Respectability and Abnormal Sexuality in Modern Europe.* New York: Howard Fertig, 1985.

Mowat, Farley. *And No Birds Sang.* Boston: Little, Brown, 1979.

Quaife, Milo M. "The Panic of 1862 in Wisconsin." *Wisconsin Magazine of History* 4 (December 1929): 166–95.

Quiner, Edwin B. *The Military History of Wisconsin: A Record of the Civil and Military Patriotism of the State in the War for the Union, With a History of Campaigns in which Wisconsin Soldiers have been Conspicuous—Regimental Histories—Sketches of Distinguished Officers—the Roll of the Illustrious Dead—Movements of the Legislature and State Officers etc.* Chicago: Clarke, 1866.

Remarque, Erich Maria. *All Quiet on the Western Front.* Greenwich, Conn.: Fawcett Crest, 1959.

Smout, T. C. *A Century of the Scottish People, 1830–1950.* London: Collins, 1986.

Stern, Philip VanDoren, ed. *Soldier Life in the Union and Confederate Armies.* New York: Bonanza Books, 1961.

Thomas, Teresa A. "For the Union, Not for Glory: Memory and the Civil War Volunteers of Lancaster, Massachusetts." *Civil War History* 40 (March 1994): 25–47.

Tolstoy, Leo. *The Sebastopol Sketches.* Trans. and intro. David McDuff. London: Penguin Books, 1986.

Trask, Kerry A. "Fire on the Lake: James H. Leonard and the Sinking of the *Sea Bird.*" *Manitowoc Maritime Museum: Anchor News* 25 (1991): 92–95, 112–14.

———. "The First Full Measure: Manitowoc Enters the Civil War." *Voyageur* 3 (1986): 5–14.

Twain, Mark. "The Private History of the Campaign That Failed." In *The Portable Mark Twain,* edited by Bernard DeVoto, 119–42. New York: Viking, 1946.

Vogl, Walter. "Forest Fires in Manitowoc County—1871." Occupational Monograph 58. Manitowoc: Manitowoc County Historical Society, 1986.

Vollmar, William J. "The Negro in a Midwest Frontier City: Milwaukee, 1835–1870." Master's thesis, Marquette University, 1968.

Wiley, Bell I. *The Life of Billy Yank: The Common Soldier of the Union.* Indianapolis: Bobbs-Merrill, 1952.

Index

Designed by Will Underwood;
composed in 11/13 Adobe Garamond by IIS, Inc.;
printed by Thomson-Shore, Inc.;
published by
The Kent State University Press
KENT, OHIO 44242